My Father's Love draws the reader into the reality of sexual abuse. Millions of people's lives are seriously sabotaged because they have been caught in that trap. Thanks, Jim Talley and Jane Baker, for bringing God's power into the picture and for directing us to His healing. That is a part of reality too.

> James G. Friesen, Ph.D.
> Psychologist
> Author of *Uncovering the Mystery of MPD* and *More Than Survivors*

Reading *My Father's Love* was a gripping and emotional experience. Finally, there is a book which openly deals with the hurt, pain, shame and dysfunction caused by incest. Dr. Talley has done a great service for the hurting and the care givers who seek to help them. The section at the end of each chapter makes this a must reference book for ministers and counselors.

> Anthony Jordan, Senior Pastor
> Northwest Baptist Church
> Oklahoma City

MY FATHER'S LOVE

DR. JIM A. TALLEY
JANE CARLILE BAKER

Here's Life Publishers

First Printing, May 1992

Published by
HERE'S LIFE PUBLISHERS, INC.
P. O. Box 1576
San Bernardino, CA 92402

Library of Congress Cataloging-in-Publication Data
Talley, Jim A.
    My father's love / Jim Talley and Jane Carlile Baker.
       p.   cm.
    ISBN 0-89840-360-X
    1. Child molesting—United States—Case studies. 2. Adult child sexual abuse
victims—United States—Mental health. I. Baker, Jane Carlile. II. Title.
HV6570.2.T35   1992
362.7'6—dc20   92-5789
                             CIP

Cover design by David Marty Design

Upon the release of each new book, Here's Life Publishers sponsors the planting of a tree
through Global ReLeaf™, a program of the American Forestry Association.

For More Information, Write:
L.I.F.E.—P.O. Box A399, Sydney South 2000, Australia
Campus Crusade for Christ of Canada—Box 300, Vancouver, B.C., V6C 2X3, Canada
Campus Crusade for Christ—Pearl Assurance House, 4 Tempie Row, Birmingham, B2 5HG, England
Lay Institute for Evangelism—P.O. Box 8786, Auckland 3, New Zealand
Campus Crusade for Christ—P.O. Box 240, Raffles City Post Office, Singapore 9117
Great Commission Movement of Nigeria—P.O. Box 500, Jos, Plateau State Nigeria, West Africa
Campus Crusade for Christ International—100 Sunport Lane, Orlando, FL 32809, U.S.A.

To Pete and George, who rescued one of God's sheep, and all like them, who will give their lives for others.

Acknowledgments

We gratefully acknowledge the contributions of:

The members of Stepping Stones whose lives, when touched by God, motivated us to continue

Ann and her critique group who helped Ella and Jane write and grow

Marie Sontag and Pauline Youd who supported us throughout and especially in the crunches

Art, for his patient wisdom

John, Maryann and Laura, who sacrificed time with their mother

Kery, Jessi, Myrna and Cal for the blessing they gave to the writing

All who supported, encouraged and motivated

Thank you.

Contents

Introduction

God Will Go With You

We met Ella Wainwright Allen a few years before we, through our church, began a support group for adults who were abused as children. Her life and the issues she's had to work through are characteristic of most adults abused as children. As Ella follows God through her recovery, the truths you need to know and the actions you may come to imitate will be revealed by God one at a time. If you are a man who was abused, change the character to Ed as you follow the story.

We share Ella's recovery with you, with her full cooperation and blessing, in hopes that you will realize through it that you are not alone. You should not read this book in one sitting. Each chapter will take you forward on a very difficult and emotional journey. Take the time to allow God to mend and restore your life. God has great plans for you, and they include your recovery from abuse.

All the places and names in Ella's story have been changed— until you come to First Baptist Church of Modesto, California, and meet Jim, Jane and Jane's family. This was not done because Ella is ashamed of being abused, but because she wishes only to share her story so that others may heal, not to take revenge upon her abusers.

Healing the wounds of abuse demands serious work. Let us say that again: Healing the wounds of abuse demands serious work. You may struggle for years cleaning out your wound. You may find yourself capable of concentrating on your recovery only in spurts. But regardless of the manner in which you choose to heal, God will go with you. Those who have not been abused themselves, but who want to learn the dynamics of abuse and recovery to help someone else, should pay special attention to the Helper's Focus at the end of each chapter. Whether you are an adult abused as a child or a person who wants to help one who was, God has promised that His plans for you are good. The Self-Assessment Guide at the end of each chapter offers a progressive path to wholeness for those abused as children. We encourage you to give God your fear and take your first step. Follow closely as Ella relates how God brought her up from the pit of abuse.

JIM A. TALLEY
JANE CARLILE BAKER

Chapter One

What's Wrong With This Picture?

Light shining from the television screen flickered on the walls and furniture as I glanced out at the overcast sky. I was listening to a talk show for company while cleaning the house when the word *incest* jerked me out of "automatic pilot." A woman with a pointed chin and short hair, wearing a tailored suit, had said, "All incest victims are angry, guilty women who have lost trust in people. Most live in misery, hiding their victimization, unaware that there are therapy groups to help them function. Therapy is the only way they can lead normal lives again. I am an incest survivor today because of a therapy group."

I had never heard anything like this before, and I sat down on our child-proofed tweed sofa to watch.

The woman on the screen boldly looked the interviewer in the eye and said, "I know you do research on your topics prior to the show. Did you know that one out of every four girls will be molested before she's an adult? And that only counts the ones brave enough to report their abuse."

The interviewer's temple vein throbbed noticeably. He said nothing.

The rear of the stage was back-lit so that only the silhouettes of a man and woman sitting slump-shouldered could be seen. The woman continued with intensity, "Incest crosses social lines, income lines and race lines because incest is any adult relative meeting his (or her) needs with a child he can manipulate. Yet each victim will feel that she is the only one this has ever happened to and that she deserved it somehow. She'll hide it because of those feelings and will probably never seek help. Did you know that incest victims hide from other people? They can't make close friendships or share themselves with others. They teach themselves not to feel."

The interviewer had recovered from the shock of these statistics enough to comment, "You must agree, however, that there are those who say that some victims bring incest on themselves by being careless about how they dress or acting seductively."

"Don't give me that!" the woman cried. "Surely you can't believe that tripe. There are also men who say children should have sexual intercourse before they're eight years old! Where do you draw the line? We're talking about adult men and little girls, and sometimes even adult women and little boys, sir. We're talking about men who have the power to interpret a child's hug however they want. We're talking about men who have the responsibility to protect their daughters, sons, step-daughters, stepsons, granddaughters, grandsons, nieces and nephews—and don't. Instead they hurt them, often indelibly. Don't try to tell me a child is responsible when an adult manipulates her. No way!"

She looked angrily at the man in the shadows and said, "Isn't that right, Daddy?"

The host interrupted, "Our guest's mother and father have agreed to be interviewed so that we may have the parents' point of view today."

The woman's father said, "Yes, you are right. I was responsible."

"There is a common characteristic of incest victims, however," the woman continued. "All incest victims have rotten relationships with their mothers, or at least unhappy ones. These relationships may have been bad previously or just at the time surrounding the incest. And all marriages where incest occurs were in trouble before incest happened. My mom didn't have time for me because of the job she took to get away from my father. When my brother told Mom what my father was doing to me, she did nothing. In fact, my mother told me to keep my father settled down!"

Turning to the shadowed woman, she spit, "Would you say that's accurate, Mother?"

"I didn't know, honestly. I was away at work. We needed money. How could I think the man I loved was abusing our daughter?"

Petey, my three-year-old, grabbed my attention as he ran his yellow Hot Wheels Corvette over my arm and leg as if my limbs were mountains. My son was a curly-headed boy with big knees, too young to understand what incest meant. I struggled to refocus my attention on the television program.

What the woman had said about therapy groups and how many victims there are made me realize for the first time that I was not alone or peculiar. I had felt isolated with my secrets, except for the help I got from my husband, Pete, and my sister, Jessi. This woman's openness on TV contrasted starkly with my secret-keeping. Nobody outside my family knew my stepfather had wasted my teen years with incest.

I appreciated the woman for going public about incest. But I couldn't help saying aloud as if she could hear me, "You are permeated with bitterness. Publicly berating your parents seems vindictive. Haven't you already asked them these things in private? Educating the audience doesn't seem a good enough reason to focus your sarcastic criticism publicly on your parents. Your problem is with their behavior. Don't you think you could discuss their dysfunction privately—or with a therapist? Why subject them to your rage on national television?"

I couldn't do that to Mom or Cal, my stepfather, no matter what they'd done to me. They were people. People should be treated with dignity, even those who choose to hurt others. I even thought that subjecting them to public scorn might do me harm, as well as them. Hate probably didn't help this woman any, either. The program broke for a commercial.

"Who are you talking to, Mommy?" Petey asked.

"This lady on TV, Petey. Mommy's kind of weird, huh? Why don't you play in your room for a while?"

"Could I make a race track in the barn?" he asked.

"Sure, but don't go anyplace else without telling me," I answered with the automated response of a mother whose attention has drifted.

Petey ran his car across the paneled living room wall, the refrigerator and over the door jamb on his way outside.

I started mumbling my feelings out loud before the show came back on. "I can understand your anger, even though I can't agree with your actions." I had never gotten involved enough in a TV show to talk back before, and especially not during the commercial. But somehow it felt good to let my emotions out a little bit after so long.

The show came back on and the woman continued, "I know the fear of trusting, of men; and I know the bitterness that changes a woman's life after incest."

"Yes, you do, and so do I," I said. There I was, a thirty-one-year-old wife and mother, with tears running down my face over something that had started nearly twenty years ago. My stepfather, Cal, had begun to molest me soon after he married my mother. I was twelve then.

The woman said to her father, "I'm a lesbian today, thanks to you."

I wonder why my bitterness seems sporadic and not nearly as keen as hers? I thought.

The show continued. "I've talked to many women who chose prostitution as a means to get love. They don't know what real love is, because they've never experienced it. You did that for me too, Dad. Thanks." Her bitterness exploded from the screen.

The man in the shadows said nothing. I could see him drop his head, and I imagined his meek look. Cal could have looked that humiliated too. I had always thought Cal seemed so "nice" that no one would ever believe me if I told the truth about what he was doing to me.

Recognizing her caustic demeanor as a defense mechanism, I wanted to touch the woman on the screen and tell her, "I don't know why God didn't save us from incest before it happened. But I know He saved me during incest and helped me end it. He can save you from lesbianism or prostitution, or anything."

The host jolted me back to the program, "I suppose with all that's happened to you, you want revenge. Is that why you've brought your parents here?"

"At first my dear old dad wouldn't even go to therapy with me. He tried to say it didn't happen. So if anyone deserves revenge, I do."

Talking to a portable television seemed so futile; she couldn't hear me. As the show ended I found myself mumbling again, "I wish I could tell her, and others, that we can be victors instead of victims. We don't even have to settle for being survivors." I didn't realize it then, but God was far from finished with my own healing.

I had come a long way. Jesus had found me, so in trouble and so without hope. I had thought the affair with Cal was my fault, because my life had been so filled with anger at Mom since the day she sent my daddy away. This woman's view was that the adult sexually involved with a child was at fault no matter what the circumstances were. I thought back, wondering how my abuse got started. My thoughts drifted back across the years to that day Mom sent my dad away, when I was eleven.

❦   ❦   ❦

I was currying my horse, Eb, when Daddy drove in.

I was too short to catch a glimpse of the driveway over Eb's back. Instead I ducked under his neck to see that the gravel I heard crunching came from Daddy's blue Pontiac. I charged for the driver's door and hit him head-on before he got it shut. He got that exuberant greeting every time he came home. We never said "I love you" much—the way we treated each other was how we showed our love. This day he didn't throw me in the air the way he used to when I was younger. He'd said I had grown too big now that I'd turned eleven, and I'd hurt his "poor ol' back." Instead he played his new part in our ritual, bending to kiss my cheek and say, "How's your 'coborosity'?" I've never known the correct definition for 'coborosity.' Maybe Daddy doesn't know an exact definition, or maybe I never asked. Anyway, it had something to do with how the world treated me. His question felt as good as getting tossed into the air, because his concern for my life made me feel a little bit more grown up.

"I got the saddle on Eb a whole bunch of times, Daddy. I'm ready to ride him, with you leading, like you said. I even laid over him and let him walk around with me," I bragged.

Daddy looked toward Eb's shed. "Is that so? How old did you say Eb was?" Grin lines crinkled around his eyes. He already knew Eb was three, a beautiful black Morgan gelding. He filled my life, if you left out family and school.

"He's three. Just turned, first of the month."

Daddy looked toward our white clapboard house. "Well, you saddle him and we'll see if he can dump you in the dirt." I hugged him hard. "Thank you, thank you!" I cried. He picked up his suitcase and walked off. Drinking made his stomach stick out a little. But other than that he was really handsome for a dad. Mom's friends teased her about having the best looking, most successful husband in the neighborhood.

Daddy usually wore suits and ties when he worked, like now. But as soon as he got home he changed into Bermuda shorts in summer or paint-streaked overalls in winter. He came from the Midwest and I thought he brought the country with him. He told me he pressed himself to succeed in business in order for Mom to have the money she wanted. But his real love was working around our farm. Then we got to talk about things. He said to never tell lies, because matching a current lie to one you told before gets complicated. He taught me to expect a little good from everybody. He loved the land and I caught that. And we worked hard because it feels better than loafing.

"Let's make Eb our first priority while I'm home," he called to me as he passed under the grape arbor. "I've got to go back and see Jack Houston at the Imperial in a few days. They're going to throw a big anniversary bash, and we're doing all the publicity, soup to nuts." His brown hair just missed the door frame as he went through.

People said I looked like Daddy, which was okay with me except for my feet. We both have big, wide duck feet. But who cares much about feet? I have his strong chin and big eyes, and I like those.

"Yeah, Dad!" I yelled as he banged the screen door. I raced into Eb's shed. Someone had built the shed of thin boards spaced so that air could get through because they used it to brood baby chickens. The corrugated tin roof amplified raindrops in the winter. Inside, a board fence held Eb's feed trough and kept him out of the feed sacks stacked in the corner. While I finished currying Eb, I daydreamed about galloping him through the meadows. In my daydreams I always made the meadows smooth, with no gopher holes for him to trip in.

Maybe because of my daydreaming, I hadn't heard any sounds from the house. Then out of the corner of my eye, I saw Daddy walking toward me, still carrying his suitcase. Tears coursed down his cheeks and his shoulders slumped as he walked. He kept brushing his arm across his face.

I suddenly remembered last Wednesday.

"Ella, what would you think if your dad and I split up?"

How could I answer Mom's question? I'd rather they stayed together. But I hated the screaming every night he was home.

"Whatever would make you happy," I answered. I thought I'd go with Daddy if they split up.

"I can't stand him embarrassing you in front of your friends the way he does when he's drinking," Mom said. "And he never wants to have any fun when he's home."

I remembered him embarrassing me only once. His love made up for little times like that. Besides, her money requirements were what made him work so hard. She couldn't have everything. "Well, this place and his job are a lot of work," I ventured. I didn't add that his work and how tired he got were the result of taking care of us. She probably couldn't take that much honesty.

As usual, when I dared to disagree with her, she flashed an angry look at me. "This farm was *his* idea. I work as hard as he does. I want to have some fun on the weekends." She turned and walked away.

The sound of his dropped suitcase shocked me back to reality. I guessed that Mom had told Daddy to leave us today. I stumbled to him silently. My running back and forth with soothing words couldn't mend my folks' marriage anymore. She had told him it was over.

I stood looking at his face, trying to memorize it. Daddy knelt, leveling his green eyes, full of tears, with mine. I could smell his Old Spice. He never used anything else. The smell of Old Spice meant Daddy to me.

"Ella, your mother has asked me to leave." His voice trembled. The muscles in his face clenched and unclenched so that his face looked like it was coming apart. He turned and gazed back at the house like he thought he might be dreaming.

I put my fingers on the back of his hand. His pulse was as regular as ever.

He grasped my shoulders and looked me as squarely in the eyes as he could through his tears. "No matter what happens, I'll always be your papa. I want you to remember that you can always talk to me, about anything. I've done every kind of wrong you'll ever think of, and more. So if you get into trouble, tell me the truth and I'll stand with you. But the truth, okay?"

I nodded.

"And Ella," he looked deep into my eyes, "don't marry anybody until I meet him. I'll come and get you and Jessi for a visit real often." Jessi, my little sister, was six, five years younger than me.

"I love you," I whimpered. "I'll go with you. Let me get my clothes."

"You can't," he whispered, looking away. "The court will give you to your mother." He picked up his suitcase, walked to the car, threw his bag in the back seat, and was gone in a moment. Even after the dust settled, I still stood there hoping he wasn't gone. Where would he go anyway? This was home. Surely he'd drive back in, the way he always did. But he didn't.

As I ran for my room, Mom leaned against the kitchen door. I stopped only long enough to scream, "Why? Why did you make my daddy leave? *I hate you!*"

Stomping Jessi's bear on the way to my room, I locked my door and fell across my bed. Pain oozed out of my chest along with the tears from my eyes. *It will be real hard for Daddy to love me from far away*, I thought. I cried so hard that I lurched like our old truck when Daddy let the clutch out too fast.

After a while my eyes had no more tears. They felt dry, kind of like my throat did when I needed a drink of water badly. I looked out my window at our place. It stood blackened—sad trees, sad dirt, sad house. I turned away.

Mom had painted my room vanilla white. She bought me pink curtains for the windows and closet door, and a pink bedspread. Mom said she had to love Jessi most because Daddy loved me most. Daddy had told me he didn't; it was only that I'd been around five years longer. Anyhow, sometimes Mom did things, like the bedspread and curtains, that made me think she loved me a little.

She knocked on the door. "Ella, are you all right?"

"Yeah," I answered, staring out the window, watching a mother bird put worms in her babies' gaping beaks. They lived in a nest molded in the tree branches.

I could hear Mom's feet shift in the hall as she spoke through the door. "Do you want to eat now?"

I stared at my side of the door. I didn't feel hungry. I'd never need to eat again; my stomach was metal.

"No," I said.

"Jessica went to play at Mary Ellen's. I'll leave you TV dinners in the oven. You can eat when you're ready." I felt her hesitation. "Some of my friends are getting together over at Phillips's, and I'm going over for a while," she said finally.

So that's it, I thought. "Okay," I answered. After a moment she walked away.

"Phillips's again," I hissed. "She spends more time with them than she does with us. Just because Ol' Spider Legs's daddy likes to dance and my daddy doesn't." I called Cal Phillips's daughter Spider Legs. She was a grade ahead of me and two years older. She got her nickname because her legs were skinny and she was a snot. When I was sure Mom was gone, I went downstairs and started gobbling cookies. I didn't want her crummy dinner. And I didn't want to love anybody anymore. I would be strong all by myself. Nobody would squeeze love out of my heart again, ever, ever, ever.

❦ ❦ ❦

A couple of months later Cal left his wife. Mom came home telling us how he'd rented this creepy apartment in town and was eating spaghetti every night. I couldn't pay much attention to what she said because I'd ridden Eb around the corral all by myself that afternoon. But she didn't seem to hear what I was telling her about riding any better than I heard what she said. We both talked and neither listened. Anyhow, Jessi and I had to move out of our rooms into the downstairs, because Mom wanted to rent our rooms to Cal for enough money to keep the place. But that was only the beginning. First we lost our rooms, and before the year was out we lost the farm. Mom and Cal got married. A few months later they decided to buy out his wife and move to his old house.

The day they made us move to Cal's he acted like his normal, irritating self. "Horse looks kind of skinny to me," he observed, his elbows on the rail of Eb's stall, his blue eyes watching my reaction.

"He's not skinny, he's sleek," I snapped. "Just because you married my mother doesn't mean you can talk about my horse." I would have reacted to Mom with silence if she'd called Eb skinny. But Cal didn't belong in our family. He made me angry when he even thought about things that were only between Daddy and me.

He ignored me. "I've got a friend, one of the owners of Wilhite's. He'd sell me oats wholesale, if you want to fatten him up a little," he said, heaving Eb's tack box onto his shoulder.

"Eb's between Daddy and me, not you!" I yelled as he lugged the box to his truck. Sweat streaked the back of his shirt. Mom wasn't there to correct my back talk, and Cal never made me do anything, right or wrong. He always bugged me, though, seemed like only to make me mad. He deserved to be talked back to.

I opened Eb's gate and glanced around the shed. Eb's hoof shavings lay scattered in the corner. They looked like dull half moons. The day those shavings came off, Daddy had stood over the blacksmith to make sure Eb's first shoes went on right. I'd purposely missed the shavings each time I cleaned the stall, even though they smelled decayed. If they weren't gone, Daddy wasn't gone.

But he was. He'd moved to Chicago saying he'd found a better job. But I thought it was because it hurt him too much to see Mom with Cal and to see me and Jessi only on weekends. Jessi and I would go visit him in August. We'd ride the bus and stay for two weeks. He told us on the phone that he'd take us fishing and to a history museum.

I picked up one of the pieces of hoof, broke it in two and stuck one half in my jeans pocket. Looking only at Eb, refusing to see the end of my life in this place, I led Eb out of the shed to live at my enemy's house.

"Don't think Eb's gonna be happy on a little place like yours," I said, trying to find a way to humiliate Cal.

Cal tightened Eb's cinch. "It's that or a boarding stable. He'll manage." It made me mad that nothing I said ever got to Cal. I put my foot in the stirrup and swung up.

Turning Eb toward the driveway, I said, "I'm gonna ride around for a while."

"Get home in time to start dinner, or your mother will be mad," Cal shouted as Eb's feet crunched the gravel.

"Home," I sneered. "I'm riding away from *my* home." I urged Eb to gallop and we shot down the driveway, my hair flipping in the wind. I refused to look at my bedroom window or smell the lilacs; I just left. At the end of the drive I turned Eb the opposite direction from Cal's house and slowed him to a walk. "Eb, I hate that man. He married Mom, but he's never going to be my father." Wrapping the reins around the saddle horn, I sought comfort from my horse. We headed for a store on the corner, where the candy bars would soothe my pain, at least for a little while, until I got home.

❦ ❦ ❦

I was tasting the spaghetti sauce to see if it needed more garlic when Mom came in from work. As hostess at the Elegant Steer, she wore long gingham and calico dresses that Aunt Nancy had made for her. Today she had on a deep blue calico with tiny red flowers and a skirt that showed off her small waist. Taking out the pins that held her long, brown hair in a net, she sighed. "It was a rat race tonight, Ella. I'm so tired."

I poured the spaghetti sauce into a bowl and said, "Well, dinner's ready."

"Cal, Jessica, come on," Mom called.

At the table, Jessi and I slurped up long strings of spaghetti. The sauce painted rings around our pressed lips, and we licked them off.

Frowning, Cal watched us slurp spaghetti. Finally he said, "Can't you two at least wind it up on your forks? You look like pigs at a trough."

"Cal!" Mom snapped.

"You oughta know," I muttered.

"Ella!" Mom glared at me.

We managed to finish dinner without screaming at each other anymore. After dinner Jessi left for Mary Ellen's to play with her best friend, and Cal went out to feed the calves. When he came back, he said, "Jessi left her bike in the driveway. Go move it, would you, Ella?"

"It's Jessi's bike. Tell *her* to move it," I sassed.

"Ella!" Cal said, his voice hard.

I turned and stared at him defiantly.

"I said, you move the bike." His voice had become very quiet, but anger burned in his eyes.

"Listen, my daddy isn't here. You aren't him and you can't order me around! Daddy pays my bills. You're just my mother's husband." What made him think I had to do what he said?

Cal grabbed at me. But Mom screamed, "I can't stand it! If you two don't stop fighting, I'm going to lose another marriage!"

He stopped and gave her a look of amazement. Waving her hand at me, Mom continued, "Cal pays as many, probably more, of your bills as your dad does, Ella. Go move that bike! Then finish dusting my room."

I burned a hole in the linoleum with the look meant for her.

As I went out to move the bike, I heard Cal say, "Myrna, I want to talk to you about Darlene." Darlene was Spider Legs's real name.

That should start a hot one, I thought. I kicked the screen door open. "Jessi!" I yelled. No answer. "First I have to dust their love den. And now she's making me obey him. She can't love me and him, and she doesn't love me that much anyhow. It was easy for her to switch to him. She's Cal's, and she's made Jessi and me nobodies. 'Just do what you're told and keep the house clean, Cinderella,'" I hissed quietly as I jerked Jessi's bike off the driveway.

"And Mom doesn't love *him* enough to be nice to him. I wouldn't be sorry if she did lose this marriage. Then maybe she'd go back to Daddy where she belongs!" I threw Jessi's bike at the fence. It crashed down with a sound of grating metal.

"If you two don't stop fighting, I'll lose another marriage," I mimicked sarcastically. *Sure,* I thought.

I didn't lose your first marriage, you did. You sent my daddy away, and you don't care about me either, just yourself. I'll show you. I'll stop fighting. I'll help Cal see how phony you are. Pretty soon Cal will want to have fun with me more than you.

When I walked back into the house, Mom screamed at Cal from the dining room, "No money, not one dime, for an abortion. She danced, let her pay the piper for once in her life." Her jeans and shirt were on the floor in her room. I picked them up and took them to the hamper.

I had knelt to dust the sides of Cal's nightstand when Mom rushed in trying to fasten her earring and looking for her shoes. Cal followed her. She shouted, "Is every stupid unmarried girl in this country trying to get pregnant? If you think I'm going to work my fanny off down at that lousy restaurant to pay for your little whore's abortion, you've got another think comin'!" She stopped suddenly and glared up at him, her hands on her hips.

A few months ago, Spider Legs's mother had wanted Cal to take her to live with us, thinking that would straighten her out. But Mom wouldn't let him because she said Spider Legs would be a bad influence on Jessi and me. I figured that could be the small half of the truth. The big half was that Mom probably didn't want the work of an extra person. Whenever Cal wanted to let Spider Legs visit, Mom said no and made him take her somewhere else. I wouldn't have copied Spider Legs, though. The boys who liked her acted as yucky as she did.

Cal turned around and hit the wall with his open palm. "All right! I don't know what you think she's supposed to do, but all right! And while I'm at it I'll cross my name off her birth certificate. Will that make you happy?" He charged out. I heard the screen door slam as he walked toward the car.

"Baloney. That girl wanted it and she got it. I'm not paying her piper. Black is black and white is white. Right is right and wrong is wrong. And being pregnant before you're married is wrong. People do what they want to do, but I don't have to pay for them!" Looking at me in the mirror, she asked, "Do you think I'm right, Ella?"

Here we go again, I thought. *How am I supposed to know?* "Sure, Mom," I said. It took too much thinking to figure out Mom's life. And she usually disagreed with whatever I said or got mad, anyway. I had started just agreeing with her a long time ago.

"I've told you, haven't I, that at twelve you are accountable to God for what you do? Right now I'm responsible for the things you do wrong. I'm supposed to teach you. But at twelve, if you decide to act badly, God deals with you, not me. You'll soon be twelve, Ella. Watch yourself. Boys will try to get in your pants." I hated the crude way she talked about sex. She peered at her face in the mirror, poking at something she didn't like on her cheek. "The age of accountability, you can find it in the Bible."

"Did you do wrong things after you were twelve, Mom?"

"No. My hometown was small, and so many family members watched me that I couldn't have done anything wrong even if I had thought of something. I couldn't sneeze when I was growing up without it being reported to my mother. Besides, I've always wanted to please God. So I've tried to do what was right. I wish your father had let me take you girls to church more."

That sounded phony to me. Daddy had let us go to church plenty of Easters and Christmases when Mom wanted to take us. He didn't care. He just didn't want to go himself. The part that hit me weird was that she had never gotten up early enough on Sundays to go to church. This was the first time I'd heard anything about her caring. Maybe once every six months she dropped us off at Sunday school. But it wasn't fun hanging around with a whole bunch of dressed-up strangers. We would come home and there Daddy would be with no shirt on, mowing the lawn, back and forth. I would rather have stayed with him.

I suspected she'd stretched the truth about her childhood too. Before today, Mom had told Jessi and me stories like the time she sneaked out her bedroom window at night to have fun at the boardwalk with her cousin and some sailors.

But I didn't say anything; it would only give her an excuse for a rage. "I wish I could be like you were and never do things wrong," I lied.

"Oh, you are, Ella." She grasped my shoulders. Her eyes met mine. "You're a good girl, Ella, and I appreciate that."

Does she believe her own words about me—or about herself? Most of the time she yelled at me about practicing the piano more, or some wrong that I'd done. *I'm not sure she actually knows what she thinks. Or maybe she changes it to fit the occasion.* But I didn't forget the responsibility that she told me I'd soon carry for everything I did. I wished I could stay eleven forever.

"Well, listen Ella, put the leftovers in the fridge. And finish the laundry. I need the work dresses in the wash; you could iron them if you're in the mood." She grinned a silly face that was supposed to be persuasive. "Got any homework?"

I put the lid back on the furniture polish. I hated to iron and she knew it. "Just a book report; I'll have time," I said. Worse than anything, I hated to feel weak. Though I did have to obey her, I never let her see that her demands upset me. That way I felt I at least controlled my thought life.

"Okay. I'll see you about 9:30." She pecked me on the forehead as she swooshed out the door for bowling night.

Cal and I didn't argue so much after I decided to make him like me more than he liked Mom. When he asked me to do something, I smiled and did it. He even started teaching me how to mow the lawn and plant flowers. Next to Eb, I loved green, growing things best. When Cal helped me plant petunias and the pale green shoots pushed through the dirt, I felt like a mother. I pulled Cal by the hand to come and see. He smiled at me, and I knew he understood how sacred their growth was to me. A look in his eyes said we were friends. It was almost like when Daddy was still with us.

My plan worked to get him to like me, and yet I had a hard time not liking him back. I hadn't planned to like him. I meant to keep my commitment not to care about someone so much that they could hurt me. Besides, I only wanted revenge at Mom. More important, liking Cal would be cutting Daddy's throat.

We took turns mowing the grass. Usually Cal got more turns because I got in too big a hurry and killed the lawn mower in tall grass. But I made up for it by fixing iced glasses of soda while Cal mowed. He taught me all kinds of things. He seemed to know everything. He also seemed to care more about me than Mom did.

"Hey, Ella," he would say, "I've gotta get some nails to fix the table. Wanna come?" Or, "Wanna help me put up fence?" One day Cal said, "Ella, come out and help me. I'll teach you how to change a tire. Myrna, you want to learn?"

Mom shook her head without looking up from her book. "No, I'm at a good part," she replied.

"I'll come," Jessi said, bouncing off a stool.

Cal shrugged his shoulders. He didn't like to have Jessi around much. I guessed it was because she talked all the time and asked a million questions. Generally, she got in the way and messed up Cal's tools.

"This thing's a lug nut," Cal said, handing me a tool with an end the shape of the nut he wanted me to unscrew. I fit the tool on the nut and heaved and pulled, but nothing happened.

"Here," Cal said, putting his arms around mine and laughing. "I'll help you get 'er started." He didn't seem to push much, but the nut loosened instantly. I could feel his muscles straining and I felt a little bit uncomfortable. I wished he had stood beside me instead of in back of me.

"Cal, I wanna do it, too," Jessi whined.

"You're not strong enough," Cal answered, fitting the tool on another nut.

"You let Ella do *everything*. She's not strong either!" Jessi said, stamping her foot.

"Jessi, go in the house," Cal demanded.

"I don't wanna," Jessi answered, sticking out her lip.

Cal didn't yell. But he ignored her as if she didn't exist. I glanced at Jessi and she pointed at the lug nuts again. She would push Cal into getting mad at her, so I said, "Jessi, go find out what we're having for dinner." Her eyes looked hurt, but she went.

"I don't know why your mother likes her best. She's a pain in the rear most of the time."

I loved Jessi. Mom liking her best didn't make me jealous. Jessi couldn't help how Mom felt. I wished she were older so she wouldn't irritate Cal, though. After the time with the tire Jessi didn't ask to go places with Cal and me anymore.

About then I had to admit to myself that my revenge against Mom had backfired. I had begun to feel genuine affection for Cal. More often now I couldn't picture Daddy's face in my mind. The image from his picture in my room didn't even last long in my memory. I hated to forget his face because I still loved him. Without Jessi and me, he had nobody.

For my twelfth birthday, Cal and Mom took us to spend a week at the beach where my best friend, Nan, had moved.

"Why don't you ride with Cal, Ella? He's never been to Nan's beach house before. You can show him the way," Mom suggested as I was about to get in the car.

I loved riding in Cal's truck. It felt free, like riding Eb, except higher. I could see out over the houses and fields. I flipped radio stations to one with a smooth, lazy style I thought Cal would enjoy, then leaned my head over the back of the seat, humming. I felt warm and electric listening to that kind of music, maybe like a tree in the spring when the sap starts to run.

Cal said, "Hey, babe, what are you going to be?"

I looked over at him. *'Babe'—what a difference from a couple of months ago,* I thought. "Daddy's going to send me to college," I said, but not to point out Daddy's superiority this time. "I want a job that's outside, but I haven't decided what yet." I closed my eyes. The hot wind blew in the open windows and tangled my hair.

"Know what I'd like to do?" Cal asked. When I opened my eyes I noticed him looking at my bust. It made my blouse push out now. I felt so self-conscious that I usually walked with my shoulders forward. If only I was one of those skinny girls who didn't have anything yet. But I liked chocolate too much to be skinny. Mom was always yelling at me for eating Oreos without asking, but cookies were comforting when I was bored or sad.

Was Cal thinking so hard that he didn't realize what he was looking at? I thought of slouching forward now, but if he was only thinking, I'd draw his attention for no reason. I stayed put.

"What?" I responded to his question.

He gestured with his arm toward the mountains. "I'd like a ranch in the mountains. Pine trees, a creek, one of those little red mountain cabins where you pump water from a well. Man, that would be heaven." The truck drifted over the line.

"Cal!" I grabbed the wheel.

"Oh, sorry," he gasped. Taking the wheel, he put his hand over mine. I looked up at him and he let go, slowly, watching me.

What's happening? I wondered.

We got to Nan's, changed to swimming suits and hotfooted through the burning sand to the surf. The smell of salt air, the sky meeting the ocean so far away and the crashing of the surf made a perfect birthday. Cal, Jessi, Nan and I played all day, riding Nan's inner tubes and heaving seaweed at each other. He threw us off his shoulders as many times as we wanted.

Too soon Sunday arrived and Cal left to go back to work at the lumberyard. Later, while we sat around a beach fire, Mom said, "I'm glad you and Cal are getting along better."

"He's okay," I said, making a pile of sand over my feet. "Just takes some getting used to." I felt closer to Cal now than to Mom, almost as if we had formed a conspiracy to survive her ways. The conspiracy made me feel less powerless in her world. And yet, I wished she would behave like a regular mom. I wished I could count on her to tell the truth in everything. I wanted her to do the jobs a mom does and not slough them off on me. I wished she loved me just because I was me.

Mom smiled. "Listen, Ella. Tomorrow I'm going to sleep late. You watch Jessi in the water, okay?"

"Okay," I grunted. *As usual*, I thought. Mom was funny. She got away with as little work as possible, but only when Cal couldn't see. As I grew, she added more of her responsibilities to my list of chores. *I'm going to let Cal know how much work she does and how much I do*, I decided.

The rest of that week we tanned ourselves, swam and went to the amusement park at the end of the beach. Nan and I talked as if we had never been apart. I sort of wanted to tell Nan about Cal putting his hand on mine in the truck to see what she thought. She had helped me figure out things before. But he probably did it by accident. I shouldn't make a big deal out of it. Maybe he was only trying to make up for Daddy being gone, or something like that. Mom and Cal would probably get into another argument if Nan told Mom. I hated listening to them yell. Besides, Nan would probably think I was a creep to desert Daddy by liking Cal. I buried the hand incident in my mind and talked to her about Eb and the kids at school.

On Saturday when Cal came back, he asked, "Myrna, can Ella ride back with me? It was good having someone to talk to."

"Sure. Ella, you like that truck, huh?"

"Yeah, it's high and windy," I answered, looking out Nan's window at the blue half-ton.

"I wanna ride too!" Jessi screamed from the porch. "And we can play the road sign game, Ella," she added, coming in the door.

"I don't want to play car games, Jessi."

"Jessica will enjoy the landscape on the way home from up high in the truck. She can go with Cal, too."

"Maybe not this time, Myrna," Cal said.

Where did he get the courage to say that? He never contradicted Mom.

"Ella doesn't have too many special times just for herself. It's her birthday. I'll let Jessi ride another time."

They exchanged a glance.

"Okay. But don't make it too long before Jessica gets a ride!"

"Never mind. I only wanted to ride because Ella was." Jessi frowned at Cal.

We drove through purpling night as we left the coast. I felt a little guilty about Jessi not getting to enjoy this. But Cal and I talked about sea anemones and Nan and me, and I soon forgot Jessi. I even told him that wearing a swimming suit embarrassed me a little now that my body had begun to mature.

"You have a beautiful body," Cal said. "Don't be ashamed."

His noticing how I looked embarrassed me even more. But we started talking about Mom and how much time she spent making sure no one took advantage of her. Then I forgot being embarrassed. Cal said again that he couldn't understand why Mom favored Jessi. I said I thought it might be because Jessi looked light, like a ballerina, and I was built like a peasant. But he said she couldn't be that stupid. The hum of the truck made me sleepier and sleepier.

"Cal, could I lay my head in your lap?" I asked. "I'm getting tired."

"Sure, sweetie." He held his arm up for me to lie down. "I really enjoyed the beach with you, babe," he said. When his hand came down, the tips of his fingers were on the edge of my breast. My breast tingled. How could my body react that way to my *mother's husband?* Now I suspected what "aroused" meant in Spider Legs's *True Love* magazines. But my head felt guilty and terrible. Cal probably didn't even realize where he'd put his hand, and here I was feeling these *feelings.* Ashamed, I pinched myself to turn the feelings off. After a while I drifted off to sleep.

The next night, after Cal came home from work and we'd finished dinner, we turned on the TV. Mom got up to get a root beer during a commercial. When she had disappeared into the kitchen, Cal pulled me to him and kissed me, more than a regular kiss like at bedtime. He whispered, "You're special, Ella," and pushed me away. The darkened room kept Mom from seeing my face when she came back. Something whispered inside me that this kiss didn't mean the same thing as a goodnight kiss.

It's nice to have smiles and friendship and doing things together. But I didn't plan for touching and kissing. I guess it's too late now, I thought. *I've already gotten it all. I probably deserve it too, for trying to make him like me more than Mom.*

That short kiss led to longer kisses and then to Cal putting his hands inside my blouse. Cal began to use the times we worked together to "show" me which part of me responded to him. His kisses and his hands were soft and warm. My body responded automatically, and though I liked his affection, I felt this closeness was wrong.

"Cal, I feel like we're doing wrong. You should be touching Mom, not me," I said again one day.

He gave me his standard answer. "We love each other. No one knows. We don't hurt anyone. Stop worrying." He chucked me under the chin and handed me the hoe to make a trench for the beans we were planting. I didn't know whether to believe him and I felt helpless. I despised myself for my confusion over whether he told me the truth, because in a way I didn't want to know. This weakness from wanting someone to care about me so badly kept me from listening to my conscience. It was screaming, "Wrong, wrong, wrong."

The day quickly came when Cal moved our relationship past the petting stage. Mom had gone to work. I avoided the July heat by lying on the sofa watching television. Cal came in and I pulled my legs up for him to sit down. Instead he picked a spot on the edge of the sofa near my head.

"Do you want to do it?" he asked gently.

"It?" I asked.

He stroked my side over my waist and down to my hip. "You know, *it*," he said.

I didn't understand what "it" was, but I didn't want him to think I was childish.

"Sure," I said. I still didn't know what he meant, but I didn't want him to know. Maybe he wanted to kiss me or touch me. Why was he asking? He'd never asked before.

"Where's Jessi?

"At Mary Ellen's," I answered.

He got up and locked the door. "You have to undress if you want to," he said, smiling down at me.

Intercourse, I thought. *Cal means intercourse.* Again it was too late; I had already said yes. And I'd grown past the age of accountability that Mom had warned me about. I was thirteen.

Self-Assessment Guide

1. Compare and contrast how your abuse began with how Ella's began. There is no word limit. Think back and let yourself relive it in order to regain your feelings. Be descriptive;

include how things looked, smelled, sounded, felt. Include how *you* felt, what your reactions were.

This is a step you can't skip. If you don't consider from an adult perspective what happened to you as a child, the result will be the same as putting a Band-Aid on an infected wound without cleansing it. If it helps, pretend you are an uninvolved neighbor watching your childhood and ask yourself if what you are seeing is normal.

2. Choose one of the books in the bibliography and read it at the same time you read *My Father's Love*. Outline each chapter using the Book Outline Form in the appendix.

3. Ella's self-protection device was passive resistance. Is yours the same, or active rebellion or something else? Describe the incident during your abuse that is the best example of your method of self-protection.

4. Can you identify incorrect information that you were given, like "the age of accountability," that assisted in your vulnerability to abuse?

5. Thinking she was responsible for Cal turning affection into sex made Ella feel guilty. What made you feel guilty?

6. Study the word "guilt" in the Bible. You'll need a concordance. Before you quit studying, make sure you know what guilt is and when it is (and is not) appropriate.

Helper's Focus

If you suspect or are certain that you know an abused person, you are probably feeling unsure of yourself. The consequences of abuse in a family are devastating. Making the accusation or helping an adult who was abused as a child to recover are serious commitments. You are probably wondering how you can be sure your suspicion is correct. There are signs of abuse in both children and adults. Remember to talk about your thoughts with God and listen to His answer. God is truth.

These are some of the symptoms of an abused child:

1. The child has a stepfather. In a recent study of perpetrators of incest who were natural fathers versus stepfathers, Diana Russell, Ph.D., Professor of Sociology at Mills College in Oakland, California, found the following: One in forty women who lived with a biological father in childhood was sexually abused by him, compared to one in approximately every six women who lived a significant part of her childhood with a stepfather.

2. The child is withdrawn and sad.

3. The child apologizes often and for things that are not wrong.

4. Lack of balance in opposite-sex relationships. The aggressive child may be promiscuous. The passive child may avoid relationships with men.

5. The child has no close friends.

6. The child is acting out, running away, abusing substances, making poor choices of friends, and so on.

7. The child has age-inappropriate sexual knowledge, has a vaginal infection, frequently masturbates, or is pregnant.

8. The child spends an inordinate amount of time alone with an adult of the opposite sex.

9. The child has frequent nightmares.

10. The child attempts to avoid being alone with a specific adult of the opposite sex.

These are some of the signs of an adult who was abused as a child:

1. Inability to make decisions.
2. Lack of trust of anyone in authority.
3. Suppressed or expressed anger that the person seems incapable of dealing with logically.
4. Scorn for the idea of God as a loving father.
5. Fear of close relationships, especially with someone of the opposite sex.
6. Sexual dysfunction either inside or outside of marriage.
7. Compulsive behaviors such as overeating, substance abuse or codependency.
8. Emotional instability, triggered by memories of childhood, at times in the life cycle such as birth of a child, marriage, adolescence of a child.
9. Feelings of guilt and shame that can't be overcome.
10. Physical problems such as headaches, nervous disorders or vomiting.

These lists are not exhaustive, but they give some insight into signs to look for. If some of these signs exist in a neighbor or in someone you know or are ministering to, find a gentle way to talk with that person.

If the person is a child, you might consider asking, "Is an adult (be specific if you suspect the identity of the abuser, such as "your stepfather") bothering you?" If the answer is yes, ask the child to tell you about it. Be careful to ask open-ended questions that will not lead the child. Get as many details as you can: who the abuser is, what sort of abuse is happening, whether the abuse is happening now, and so on. Then you *must* report the abuse to the authorities in your town. Secrecy is

Satan's great tool in an abusive situation. Until a molester is reported, he will not stop. Until he is reported, he will not get help. In an abusive situation, to love is to tell.

If the person is an adult, it is likely that you have begun to suspect abuse because the person, in talking with you, seems to dance around a hidden issue. Guess. Say something like, "Donna, I could be wrong, but I get the impression that something happened in your past that you might like to talk about with someone. Is that right?" If you feel you can devote hours to listening to this woman, offer to. If not, offer to help her find the assistance she needs. In future chapters we will discuss how to begin a support group for abused adults.

> Whatever you did for one of the least of these brothers
> of mine, you did for Me. (Matthew 25:40)

Chapter Two

The Light at the End of the Tunnel

Femininity. Who needs it?

First it had been deodorant. "How long have your underarms been smelling like that!" Mom had gasped one day in the car as I sat next to her with my arm draped over the back of the seat.

Next it was a bra that felt like someone had cinched a rope around my ribs. And now this. Mom had prepared me for my periods, telling me they would start when I was thirteen or fourteen. She said women had no choice about periods, they were our curse. I could have lived without any of it.

I wondered now whether this meant the end of my tree house days. This "becoming a woman" business made me feel like I was trying to balance on the support board of a picket fence. The fun days of a tomboy lay on one side and the exciting new feelings of a woman waited on the other. The woman side hovered, unknown and frightening, especially the sexual side of it. All the stuff with Cal had happened so fast, and I didn't even know why. So what was being an adult woman going to be like? I wished I could perch on the pickets forever.

Only a month ago I had had my first boy-girl party to celebrate my thirteenth birthday. I had fallen in love with Seth that night.

When I answered the doorbell there he stood, shyly offering me a bunch of daisies. "Maybe you should put them in some watah," he drawled, looking at me under long, dark Southern lashes. My heart ballooned dizzily. The multi-colored daisies bore a pink florist's ribbon and a card that read, "Happy Birthday, *Love*, Seth." I stared at them, amazed. No other boy I knew would do something so romantic.

We danced every slow song together, my cheek against his sweater. With the scent of his after-shave and the soft lights I felt like a princess or a heroine in a book. Everyone seemed to float on air. We told each other everything about ourselves. He came from Georgia and planned to play basketball when we were freshmen next September. He didn't like to swim because he felt self-conscious about being tall and thin. At the end of the party he kissed my cheek. The spot was still burning when I fell asleep.

Tonight we were going to the movies. His mom would drive and pick us up. But now my stomach hurt. I wondered if he would be able to tell that I had changed since school yesterday.

Jessi's scream instantly followed a loud clang in the kitchen. "Ella, help me," she cried as I ran through the door. She already clutched her left hand with her right. Our Pyrex casserole dish lay in pieces in the sink. Blood ran through her fingers.

"Get off the chair and come into the bathroom," I ordered, helping her down. Shoving her arms up level with her shoulders, I commanded, "Hold them there. It'll help stop the bleeding." The water in the bathroom sink turned pink. "Get some of that blood off and I'll put a Band-Aid on it," I said, trying to sound calm. But her hand, cut between her thumb and index finger, bled so hard that the water didn't wash away enough blood to keep up. I glanced at Jessi's gray face, feeling sick to my stomach.

"I told you that dish was too big," she whimpered.

"Here, hold your fingers hard on your wrist, like this," I directed, putting her fingers in the spot over the veins. She kept bleeding. *What will I do if it won't stop?* I thought. *Jessi could die if it doesn't stop bleeding. I'm not sure how to do tourniquets.*

"It's all right, Jessi," I soothed. "It'll stop bleeding in a little while."

The front door opened. I rushed to the bathroom door. "Oh, Cal," I begged, "please help me. Jessi's bleeding!" He came calmly into the bathroom, grasped Jessi's wrist where she'd held it and lifted her hand above her head.

"Give me a wash cloth, Ella," he said. I handed him one, and he put it over the cut. "You'll be all right, Jessi. What happened?" he asked.

"Ella made me wash that big dish. Mom said I didn't have to, but Ella *made* me," Jessi blubbered, now that she wasn't so frightened.

Since she was being a snot, I took off to the irrigation ditch. Nobody used it anymore, and I could almost disappear in it. I sat down and pulled my knees up to my chest, feeling too young and stupid and weird; I wished Mom didn't have to work.

"How'd I know she'd cut herself? I thought she was just being lazy," I sniffed, trying to hold back tears by snatching grass clumps out of the bank. "And besides, I have to worry about her all the time. Nobody cares that my body's coming apart, breaking out in breasts and blood. And I don't want to be a woman." Tears came anyway. I hit the bank with my fist.

Nobody knew I hid in the irrigation ditch except Cal. Now he stooped on the bank. "You didn't do anything wrong, Ella. Jessi will get over it. Why don't you come back to the house with me?" he suggested, holding his hand out to help me up.

As I looked up at him, more tears flowed. "Come on," he coaxed. He lifted me out and put his arm around me as we walked back.

"Your periods have started, huh?" he asked. I nodded, a lump in my throat.

"How'd you know?" I asked.

"I heard you talking to yourself. I'll start using something so you won't get pregnant." He smiled and hugged me tighter, but it didn't feel good.

When Mom got home and Jessi finished telling her how I'd nearly cut her hand off, Cal said, "You guys come into the living room. I want to talk to you."

Cal and Mom sat together on the sofa. Something was up. She smiled at him and he began, "Your mother and I have been looking at a farm outside Maplewood Springs. It's what I've always wanted and the price is right. You two got any objections to moving to the mountains?"

"I don't want to leave my friends. Mama, we don't have to, do we?" Jessi began pleading. The same thought had crossed my mind, but Jessi beat me to it. We had already lost our dad and the farm. I didn't want another change. I finally had a boyfriend. I didn't want to lose Seth when I had just met him. *Could Cal be moving now just to get me away from Seth?* I wondered.

"There's a creek to swim in and a tire swing at the farm, Jessi. And deer come right down to the house," Mom said.

"Yeah?" Jessi's eyes got wide.

Cal looked at me. "Ella, you haven't said anything," he said. "There's lots of room for Eb."

I rubbed one thumbnail with my index finger. "Well, I need some time to think about it," I hedged. Everybody but me seemed to like the idea. I didn't want to be the only one to cast a negative vote. "Mind if I go finish getting ready? Seth will be here pretty soon."

"No, you go ahead." Mom looked silly. "Wouldn't want a hair out of place for your first date."

Seth knocked right on time, and I hurried to the living room. Cal wouldn't talk to Seth and his silence made me edgy. At my birthday party, Cal had watched us every minute. But I had no intention of having the kind of relationship with Seth that I had with Cal. If Seth moved too fast, I would tell him to stop, and I wouldn't waste any time finding something else to do. But so far Seth had treated me only with gentle courtesy.

Seth kissed me twice that night. I felt like our destinies were intertwined for eternity as we walked toward his mother's car after the movie. I, who had planned never to love anyone after Daddy. *Maybe people aren't capable of keeping love out of their lives*, I thought. *Maybe I made an impossible promise to myself.*

Cal left me alone as far as sex was concerned that week. It was fun to do things like before, without the pressure of sex. But the day after my period ended, as soon as Mom had gone to work and I saw Jessi running down the road toward Mary Ellen's, Cal stood near, gazing at me.

"Cal, we have to stop. It's not right. You're married to Mom. Seth loves me, *and I love him*," I pleaded for him to understand. I started for the kitchen to make dinner.

But he followed me, saying, "But you love me too. You can love Seth and me. Your mother doesn't know; she's not hurt. And she's so stiff. Please don't turn away, I need you," he begged, catching my arm. "We matter to each other."

"I do love you, but it's wrong, Cal. It makes me feel dirty. Good women don't do this. They don't even have intercourse until after they're married. They save it for their husbands. I'd at least like to try to save myself from now on," I said.

He turned to lean on the kitchen counter. "You and Seth must be having a pretty good time." He didn't look at me.

I felt sick to my stomach. "We aren't! Just shut up!" I screamed. Cal had never talked to me like this before. "Seth isn't like you. He cares about me because he thinks I'm a nice person and that's all." I felt dirty, guilty and alone again. Cal would probably separate me from Seth with this ugliness—either by making me feel so worthless that I couldn't inflict myself on Seth, or worse, by telling Seth something about me. I would end up with no one, at least no one I wanted.

"Okay. I'm sorry," Cal said, finally meeting my eyes.

Words are easy to fling around, I thought.

He lit a cigarette. "You think your mother's a good woman?"

"Yes, you know how she is. What you and I do isn't fair to her."

Cal put his arm around me and told me that my mother had compromised her principles with him. The principles that she'd sworn to me were right, that she demanded I follow.

I pulled away. "No, that's not true, she wouldn't," I cried, the firm right and wrong of my mother's world collapsing to meet the ashes of my own. "Oh, Cal please, if it's a lie, don't lie," I whimpered. I began to grope for a secure ground of reality. But all I could hear was Cal.

"It's not a lie," he said, catching my arm again, pulling me close, that look in his eye.

Maybe nothing people do really matters at all, for right or for wrong. I drifted away in my mind for the time he took, mentally playing the piano louder and louder, concentrating on my fingers making the keys dance, turning myself into a whole orchestra, until Cal slumped on me.

Even though I missed Seth so bad that my heart felt squeezed when I thought of him, I did like the farm in Maplewood Springs. Jessi was crazy about the tire swing and the deer. I liked the sound of the pine trees when the breeze blew. Eb and I could ride forever without seeing a road.

One night a few months after we moved, Cal and I were down at the barn milking our new cow, Holly. The lady who lived there before us had painted a cow looking over a fence on the door to the milking side and three horse's heads where you went into the horse stalls. Up at the top was a sunburst of yellow, white and orange. I poured Holly's grain in the box while Cal wiped down her udder. She had big, nearly black eyes and a soft, warm, tan hide that moved back and forth when flies landed on her. She loved me to scratch the flat part of her head between her eyes while Cal was milking her.

"Ella," Cal called. "I was thinking of mating Holly with Abner after we're done milking her. Can you open the gate and let Abner in?

Abner was small for a bull, but very muscular, and his head was tremendous. As I opened the gate, Holly mooed her soft, low moo, and Abner went through without me even jumping off. I didn't want to be there, so I said, "I'm going to feed Eb."

I scooped up Eb's oats and ran out to the corral. He was stamping one foot and then the other, shaking a swarm of flies loose each time. "Eb, there's sex everywhere. Cal says I'm oversexed. Only he's the one who always bugs me. But his kisses do make my body feel warm, even though my head doesn't want to. Is that oversexed, Eb?" Eb moved the oats in the scoop around with his whiskery lips. He always acted like I had hidden the best one right at the bottom.

"Now he's got me cloistered up here and he's after me every other day. I don't have any friends. Everything's a mess. And Seth hasn't written in two weeks; he's already forgetting me." Eb raised his head, his eyes seeing behind me.

Cal had decided we should "try out" the loft. He had one of my grandmother's, *Daddy's* mother's, quilts up there. I felt dirtier. He was tucking in his shirt when Mom called.

"Cal! Ella!" she shouted. She was coming right under the loft window.

I froze.

Cal whispered, "Stay up here and don't move." Fastening the buttons on his jeans, he hollered, "I'm up here, Myrna! Be careful!" And he shoved a bale of straw off the loft.

The barn door slid open. "Where's Ella? Dinner's been ready for forty-five minutes!"

I held my breath.

"She said she was going to feed Eb," Cal said offhandedly as he climbed down the ladder.

"Ella!" Mom shouted toward the corral.

Don't move echoed in my head.

"Elllllaaaaaa!" Mom shouted again.

In my mind I could see her face appearing over the edge of the loft.

"Let's go eat," Cal said. "She probably got carried away with exploring. She'll turn up before dark." The door slid shut.

"She spends more time outside with you than you and I spend anywhere," Mom complained as they turned Holly and Abner out.

"You don't like the outdoors the way she does, and you know it," Cal said good naturedly.

I rolled over and looked out the window as they disappeared up the hill. *I wonder how many times Cal has been in this position. He seems to think of what to do awfully fast. I ought to tell her. No, I can't. It would hurt her too much. Everyone she loves would become an enemy. It's too much.*

Halfway down the ladder, I jumped off. I let Eb out of the corral and he followed me down to the creek. The water was cold. I loved the gurgling water and the sun dappling the leaves of the trees and ferns there. The creek had replaced the irrigation ditch as my place to go when I felt emotional, especially unhappy. Now I wondered how beauty like this could exist alongside the ugliness of my life.

"I sure hope Cal's right about being sterile because of that kidney infection," I said to Eb. Cal had stopped using condoms when we moved.

The next day, Mom sat in her pink sweatshirt and jeans drinking coffee at the kitchen table with her friend, Pearl, when I came up from the garden with my shirt front full of vegetables.

"It's no denomination," Pearl said. "Just a little church the hill people started so we can worship." Pearl had gray hair even though she was the same age as Mom.

"Ella, wash those and put them away. I hate it when you bring vegetables when I'm not ready," Mom said as I dumped my shirt out on the pink formica drainboard.

"Cal told me to," I replied, separating the carrots, Swiss chard, onions and tomatoes. Out the window I could see Jessi goofing off up the hill, twirling madly in the tire swing. *At least I help*, I thought. *Why doesn't Mom appreciate me?*

"I'd like for Jessica and Ella to go. It's been ages since they went to Sunday school," Mom said, turning back to Pearl. She had a way of saying critical things to someone else that were really intended for people she wasn't talking to. And this one didn't make sense because I wasn't responsible for driving us to church; I didn't have a license yet.

"You'd be in my class, Ella," Pearl said, smiling at me. "And we sure could use a pianist. Think you could play for church?"

I started washing dirt off the carrots and putting them in the dish drainer to dry. "I guess. What do you wear?" The people at churches we'd been to in Newkirk were always dressed up real fancy. Jessi and I didn't go often. It seemed to me that the people only went to see who had the prettiest clothes. We never went to Sunday school because we didn't know the answers to the questions the teacher asked.

"Oh, whatever you feel comfortable in," Pearl answered. "The hill folks's best mostly consists of overalls and clean shirts." That sounded great to me—I liked jeans much better than dresses.

I started at Maplewood Springs High School in September and forgot about the little church Pearl went to, until Christmas. On the Sunday before Christmas, Mom, Cal, Jessi and I got dressed and met Pearl in front of the whitewashed, one-room church. Snow clung to the branches of the pines near the church, making them look like a St. Bernard's paws. Pearl *was* my Sunday school teacher like she had said. I was the only one in her class that day.

She started off with, "Do you know why Jesus was born, Ella?"

I tried to think of an answer. "No," I said finally. *This is going to be exactly like Newkirk*, I thought.

"Well, let's see, do you know Who His Father was?" Pearl asked.

"Joseph," I said, feeling relieved that I at least knew something.

"Sort of," Pearl said. "Actually God was Jesus' Father. Joseph was sort of a human stand-in, like in a play when the real actor can't be there and they put in someone else to take his place."

"Why did God do that, Pearl?" I asked.

Pearl looked at me for a while, like she wondered if I really wanted to know. Then she said, "The world hasn't changed much since Jesus was born. Everyone still looks out for himself and doesn't care about anybody else, about the same as in the days when the people in the Bible were living. They'd forgotten the Ten Commandments and everything else God said, just like us."

I hoped she wouldn't ask me what the Ten Commandments were.

Pearl shut the little Sunday school booklet. "God let Jesus be born as a human, but He was also still God. He wanted to remind people of Who He is and what He put us here for."

"But Pearl, why didn't God just be Jesus' Father Himself?"

"Oh, I see what you want to know. Because Mary was an unwed mother and she needed Joseph to protect her, and later Jesus needed Joseph's instruction in growing up. God is a spirit, and though He's with us, people don't see Him, so He often uses people to do the things He wants done." She paused. "Ella, you seem to need to go at your own speed instead of out of the lesson book. How about if we start in Matthew and read? Call me each Friday and on Sunday we'll talk about the questions you give me."

I was elated! I really wanted to understand who Jesus was. It had simply been embarrassing before.

We all sat close to the heater during the preaching. Everybody smiled and I felt cozy, in a *church*. The minister—a short, skinny man with a bald spot and kind eyes—repeated again and again, in different words, how Jesus was knocking on our hearts and we should be saved. Even though he kept repeating the same thought, he was better than the preacher in Newkirk. I hadn't even been able to understand what that one was talking about.

Everyone seemed to have been saved except me. The preacher kept saying that God loves each of us and wants us to know Him. I had always thought God's job wasn't loving me, but watching me, making sure I wasn't doing wrong. And lately I was surprised He hadn't zapped me, since I thought He was mostly concerned with punishing bad people. This God was a different God than I had thought He was.

When the service was over, the minister shook hands with people in a little room at the back door. Shaking my hand, he said, "Pearl tells me you play the piano, Miss Wainwright."

"Yes, sir," I said, looking at a bunch of magazines lying on a table so I wouldn't have to look at him. I had an idea he might be able to look through my eyes and know what Cal and I were doing.

"Would you consider playing for us next Sunday?" he asked. "If I could have time to learn the songs," I said. He picked up a hymnal and chose three songs. Writing the numbers on a piece of paper, he handed the book to me.

A heavy, gray-headed lady in a plaid cotton dress, who stood waiting to shake hands with the minister, hugged me and said, "Oh, it'll be just fine to have music again." She smelled like vanilla and I liked her right away.

School started again and I moved into a weekly routine of school and church. Cal successfully ran off any boys who showed interest in me and we continued to have sex about every other day, as if we were married.

I moved through my sophomore and junior years in the same routine, without making any good friends at school. Everybody's friendships had begun in elementary school and I was a fifth wheel. Besides, friends shared confidences. Thinking of my secrets, I avoided making close friends. There were people who liked me pretty well, and I was president of a lot of clubs. But that was mostly because nobody else wanted to do the work a president had to do. All my school relationships stayed superficial.

One boy that Cal didn't know about always saved me a seat on the bus, and would sing funny Roger Miller songs all the way to school and home again. One day at the beginning of our senior year, he said, "Ella, are you eating too much? You're gaining weight."

"No," I answered, and changed the subject. But fear rose in the pit of my stomach. I was trying not to admit, even to myself, that I might be pregnant.

I pretended I didn't see that boy afterward and sat with somebody, anybody else. I'd missed four periods, and my stomach had a little paunch—not much, but noticeable.

I'd been trying to tell myself that I was working too hard on the club activities. That's why I tired easily and slept often. After the boy noticed the weight gain, I couldn't deny my fear anymore. But every time I tried to decide what to do, I came to ugly futures, so I pushed the thoughts out of my head.

I tumbled with a vengeance during gym class after that. When I jumped off Eb, I hit the ground hard. But my efforts to stop the pregnancy only resulted in an expanding waistline.

At church I felt like a first-class hypocrite. Pearl had told me that Jesus wanted me to know Him personally. My acceptance of a friendship with Jesus was what the minister meant about "knocking on my heart" and "saved." The more I read about Jesus, the nicer He seemed. He liked children and He told people to love each other and think of others first. But I didn't think He would want to know me, no matter what Pearl said. He was sinless and my body was beginning to show proof that I wasn't, by a long shot.

Finally, one day when Cal and I were harrowing the garden, I made up my mind to tell him. While Cal pulled with the tractor, my job was to ride the harrow so it would dig deeply into the soil. When we were finished and Cal turned the engine off, I said, "Cal, I need to talk to you about something."

"Yeah?"

"Um, I don't think you're sterile."

He looked at me sharply. "I *thought* it had been a long time since your last period. Have you been with someone at school?"

I jumped off the harrow and ran, swiping at the dirt on my face that was blowing into my eyes. My eyes were so full of tears that I couldn't see where I was going. The tractor started and I ran harder.

"Ella!" Cal yelled over the engine. He was catching up with me.

I tripped over a tree root and fell. The engine stopped, but I pushed up and ran again.

He caught me as I got to the trees on Digger's Ridge. "Stop!" he yelled. "I'm sorry! Listen to me! I'm sorry." He pulled me down in the pine needles and held onto me until I stopped trying to get away.

When he caught his breath, he asked, "Are you sure you're pregnant?"

I kept my head down. He wouldn't see me cry; I wouldn't let him. When my tears stopped, I wiped my face again and said, "I haven't been to a doctor, but I haven't had a period in five months and my stomach expands every day." I bit my words off. After every-other-day for years, how could he try to blame someone else, to blame *me?* How could he?!

Telling Cal forced me to face the fact that I was actually, unchangeably, going to have his baby. If any shred of confusion was left in me about the morality of sexual involvement with my stepfather, he banished it with his explanation of what my pregnancy meant.

"Ella, if your mother, or anyone, finds out about us, I'll go to jail." He spoke so directly.

What happened to "It doesn't hurt anyone. It's only between us. Love is good"?

"How far along are you? His question interrupted my thoughts.

"I think five months," I answered. "Cal, I don't know what to do. What do I do with a baby? I can't keep this from Mom. The baby will *come.*"

He sat weakly fingering pine needles. I felt miserable. At last he suggested, "You can say you were raped. Say that you waited so long to tell because he threatened to hurt Jessi. That way, you won't be in trouble either." He stopped and put his hand on mine. "Or we could go away. I could get you a ring and we could start a new life somewhere else."

I looked closely at him. He was serious! He was willing to tear up our whole family for me. More fear and deception, more hiding and dark future. Or, I could choose to be an unwed mother, a phony victim of rape. On one hand I was scared to be alone with a secret, facing a baby. On the other hand, he couldn't ignore his obligation to Mom and Jessi and leave them. I had wanted Cal as a friend, not as a husband or whatever.

"I can't, Cal. I mean, I'll lie about rape, but you can't leave Mom." I looked away. His eyes looked disappointed. "Cal, I'm not sure I can make Mom believe me. I'm a bad liar."

"Well, we'll work it out," he said. He smiled wanly, trying to make the pregnancy seem less a catastrophe, I guess. "Now, go wash your face. You look like a mud pie," he said.

Cal helped me devise the whole story. He thought Mom would keep it in the family to protect us all from the questions of authorities. The thought of such a lie and what Mom would do because of her "black is black and white is white" philosophy, if she knew the truth, made me cry so hard that I could hardly tell her. "A man forced me off the road on my way home from a drama club meeting," I sputtered between sobs.

"Oh, Ella," Mom cried. "Ella, honey."

And Jessi said, "I love you, Ella. And nobody better say anything bad about *my* sister."

I wanted to die.

I went to school one more week. I couldn't stand wondering if someone in gym would glimpse the stretch marks developing at the sides of my stomach. Mom told Mr. Grant, my counselor, that I had been raped. He helped Mom arrange tutoring from my English and civics teachers so that I could graduate.

The deceit had my life tied up with a neat bow. But there was still the baby. When Mom told Daddy, he suggested an abortion. I couldn't do that—this was my baby. Being his dependable self, Cal suggested letting someone adopt it and I screamed at him. Mom suggested that if I gave my baby to someone else, I would probably look for it the rest of my life. I guess that's when I realized that letting Mom and Cal adopt the baby would at least let me know it was okay and keep the responsibility where it belonged.

After dinner one night I meekly asked, "Mom, will you adopt my baby?"

"I'll adopt it if you understand that the baby will remain mine and Cal's. I couldn't stand it if you gave it to me and then took it back."

I agreed.

At each visit to the doctor's waiting room I sat with my right hand over my left for three months, thinking people might not realize I wasn't married. In the examining room I ignored the doctor's innuendos about my rape being odd when there was evidence that I was continuing to have sex. Though I feared he was supposed to, he never confronted me directly about who I was having sex with.

The day I delivered my daughter, I ignored the first pain, a light tremor. We had driven the thirty miles to Springville to have dinner out in celebration of my eighteenth birthday. I was only ten minutes from the hospital, and our enchiladas hadn't come yet. The baby could wait, if this wasn't another false alarm.

The baby, and my whole life, seemed like an illustration in a thick, blue book on sex that Mom kept at home. It explained the physiology of sex, but one page had an illustration of two stairways that frightened me. A girl stood at the bottom where both stairways started. She could climb either set. One set illustrated a woman partying and living loosely through her life, not a woman you could trust. The other woman became a mother, with one man and housework. At the end of the partying stairway sat the woman, now a lonely, wrinkled old hag. At the end of the motherhood stairway the woman had become a grandmother, playing with her grandchildren. *I'm halfway up toward the hag*, I thought. I felt again the despair that my life would never amount to anything, sitting there waiting for my baby to come.

Mom asked me something about diapers.

"What, Mom?"

"I'm not sure we bought enough diapers. Do you think we should get another dozen while we're in town?" she asked.

I watched the Mexican waitress carrying steaming dishes to other people's tables. She looked young and carefree, a mocking contrast to me. I wished silently that Mom would figure out the stupid diapers for herself. Shouldn't responsibility go with reward? On the other hand, it could be that Mom was merely trying to make me feel included again. Mentally slapping myself, I tried to balance my thinking. *It's great of her to take this baby. I asked her to adopt it. Why do I feel so resentful of her?* I wondered.

Deep inside me a suspicion clawed. How could she see all the time Cal and I spent together and the way we treated each other and not guess? Once Nan's father had even told her that he thought Cal and I were too "friendly." Mom had become really angry, but asked no questions.

No. My mind staggered. Oh, no. Mom couldn't suspect that Cal and I had sex or where the baby came from. She trusted me and she trusted him. I couldn't allow myself to think these thoughts.

My delivery interrupted my birthday dinner nevertheless. We left the restaurant and drove quickly to the hospital. I was glad Jessi had chosen to spend the night with a friend.

The nurse who took me to the obstetrical ward wore a white cap, white dress, white shoes, and she herself looked stern and white. I wondered whether she already "knew" about me. She made me sit in a wheel chair. "Hospital rules," she said, not seeing me. As she rolled me away, I lost track of Mom and Cal.

I shouldn't be living this, I thought somewhere in the midst of the pains and delivery preparations. *I'm not old enough. I'm not ready. I have no husband.* A stronger pain banished my thoughts.

I gripped the sides of the mattress. Panting, I tried to think of something other than this pain, but I couldn't escape it. *They're looking at me. I have to get control.*

I don't remember what happened in delivery. They told me my daughter came breach, feet first. It seemed appropriate. A backward birth to match her conception. Through the night a friendly black nurse named Rachel kept taking my temperature and checking the I.V. bottle. Straightening my covers, she said, "Y'oughta sleep, honey, dat lidda gul gonna be keepin' everybody up soons' ya'll get ha' home. Wanna pill fo' it?"

"No thanks, I'll try on my own. When does the I.V. come out?"

"When it's empty, suga', notha' twenny minutes. Gets yoah strength back up. Go'on ta sleep now."

In the morning I was glad when it was Rachel who brought Kathryn to me. The other nurses called me "Mrs. Wainwright," while they stared at their shoes. Rachel called me "Ella." She unwrapped Kathryn and placed her in my arms. "You has a bootiful lidda daughta', Ella," she said. She put a bottle of formula on the bed table. Tears filled my eyes. Looking at Kathryn's tiny face, I said, "Thank you, Rachel." She patted my shoulder and left, shutting the door quietly.

I uncovered Kathryn to see all her fingers and toes. "Baby girl, you are mine for three days, and I'm going to love you as much as I can," I told her. My heart wanted to surround Kathryn and gather her in. But inside me somewhere a yellow light came on. Hold it! If I loved Kathryn, then when Mom took her, my heart would shred as she left my arms. Just like when Daddy left. So, Kathryn didn't belong to me, not even for these three days.

I wrapped her back into her blanket. She gazed at me with her milk-blue eyes. I swished my lips across her cheek. It felt softer than anything I'd ever touched. She nuzzled at my breast the way a baby calf does his mother's udder. I knew I shouldn't —it would be almost sinful because I wouldn't be her mother for long—but I unbuttoned my gown anyway and let her nurse. She made little murmurs, her eyes almost shut.

The door opened and a doctor sauntered in. I covered Kathryn and me. "I'm Dr. Wyatt, your baby's pediatrician. I've checked your daughter and she's perfect."

"I'm glad," I replied.

He sat on the edge of the bed. "Have you thought about what you're going to do with her?"

"My mother and stepfather are going to adopt her."

"I'm going to be blunt." He looked disapproving. "Isn't it a little selfish and somewhat lacking in courage to give her away? Your mother certainly can't nurse her like that, and you'd look strange doing it as her sister."

"I'm just barely eighteen and I don't have a job. I can't give her anything. I have a younger sister who would be affected." My breath was starting to come in gasps. "I really thought about it. Giving her to Mom and Cal seemed the best for her." Close to tears, I loosed Kathryn from my breast under the covers and brought her out.

"How will you feel when people congratulate your mother and your head screams, 'But she's mine!'?" He looked intently at me.

"I'm going away to school," I answered almost inaudibly.

"Well, I think you should give it some more thought." He stood to go. I could only look at him.

After he left, I began to cry. I snuggled my face into Kathryn's blanket. "Little Kery, if I keep you, Cal will see me as his illegitimate wife. There'll be no future for me but adultery, forever. I can't keep you. The doctor doesn't *know*."

I put my finger inside her fist. "Kery. That's a good name for you. You can be Kathryn when you grow up."

Rachel pushed open the door. "Time to go now. You rest, Ella." She bundled Kery up. "I means it, lay back dere and shut yo' eyes," she ordered, shaking her finger at me.

A little later, I loosened a knot in the embroidery thread I was using to sew a lamb onto a bib, when a lady opened the door and said, "Mrs. Wainwright?"

"Yes," I lied. I noticed she didn't wear a white uniform and she carried a clipboard with papers on it.

"Mrs. Wainwright, we need some information for your baby's birth certificate."

"Okay."

"What is your full name?"

"Elizabeth Ellen Wainwright."

"And the father's full name?"

What shall I say? I wondered. "I don't know."

"I see, unknown." She wrote on the clipboard. "The baby's name?"

She didn't even hesitate. *Someday, when I meet a girl like me, I won't act like I expect her to have slept with so many men that she doesn't know who the father of her baby is.*

"Kathryn Lee."

"Kathryn Lee what?"

"Kathryn Lee ... Phillips."

"Phillips?"

"Yes."

"Have you had any other children?" still staring at her clipboard.

"No." I wanted to tell her that I wasn't a professional.

"Thank you, Mrs. Wainwright."

"You're welcome." It surprised me that she didn't march out. *Kery's name should be Phillips, naturally. Maybe, just maybe, Mom will realize what I'm trying to tell her, but can't.*

"Please God, just this once, let her read between the lines

and help me stop this relationship," I whispered. I wished, if God really existed, that He would help me keep Cal's love but get rid of the sex.

Mr. Grant said that Jesus and God are the same. God became a person for us, and that was Jesus. He also said that Jesus wanted each person to give control of his or her life to Him, that we don't automatically belong to God when we're born.

I hadn't heard that before we started going to the little church. *Maybe it's similar to Kery being mine, but legally Mom's. Who do I belong to now?* I wondered.

Cal and Mom arrived as I was coming out of the bathroom after my shower, feeling much better but very weak. Cal looked dejected and avoided eye contact with me.

"We saw her last night, Ella, and she's beautiful," Mom said. "We didn't bother you because you were asleep."

I had been awake until midnight, but why shoot holes in her alibi?

She placed some books where the bottle of formula had been. "Jack said all these would be good for you to read." Jack was my senior English teacher.

"You didn't mind her having brown hair?" I asked.

"No, sweetie," Mom said. She smiled the smile she lied with.

Cal's face was set; Kery's hair came from him. He said nothing.

"I put 'Phillips' on her birth certificate for her last name," I said. Cal glanced at me sharply.

But when Mom said, "Oh, you didn't need to; they seal it and give her a new one when the adoption is final," he relaxed. He turned on the TV and applause filled the room.

"Turn it down, Cal," Mom ordered. "We came to see Ella. Can't you stop watching television for a little while?"

"Myrna, maybe we better go. Ella looks tired," Cal suggested.

"Cal, we just got here," Mom fired back at him, then turned to me. "I wanted to see you while you were in labor, Ella, but they insisted they were taking you for X-rays and I should wait. Next thing we knew, they were wheeling you into delivery."

"It all happened so fast," I said.

"No kidding, three hours from the time we pulled up," Mom said. "You're a real peasant."

Another comment with Mom's famous double-entendre. Peasants tend to delivery babies easily, and to be a little portly.

"I got the crib set up in your bedroom," Cal offered.

"In *my* room?" I asked.

"Yes," Mom said. "We thought you might like to have her with you until you go to school." I was glad, but I wondered if Mom had simply found a way to miss the 2 A.M. feedings.

Mom leaned conspiratorially close to me and asked, "How are your stitches?" as if Cal didn't know about stitches, and as if I were doing a perfectly normal thing having a baby with no husband. Cal's first wife had Spider Legs before he married Mom. He knew about stitches. I just smiled and shrugged.

"Listen, honey, we'll see you tomorrow. I have some shopping to do. You'll be home soon. Read the books—that'll keep you busy. Ready, Cal? She sure is a pretty baby, Ella." Mom headed out the door. Cal came over to the bed and gave me a long kiss. Touching my cheek, he asked, "Are you all right?"

"Yes, I am. Did anybody tell Daddy?" I asked.

"I'll have your mother call him for you." He turned and left.

Self-Assessment Guide

1. When did you begin to know you were being abused? What was happening? How did you feel? Be descriptive.

2. It is sometimes difficult to admit that you come from a dysfunctional family. Describe the problems you notice in

Ella's family relationships. Then compare what you find in your relationship with your own family.

3. Look over these first two chapters and list the situations where being a *child* made Ella susceptible to abuse. Then look at your own abuse for similarities and contrasts in the imbalance of power between an adult and a child.

4. Describe your encounters with the opposite sex, other than your abuser, during your abuse. Include any thoughts on how abuse affected these relationships or how the relationships may have affected the abuse.

5. List the manifestations of fear that Ella displays in the first two chapters. What part did fear play in your abuse? Have you carried fear into your adult life? Write your feelings about this in your journal.

6. Read 1 John 4 looking for the relationship between fear and love. Use your journal to explain what the passage says about the fear-love relationship, and how what you learn affects what you believe about Jesus. What effect should this have on your life?

7. Were there complications, like pregnancy or venereal disease, to your abuse? Write about your reactions to and the outcome of these complications. Can you see any light at the end of these tunnels?

Helper's Focus

Every sexually abused person feels guilty. Generally, she (or he) has taken the gradual initial manipulation she fell for, or the fact that she didn't tell anyone, and blown it into responsibility for all that has happened.

Assuming the abuse is over, the first issue to address is this guilt. It stands in the path of all other issues the victim must work through. The first thing to say to a person who reveals she is a victim of childhood sexual abuse is, "You were not responsible. A child isn't powerful enough to prevent someone older who is bent on abuse."

You will find yourself saying this again and again. The guilt the victim feels is deeply ingrained. You would do well to connect the victim with others who will repeat, "You were not responsible. A child isn't powerful enough to prevent someone older who is bent on abuse," as many times as necessary for the victim to allow it to sink in. Involving others must be taken a step at a time, but it usually takes more than one person to convince the victim that she's not responsible for being abused.

Victims develop what we call "plastic skin." Initially, its purpose is to avoid pain. Plastic skin serves to keep out feelings and experiences that hurt. The victim doesn't realize it when she's building the defense, but plastic skin also keeps out compliments and truth. The victim's helper has to poke away at this plastic skin, like trying to bend a credit card. Eventually you will get through, but it takes a long time and a commitment to say, "You were not responsible" until the day you finally hear the victim say, "I was not responsible," usually with great emotion.

The victim will feel guilty about other issues in addition to that of her responsibility for the abuse. She may have consolidated these issues and allowed them collectively to "prove" to her that she deserves her guilt for the entire episode of abuse. These issues can range from guilt over weakness in the face of manipulation to guilt over pleasurable physical responses to abusive sexual experiences. If she has been abused by more than one person, she may even consider herself the catalyst. She may assume that she personally is the problem and embrace the guilt.

The helper listens as the victim talks these issues out. If the victim assumes responsibility that isn't hers while doing this work, the helper points out again that the victim is not responsible. An effective tool to accomplish this is to have the victim choose an event from her abuse that causes her to feel guilt. She relives this event as if she were an adult neighbor of her childhood family. When the victim watches the action from this detached adult perspective, the helper may suggest the truth if the victim still has trouble recognizing reality. With this sort of help, the victim often will see, on her own, the distortions that caused her to accept inappropriate guilt.

When the victim has become pregnant as a result of the abuse, the growing child is an ever-present reminder, no matter how hard the victim may try to disassociate her innocent child from her abuser. Feelings such as guilt over the child's existence, the embarrassment to her family, her association of the child with the abuse, her decision about what to do with the child, and so on, can be dealt with. The helper encourages the victim to make well-thought-out, responsible decisions from here on. The idea the helper espouses is, "What has been done by others is done. But what you do now is no longer influenced by them. You can choose to do the responsible, right thing."

Given that abortion is only adding another wrong to a string of wrongs, the victim facing delivery of a child has the following three alternatives, none of them completely satisfying:

- Keep the child herself
  - *Drawbacks*: Immaturity, lack of financial stability, inability to overcome connection of child to abuse

- Adoption by a family member
  - *Drawbacks*: Emotional attachment and continuing pain, inability to step aside as mother

- Adoption by an outside party
  - *Drawbacks*: Loss and possibility that she will lose track of child, dissatisfaction with adoptive family

The drawbacks to making a child available for an outside adoption are not as severe as they have been in the past. Adoptions can be arranged in which the natural mother chooses and meets the new parents. She can see her child occasionally in its early years and have a gentler leavetaking. This possibility should be thoroughly researched by the victim and the decision left to her. The helper may serve as a barrier between the victim and other interested parties to give the victim the space to consider and make this decision herself.

Ministry to the abused requires a great deal of listening and redirection of dysfunctional thinking. The person who accepts the responsibility to help will probably want to set a guideline regarding how much time can be spent weekly working with the victim. This boundary helps each person balance his or her own commitment and life. The process should be flexible, recognizing that intense emotions will come in waves. Recovery is hard. When the waves get too high, the victim should be allowed to get out of the water. When the waves are simply a little higher than the last waves, the victim should be encouraged to take God's hand and float through them. Most important, cover the recovery process with prayer, and keep short accounts with God (seek His forgiveness for sin immediately). The wisdom to heal, and healing itself, come from Him.

Chapter Three

Which Way Is Up?

After Kery and I came home from the hospital, Cal barely talked to me anymore. I spent my days looking after Jessi, and now Kery, whose needs took away the time I could spend outside. I didn't blame them for the loss of my freedom. Mom had determined that her working made me responsible for everything at home. When the responsibility grew, how to handle it became my problem. Along with ignoring my presence, Cal made no move to resume the sex that the doctor had cautioned me to stop before delivery. Although I didn't miss the sex, I now had no companion. I tried to replace the times we'd had fun with preparing to go to college. But inside I wanted someone to talk to, someone who accepted me. For whatever reason, Mom didn't accept me. Jessi loved me, but she was so young. Now that I was out of school, we were pretty much to ourselves on the farm and there was no one to relate to—until the night of Mom's baby shower.

Until that night, I had tried not to approach Cal about anything, though I felt so confused about how he acted. *He's mad that I didn't give her up for adoption*, I would think. *No, he just never really loved me and he realizes sex could mean another baby. Now that it costs him something, his game is over.* My mind had tried dozens of alternatives as the summer had progressed.

Maybe I looked for his comfort this night because I felt consumed by the loss. Keeping my promise to Mom never to take Kery back didn't quiet the scream of my emotions for my baby. All those middle-aged women exclaiming over her had exactly the effect the pediatrician had predicted. I even considered nonchalantly removing her from her little seat on the table and walking out, never to return.

When only the first guests had helped themselves to coffee, I couldn't stand it anymore. I edged between ladies, heading for my room. Jessi stood on the rock hearth of the fireplace. When she saw my face, she followed me.

"Come in and lock the door," I said, dropping on the red and blue quilt on my bed.

"You okay, Ella?" Jessi asked as she flopped down next to me, clasping her knees with her arms. Her shoes were on my quilt, and when I glanced at them, she kicked them off. "I didn't think Mom should put you through this dumb shower in the first place," she added.

I stared up at the knots in the pine ceiling. "She asked me first, Jessi. And I said okay." I started to whisper because I felt like screaming. "I didn't realize how I'd feel." I looked at her, "It's like I have two heads, one a mother and the other a sister, and they can't sit on my neck at the same time. I have to carefully hide the mother one. I want to march out there and shout, 'she's not Myrna's, she's mine!' " My tears were running into my hair, and I wiped them onto the quilt.

Jessi reached out and touched my shoulder. "I'm sorry, Ella," she said.

I looked out the window at the pines swaying in the evening breeze. "School will start soon, and I won't be so close to the problem. If only this dumb shower would end. When I let my feelings show, you're upset too," I said. "I ought to toughen up a little bit. I made the decision. Maybe not the right one, but it's made. How about if I braid your hair?" I offered. She turned her back to me and I made a French braid out of her honey blond hair. Her hair was beautiful. To keep her humble, I always told her that she was a dishwater blond. Finishing with a red ribbon that I got from my nightstand, I said, "We can't stay in here very long or it'll look funny."

Pearl called, "Come on, Myrna, open the presents," as Jessi and I settled near the fireplace.

When she said that, it reminded me of a Sunday school class when she called Jesus a "present." She explained that we didn't do anything to deserve Jesus dying for us; He died as a gift from God. I was confused, so she said Jesus needed to die because God knew we couldn't obey Him. That seemed even harder for me to understand. So she had continued to explain that God is perfect and just, and we are separated from Him because of our disobedience. The punishment for disobeying is death, separation from God. Jesus was God, but He gave up knowing everything and being everywhere to become a man, so he could die instead of us, so we wouldn't have to pay the price of our sin. Phew! Though I was pretty sure some of this had gone over my head, I could tell God loved us more than I had ever imagined. Going back to church after Kery was born had comforted me. I wanted to get more answers to the questions I had about God.

Mom passed us, her perfume following her. "Ella, could you bring me a knife?" she asked.

I squeezed between two women and got her the knife. Sometimes—especially when "that" time of the month had resumed that summer—when I looked at a sharp knife, I thought if I knew the right place to stick it into me, I could get myself out of this world. But I would have to die, not just injure myself, and I couldn't guarantee the outcome.

"Jessi, Ella, why don't you start serving before I finish these? I don't want everyone to fall asleep," Mom said with a sociable smile for her guests. She acted more charming when we had company, which wasn't very often. Mom thought that hospitality was too expensive.

"Jessi, would you serve and I'll cut and pour?" I asked, heading for the cake, a white confection covered with pink umbrellas.

"Sure," she said, picking up two pink napkins and two trays.

After we'd finished serving the women, I put a hunk of cake on a paper plate and poured a mug of coffee. "I'm going to go talk to Cal until this is over," I said.

Jessi shrugged and wandered off into the crowd of pastel ladies.

Cal was leaning back in his recliner, looking out at the pines swaying, the full moon and the stars beginning to twinkle. Fats Domino was singing "Blueberry Hill" on his "oldies" station.

"What are you thinking about?" I asked as I handed him the cake and coffee.

He gestured with the coffee mug. "See those deer in the orchard? I need to stop them from eating the apples."

I hesitated, then asked, "Cal, are you still my friend?"

He kept looking at the orchard. Finally he answered tonelessly, "I'll always love you, Ella." His face was pinched at the sides of his eyes.

I knelt beside his chair and spoke softly enough that the ladies wouldn't overhear. "But something has changed. Are you mad that I got pregnant or that I didn't let Kery be adopted by somebody else? Why can't I go with you anymore? I hate staying in the house, and Mom won't let me ride Eb yet. The sex ended. Couldn't we treat each other as honest friends?"

His eyes probed mine, as if he were trying to find something in my head. He pulled me onto his lap and offered me a bite of cake. "Ella, raising a baby at my age costs so much. Choosing adoption would have helped both you and me. This hurts you too."

My head swelled with anger. "You want free everything!" I spit the words at him. "You're responsible for her and now you want to give her to *strangers!*" I pushed myself off his lap, but he grabbed my arm.

"Settle down," he said. "I'll manage. I thought you wanted the truth."

Keeping my head turned from him, I asked, "I carried her nine months. Doesn't that matter?" Through my tears, the deer's front hooves appeared to melt into the trunks of the trees as they reached for leaves and fruit. "I can't give her away. If you don't want her, I'll think of something else."

"I'll keep her," he whispered. "For you."

For you, so full of meaning. The truth remained that Cal and I did have a relationship, cemented in Kery. Hopelessness smothered me. No one but Cal and I knew the truth, and I couldn't talk about it. Daddy was gone. I had no help to think, to stop. Didn't Cal see that nearly thirty years separated him from me? When I reached twenty-five, he'd be almost fifty-five. There was no sense in what he was saying, and he was the adult. Nothing I said made any difference. Society hated incest, even without an illegitimate baby. But our sin didn't seem to matter to Cal. He couldn't hear my conscience screaming. He had robbed me of a future with any other man because I couldn't live with hiding my past forever. I would always wonder when Cal would tell, and how horrid life would become when my husband threw me out. That look I knew so well gleamed from Cal's eyes again.

I stood up. "Better see who needs a refill," I said. I felt like running as I moved quickly toward the door. He didn't understand what I wanted. He and I were not so much the same as I once had thought. I didn't want what he wanted.

"Wait! Come here," he called to me. I turned, hoping he had reconsidered. He had moved behind me to pull me back to his chair. "You are a wonderful woman, Ella," he whispered and kissed me gently but too long.

"Please, Cal, just cheek kisses," I said, as he pulled my head against his chest. "Okay?"

"We'll try," he said.

Sex started again the next week. It made no difference that since the night of the baby shower I had hugged my side of the truck, dressed before I came out of my room so he didn't even see me in pajamas, and gave him quick kisses when I left the house.

He approached me very subtly the first time. Mom went out to water her roses, and as soon as the door shut behind her, he came up behind me at the sink. Standing close, he silently stroked my hair. When Jessi came in, he moved away as if it were nothing. It happened so quickly, and the affection without pressure felt so good, that I even hoped it might amount to nothing, that somehow we might regain a little semblance of a normal family.

After dinner Mom and I were sitting alone at the table talking while the TV blared in the living room. I kept thinking that I should tell her the whole truth. Then I'd have an adult to keep Cal honest. And yet Mom loved Cal and wouldn't want to leave him—she feared not having enough money to live comfortably. Without him I didn't know if we could even stay off welfare. She'd never go to Daddy for help. That would kill Mom. And I didn't want to live like one of those shabby kids with hunched shoulders and a hanging head, either.

Besides, if the truth all came out, I had no guarantee that Mom would believe me. She might send me away. Daddy would believe me, though. He'd believe me so well that he'd go to jail for trying to kill Cal. Cal would go to jail for sure. I didn't want jail. I didn't hate him—I just wanted to live without the sex. Our family would headline the newspaper. And what about Kery? She'd end up with strangers after all and never know any of us—never know me. Jessi would wind up in the middle, with a tarnished reputation at best. I would make a mess for every one of us. I sat listening to Mom talk about her new job in real estate, knowing I'd never tell her.

The next morning Cal came into the kitchen as I was feeding Kery her cereal, and said, "Ella, what are you doing today?"

"Going to ride Eb," I said. "Mom finally said it's okay."

He took a piece of toast left over from breakfast. "I have some fence to mend, and I could sure use some help."

Wiping cereal off Kery's chin, I answered, "I'd like to help, but I was really looking forward to a ride up Digger's Ridge."

"We'll both ride, then you can help me with the fence."

Mom and Jessi were dressing, but Mom's door was open, so I whispered, "I guess that sounds all right, but no sex, Cal. That's what we said, right?"

As he was about to take a bite of the toast, he took it out of his mouth and whispered, "You sure don't trust me very much."

"I trust you."

Kery turned her head just as I was about to spoon cereal into her mouth, and I nearly dumped it in her ear.

"Aw, shut up and finish feeding this squirt. Meet ya at the barn," Cal said and chucked Kery under the chin before he went out the front door.

"Mom, I'm going to help Cal mend the fence," I shouted.

"Another Saturday shot to crud," she retorted from the bedroom.

I brought Eb a couple of carrots and sugar cubes to celebrate our long-awaited ride. When I put his bridle on, he threw back his head and pranced. Eb wanted to go as much as I did. We rode bareback to all my favorite places, talking about Cal's plans as we went. It felt glorious to have Eb moving under me again, his muscles rhythmically expanding and contracting as we cantered along. We got to where the fence needed mending and stretched barbed wire all afternoon. The stream sparkled in the sun and blue jays squawked and dove at every little bird that flew by. Even with gloves on, I had blisters on my thumbs. Cal hadn't made one single move toward me the entire time. I hoped it meant we could live in the same place without sex. I felt cautiously happy.

"I think she'll hold, Ella," Cal finally said, pulling off his gloves.

"Boy, I like to work until I'm real tired like this," I said, smiling.

He put his arms around me. "I know you do," he said, bending to kiss me. Then he started his old routines.

I couldn't, wouldn't, allow this to happen again. Struggling free, I ran to Eb, threw his reins over his head, jumped onto his back and rode away. "No more!" I screamed, and escaped at a gallop across the meadow. Eb and I would keep going. I wouldn't return to the house to get my clothes—I would just leave. Maybe I could find a ranch that Eb and I could work on somewhere.

We came to the road and I reined Eb toward town. But they would want references. So far, Cal hadn't followed us. Where could I go after I got as far as town? I couldn't stay there because people would only send me home. Further than town were cities. Eb couldn't go to a city; maybe I would have to sell him. My head reeled. I patted Eb's neck. "Slow down, boy, nobody's coming," I soothed, for my benefit as much as his. I released the pressure I had been putting on him with my knees. *I wonder if Mom can keep Jessi and Kery safe without me*, I thought. *She won't know why I ran away. And she doesn't know about Cal. What if Cal trades Jessi for me?*

Cal was waiting for me at the hairpin curve in the road before the ranger station. He must have known a shortcut.

"Where are you going?" he asked, leaning casually on his saddle horn. His buckskin mare snorted a greeting to Eb.

"I don't know," I answered.

"I won't do it anymore," he said. "Come home."

I looked at him. He looked sincere. But how could I know for sure? He appeared sincere when he lied to Mom, encouraging her to go to town and enjoy herself, when what he really wanted was to get me alone. And he lied to me. But I had to think of Jessi and Kery.

"Promise?" I asked.

"I said it, didn't I?" He waited.

"Okay," I said, and turned Eb toward home.

Saturday night Cal asked if we'd like ice cream, and I went for my sweater so I could go to town with everyone to get it. But when I got back, Jessi and Mom had decided to finish watching a TV program and I got stuck going with Cal alone. He pulled into the yard of the feed mill, around where the lights didn't shine. I didn't say anything—it was no use. His thinking was mixed up when it came to sex. Why hadn't I seen his weakness before I became pregnant? My life lay in ruins. What would it accomplish to try to save anything? I felt my mind sliding away from my body, rejecting this happening to me, again. My body degenerated to a piece of meat.

❦   ❦   ❦

At the freshman camp, the guys fidgeted on one side of the outdoor basketball court/dance floor while the girls whispered and giggled on the other. No one danced. The scene reminded me of junior high.

I had chosen the college in Morley, about a hundred miles from Maplewood Springs, partly because it had a rural campus. It also seemed close enough to Kery and far enough away from Cal.

Summer hadn't left the mountain site that served as freshman camp and treetops swayed gently, making blinking lights of the stars. The perfume of lupin drifted to my nose. The

Beatles's "Yesterday" wafted away into the dark. I stood listening to Kelly, a girl from Maplewood Springs, but my eyes kept slipping from her face to a boy.

"Kelly, see that guy who isn't talking to anyone?" I said, pointing with my eyes.

"Yeah," Kelly said. Kelly weighed about forty pounds more than I did and had taken a lot of flak in high school because she acted like a square. But I liked her.

"I'm going to go introduce myself," I said, more confidently than I felt.

"You're gonna march into that gang of *boys?*" she squeaked.

"Yes," I said over my shoulder, walking before I lost my resolve.

He wasn't as tall as Seth, but several inches taller than me. He had sandy hair, cut short, and wore black slacks and a dark shirt that reminded me of Johnny Cash. He was on the slim side, but not skinny. When he realized that I was walking toward him, he looked startled.

"Hi. My name is Ella," I said, smiling.

"I'm Peter," he responded. He had a kind smile. His face looked very young, like a high school sophomore instead of a "college man." He had high cheek bones and deep brown eyes. His eyes were odd, though, as if he had shut a door behind them so no one could read his soul. He shifted feet uneasily when neither of us said anything else.

"My major's English. What's yours?" I asked.

"Math," he answered. "I'm starting my junior year."

"What's a junior doing at freshman camp?" I asked, smiling. He seemed ready to run and I didn't want to scare him off this quick.

He shifted his feet again. "I work at the dorm and they thought I'd like a chance to meet some of the kids."

"No kidding. I'm going to live there too. What's your job at the dorm?"

Taking his hands out of his pockets, he leaned against a pole. "I'm a student cop," he said, watching me closely.

"Do you make enough money to pay your way?"

"No. But I have a summer job at a factory near my parents' home. Covers books and fees." He had noticeably relaxed when I didn't call him a pig for being a student cop.

"Do you work?" he asked.

"No, my dad's paying my way," I said, hoping that wouldn't distance us. Two weeks ago, Jessi and I had returned from what I thought might be our last summer visit with Daddy. He lived in St. Louis now and one night we had gone out to dinner on a river boat. I missed him when I thought about that.

Some of the boys were beginning to ask girls to dance. I longed to dance, free, away from Cal. But Peter didn't ask.

"I'm going to be a preacher when I get out of school," he said. "I preach now, sometimes."

"Oh. That's nice," I answered. Seemed like a strange thing to say when he'd just met me. "You *like* math, huh?"

"Yeah."

"I'm rotten at math. General Math's on my schedule this semester, and I can hardly wait."

"It's easy if you work at it. If you ever need help, I live down at the end of the boys' wing; have someone come and get me."

"Thanks. But you may regret you ever made *that* offer." I laughed. "Do you like to dance?" *Brother, how brazen can I get?*

"I've only danced once, in seventh grade, and I mangled the girl's toes so badly that I've never tried to dance again," he said. "But if you're willing to chance your toes, I'll try anyway."

"Sure," I said. He danced stiff legged, a one-two, one-two that never varied, holding me at arm's length. I felt special instead of odd.

When the music stopped, he asked, "Ella, would you like to go to a concert next Friday?"

I was surprised. "A concert?" He didn't seem the concert type.

"Yes, it's Beethoven, at school."

"I guess so." Beethoven didn't bore me as much as some other classical composers.

❦ ❦ ❦

After the concert we walked back through the fields to the dorm in a misting rain. I finally confessed. "The truth is, Peter, I'm not usually too big on music without singing, or that lasts longer than a long-play record. But Beethoven's crashing and banging held my interest, through the whole thing, too."

Peter laughed. "I enjoy training rats and collecting stamps and all kinds of 'different' stuff," he admitted. "And I don't care about many sports, except track."

"What do you like other than music, rats, stamps and track?" I asked. Once it was out, my question sounded belittling, but Peter didn't seem to notice.

"Lately I've been studying Eastern religions."

"Which ones?"

"Buddhism, Hinduism. I'm really interested in J.D. Salinger. Do you know anything about *Catcher in the Rye* or *Franny and Zoe*?

"No." Mental note: Read *Catcher in the Rye*.

"Didn't you say you were planning to be a preacher? Eastern religions have maharishis or something, not preachers, don't they?"

"Yeah. I just want to see what other people who aren't Protestants think about God."

"I always knew about God. But I didn't learn Jesus said *He* was God until a couple of years ago. Could I call you Pete instead of Peter? Peter sounds so formal."

"Sure, whatever," Pete said. "Ella, what do you think about Jesus?"

"I'm not sure. Do you think He is God, Pete?"

"I'm sure He is." Pete looked thoughtfully at me.

"The people at a little church at home say Jesus *must* be God, or He couldn't raise Himself from the dead. I heard about Jesus at church when I was a kid, but until I started going to the little church I didn't know He brought Himself back to life. I only knew He died on a cross. Do you think He could really reincarnate Himself?"

" 'Reincarnation' means coming back in a different body. Jesus still had nail holes in his hands and feet. If He didn't bring Himself back to life, though, the whole Bible must be a lie," Pete said. "I guess we test His claim by letting Him prove He's God."

I saw a clover in the grass and picked it, twirling it between my thumb and finger.

"How do I test whether He's God?" I asked.

"Well, He answers yes to a prayer when a person admits his sin, asking Jesus to control his life. Christians call this prayer 'receiving salvation.' I guess afterward you'd watch to see if He began to take sin out of your life because of your commitment to Him."

"If I prayed the prayer honestly, I'd already have decided He really is God, wouldn't I?" I asked.

"I imagine so. That's faith. Faith is like stepping out of a plane, believing the parachute on your back will work. Faith pleases God. Nothing comes before faith or matters more to God. It takes only a tiny faith to become a Christian.

"When I read the Bible my faith becomes stronger. His Word hits me as true, so incredibly true. No man who didn't have God's help could have known so much or made himself stay so honest as to write the Bible. I made up my mind to ask Him to save me because of reading the Bible. That probably would be a first step for you too."

As we walked closer to the dorm, I could see Cal's truck parked in the dorm parking lot.

Pete reached for my hand and said, "Ella, we could talk more about Jesus if you'd like."

I glanced at his brown eyes looking down at me. That funny door remained shut behind his eyes, but he appeared sincere too.

"Sure, Pete. I'm already reading the New Testament and I have a list of questions I planned for my Sunday school teacher. But I could ask you as easily. You're sure getting extra homework out of knowing me."

"How about later tonight?" Pete suggested. "I've got homework, other than you, but I could have someone call you when I'm done."

He bent to pick a deep red rose from a bush growing near the road and handed it to me. I put one fingertip on a raindrop at the edge of its petal. Then I touched the water to my tongue, expecting it to taste sweet. "Okay," I said, holding the flower to Pete's nose so he could smell it. "I think I see my stepfather's truck. Maybe you'll get to meet him," I added, trying to sound nonchalant.

Pete reached for my hand again. "Ella, you're awfully nice," he said.

"Thanks, Pete. You're nice too." I took my hand back. There was no point in having a scene with Cal.

We met Cal pacing the lobby.

"Hi, Cal. How come you're here?" I asked. "This is Pete."

"I came down this way and thought I'd stop by and see how the world's treating you," he answered, eyeing Pete. "Hi. Pete, did you say?" he questioned.

Pete held out his hand to shake with Cal. "Hi. Pete Allen. Nice to meet you. See you later, Ella," he said, disappearing down the boys' wing. I wondered if he had noticed Cal's look.

"Would you like to have dinner out?" Cal asked, turning his suspicious look on me.

"I have a lot of homework."

"Have to eat sometime," he observed.

"I'm trying to lose weight," I countered.

He looked me over. "Doing a nice job of it too," he said suggestively. "Come on, Ella. Do I have to hit you over the head with a board? What would we do down here?" He grinned innocently.

Everything, I thought. "Oh, all right," I said, knowing he wouldn't let me refuse anyway.

He took me to dinner, as he promised, but on the way back to the dorm, true to form, he turned right at the corner before we got there, into the farm country.

"Cal, where are we going?" I asked sharply.

"Just for a little drive. I thought you might feel a little cooped up in the dorm." He made a left off the main road.

"It's got to stop," I pleaded, my voice shaking.

"I brought protection," he said.

"Cal, let me out!" I demanded, putting both hands on the door handle. He turned again, onto a one-lane road.

"Peter's better than me, huh, Ella?"

I began to turn the handle. Cal braked and turned the key off. We had stopped far away from anything but cows. When he tried to touch me, I screamed, "I hate you! Leave me alone!"

"Okay. If that's how you want it." His jaw set and he wordlessly turned and jammed the truck into gear.

"I shouldn't have come with you," I muttered. "I'm sorry. I know how things go between us. I don't want sex. Are you really mad at me, Cal?"

He kept driving. When he stopped in front of the dorm, I got out and said "Bye." He didn't even turn his head. The tires squealed as he wheeled out of the parking lot. I felt empty and tired.

Later, when a girl came to say Pete was asking for me, I told her to say that I had come down with something. I didn't blame Pete for Cal, but I just couldn't take the sudden contrast.

The next morning as we chose our breakfasts in the cafeteria line, Pete asked, "You okay, Ella?"

"Yeah, I guess I had indigestion. I'm all right now," I said, keeping my eyes down. *You're a rotten liar,* I thought.

Because college demanded so much homework, the days passed quickly. At Thanksgiving Daddy came to visit, so I stayed at the dorm instead of going home. Sunday we were playing catch in the parking lot and I ran out for a high toss, nearly smashing into Pete coming down the sidewalk. He caught me or I would have fallen. His face turned bright red. Balancing me he muttered, "I'm sorry, I didn't see you."

"No, I wasn't watching where I was going," I replied, and asked, "Want to meet my dad?"

"I thought I met him in September," he said.

"No. You met my stepdad. You need to meet my real dad. He's great."

"Got to watch her," Daddy said, coming up to us, extending his hand to Pete. "She dreams she's a halfback."

"Oh, Daddy!" I couldn't believe he made me sound like a football player, and to *Pete.*

"I'm George Wainwright."

"Hello, Mr. Wainwright. I'm Peter, uh, Pete Allen. Glad to meet you."

Daddy shook Pete's hand. "Call me George," he said. "Like to play some catch?"

"I'd like to, but I have to work," Pete said. "It was nice to meet you, though."

As Pete disappeared into the dorm, Daddy said, "I like him better than the other boys you've introduced me to. Why don't you pay him a little attention?"

"Oh, Daddy." I had become most articulate today. "He's kind of nice, I guess." Daddy liked him, so...

Pete and I got together on Monday to work on my math. After an hour he said, "Ella, let's give your head a break and do something else."

"How about letting me ask you some New Testament questions?" I suggested.

"Shoot," he said.

"Well, why did Jesus have to die at all? Couldn't God *make* everyone act right? I mean Jesus died because of sin, right? And why did someone have to die, and why Jesus?

"Slow down," Pete said, grabbing his head and grimacing. "Too many questions at once give me a headache." He stood and offered me his hand. "Let's move to the sofa, away from the math books. I don't want your opinion of Jesus influenced by your opinion of math."

"Ha!" I said. I curled my legs under me as we sat on the brown and beige plaid sofa, a dorm standard. It looked like he would need quite a while to explain, so I might as well get comfortable.

Pete grinned. "Let's start with sin. Not you and me of course, but sin in general."

"Yeah, right." I grinned back.

"Do you know the story of Adam and Eve?" he asked.

"The one about the apple? I think so. I'm never sure about the stories I've only heard and not read myself."

"It comes down to them having the choice to obey or disobey God. They chose to disobey. Ergo, sin." He looked sheepish. " 'Ergo,' pretty classy vocabulary, wouldn't you say?"

I put my chin on my fist as if I were The Thinker, and said, "But of course."

He resumed, "Satan said we would love life after sin. Life actually turned out to be separated from God, and physical death became part of life as a portion of the punishment for sin. Adam and Eve and their children were meant to be immortal."

I put my hand on his arm. "Stop. They disobeyed God and that was sin?" I asked.

"Right."

"Could little stuff, like saying you didn't eat a cookie when you really did, be sin?" *Crud, I thought, there's probably no one who could keep from being separated from God.*

"Right. Judging your friend for acting like a jerk is a sin too," Pete answered, nodding his head approvingly.

"Pete, everyone in the whole, entire world would be separated from God if one sin does it!" I declared, somewhat loudly. Even the TV junkies in the student lounge looked up.

"Sorry," I murmured.

"But you're right," Pete agreed quietly. "Everyone exists separated from God, except for one thing. God plans way out ahead of Satan. The Bible says He planned from the beginning to save us from our sinfulness through the death of Jesus. Jesus stood as our substitute." He scooted closer to me and began making imaginary marks on the sofa for each point he made.

A dyed-in-the-wool mathematician, I thought.

"The penalty for sin isn't just physical death, though. It's also spiritual death, the separation from God that I already told you about. Satan *knew* that, too. He hates us, so he rejoiced. But God loves us and prepared a sinless part of Himself, His Son, who would pay for sin for all people for all time and reunite us with God. Because He knows everything in all eternity, He prepared even before Satan tricked Eve. But each of us, personally, decides to receive or not receive this gift of salvation from sin through Jesus' death. I can't do it for you; you can't do it for me."

"Pete, I know you understand the connections of all this, but I need to ask some dumb questions," I said.

"Fire away, I'm best at dumb questions," he replied.

"Wait a minute, I have to get my mind to quit whirling." I

changed the position of my legs and scooched into the back of the couch a little more. "Okay. Why did God give Adam and Eve a *choice* to sin?"

Pete offered me a pillow to put behind my back, then continued, "I told you He loves us, right?"

"Yes."

"Love means having the right to choose. Robots who aren't free to say yes or no don't love. And faith involves choice too. Faith pleases God, remember? Put love and faith together, and there *must* be choice. God loves us so much that He gave us choice and also gave us rescue from the foolish choices we make."

"Love includes choice. Got it. Why do all people have to be separated from God just because one couple, ages ago, made one wrong choice?" I wasn't even sure my mind would hold all this.

"Sin is terrible, Ella. Its influence is like a bad smell, like mothballs. It pervades everything. Once our ancestors, Adam and Eve, succumbed to it, it influenced every one of us. Like you said, everyone thinks wrong thoughts. One little sin counts as sin, the same as a whole bunch of big ones." Pete made quotes with his fingers around the word "big."

"Why quotes?" I asked.

"To God, sin is sin, whether it's very hurtful, like murder, or unknown, like a bad thought. One sin makes us sinful."

Unknown, like a bad thought, or like incest, I thought. I threw up my hands. "Enough!" I whispered.

"I meet with a group of kids to pray on Tuesdays," Pete said. "Would you like to go with me tomorrow?"

"I don't know. Can I bring Sherrie?" I asked. I felt kind of silly about watching people pray. What if they asked *me* to pray, out loud? At least my roommate could act as a security blanket.

"Sure. Sherrie can come."

At the prayer meeting everybody sat around a circular table. The boy named Hal, who led this group of Christian kids, said, "Okay, shoot, you guys."

"I have a tough chemistry test coming up," from a girl I hadn't met before who had flaming red hair.

Hal wrote something in a little black notebook. I glanced at Sherrie. She shrugged her shoulders.

"Joe, in 31, has a brother who has just been diagnosed with leukemia. Joe might leave school because of his brother," Pete said.

Another notebook entry.

The kids must have mentioned at least twenty people. Finally, there were no more suggestions and Hal said, "Let's pray. You new guys don't have to pray if you don't feel like it."

Phew!

They all held hands and I began to worry that this was a seance like I'd seen on TV. I thought, *I wonder why these kids pray for people they don't even know. I wonder if when they do this they can see hidden stuff about people—for instance, what's going on between Cal and me.*

The kids prayed for every single person they'd mentioned. Their prayers were worded just as if they were talking to me or anybody. Nobody said "thee" or "thou." They treated God as a *friend.* My seat felt numb by the time they finished. I expected everyone to stand up and shake themselves out.

But they didn't. They opened their eyes, but they still held hands and simply smiled at each other. I felt a very tangible peace. Someone said, "I can almost see Him here in the room with us." I could too, and I even knew who He was: Jesus. Nobody looked at me weird, so they must not have E.S.P. about Cal and me like I had thought. But the atmosphere was amazing.

As we walked down the hall, I asked, "Sherrie, did you feel Jesus in there?"

"It *was* peaceful," she answered with wondering eyes.

Pete caught up with us. "Ella, want to go to the football game with me Saturday?" he asked.

"I can't, Pete, I'm going home this weekend."

"Well, will I see you tonight to get ready for your math test?" he countered.

I couldn't resist myself. "Sure," I said, patting his arm and rolling my eyes up at him. "I know how badly you need me."

He put both his hands around my throat and shook me. "Take that, and that," he snarled facetiously.

"I'll see you guys later," Sherrie said.

Pete and I stayed up late every night that week, first working on math, then on the New Testament. Friday he walked me out to my blue Fiat.

"I'll miss you, Ella, but have a good time," he said. He bent and kissed my cheek.

"Bye, Pete," I responded. After he disappeared inside the dorm I touched the place on my cheek where I could still feel his kiss.

🐦 🐦 🐦

I had tried to time getting home so Mom would be back from work. Her car wasn't in the garage though. Jessi came running out on the porch, her arms wide, like we used to do to Daddy. "Ella! You're home," she cried, smashing into me.

"Hi, Jessi. I missed you. How's Kery?"

"She's good. She's all dressed up for you, Ella. I even put a bow in her hair. Come and look."

Kery lay on a blanket watching cartoons. It amazed me how fast babies got tuned in to television. She looked up when the door shut and started crawling toward us. She could really move. Her curly hair bounced in rhythm with her knees hitting the floor.

Picking her up, I said, "Hey, look what you can do." She hadn't been able to crawl the last time I came home.

"Aba moodo," she said.

"Right," I said. "Isn't that right, Jessi?"

"Of course," Jessi said.

Holding Kery's hand so she wouldn't succeed in putting her finger in my eye, I said, "She looks adorable, Jessi. You really outdid yourself."

"How 'bout me? Do I look adorable?" Cal asked from the doorway.

"Hi, Cal," I said, pecking him on the cheek. I wanted him to know that I wasn't angry with him, but that I didn't want sex.

"What's this?" he protested, turning my face to his and kissing me on the mouth.

"Yuck," Jessi laughed. "Ella, come and see my new bedspread. Cal bought it for me."

Cal, I thought. *Why?*

"Cal likes me better than he used to," Jessi said in her room. "Sometimes he lets me help him like you used to."

"Oh," I said. "How's Mom's work coming?" I wondered if Cal had decided that since I wouldn't have sex with him anymore, he'd switch to Jessi. The bedspread was lilac satin with pillow covers to match.

"Slow. She must not sell real estate very well."

"Have you gone to the little church?"

"No. Nobody wants to go since you're not here. Will we go this Sunday?"

"Yes. We're going to Sunday school too, so you'll have to get moving Sunday morning.

"Okay, I will. You know what, Ella?" Jessi said without looking at me. "My period started." She finally looked up, an amazed expression on her face.

"Are you glad?" I asked.

"I don't know yet," she said.

"Jessi, has Mom told you anything about sex?" Mom had kept telling me she planned to before I went to school, but hadn't that I knew of.

"Yeah, she told me a whole bunch of stuff I could hardly believe. Is it true that men have to...?" She trailed off.

"Yes, it's true, Jessi." I was familiar with how Mom would have told Jessi about intercourse.

"I'm never going to get married," Jessi said, folding her arms strategically over her chest.

Not to worry yet, I thought.

"Jessi, being a woman has a lot more going for it than Mom makes it sound like. Periods are sort of inconvenient and getting pregnant without marriage stinks. But carrying a child, a new person, inside includes you in creation. Men can never know the wonder of new life fluttering on your insides."

I sat on her new bedspread. "So making ourselves vulnerable by having intercourse with our husband isn't shameful or degrading. In fact, when you've found the man God intends as your husband, God will give you great joy in intercourse. It says that in the Bible. You should respect yourself enough to let only one man, the one you've married, be that close to you though. God plans for one man to love you. He doesn't create sinful or dirty things, and He created intercourse, so you can relax about married sex." Most of my information about God and sex came straight from Pete's mouth. "I know my rape probably made sex seem ugly and dirty to you, but some good came out of even that: Kery. Kery makes us all happy, right?"

"Uh huh," Jessi said. She sat next to me. "Mom makes sex sound so scary, Ella."

"She doesn't want you to make a mistake that will get you into trouble, so she scares you, Jessi. In some ways, she's right. Some men will try to take advantage of you. They could be people you know, even relatives. So try to be careful. But be glad you're a girl too, okay?"

"Okay. I love you, Ella."

"I love you too. Let's take Kery down to see Eb," I suggested, "as soon as I get my jeans on." I wanted to tell her how subtle the men would act who might try to seduce her. But I might scare her too much, or make her wonder how I knew.

Jessi jumped up and said, "I'll go turn down the burner under the stew."

We were "flying" Kery down the porch steps, both of us holding a hand and her picking up her feet as we swung her, when Mom drove up. We waited while she pulled into the garage and got out. She hugged me and said, "Hi, Ella. Gee, I'm glad you're home. Jessi, is dinner ready? Ella, our Jessi fixes dinners as delicious as you used to. Hi, Kery, how's Mama's baby?" She patted Kery on her bow.

"No problem—out of a can and into the pan," Jessi whispered to me. "Yeah, ready," she said to Mom.

"Jessi, you can help me put the groceries away," Mom said.

Jessi started to say, "Why doesn't Ella...," then stopped and smiled at me.

"I'm going to see Eb. Do I have time before dinner?" I asked.

"Go ahead. But don't stay long," Mom answered, a grocery bag on either hip as she climbed the steps.

I picked Kery up and hugged her. "You smell sweet, like baby powder," I said. Scooting one of her legs around my neck and holding her hands tightly, I hopped down the driveway. She giggled, which made me laugh.

"Hi," Cal said. He startled me and I nearly dropped Kery. He was leaning against the tractor shed. I could tell he had waited for me.

"Hi," I said and just stood there.

"You look like a woman who needs it," he observed, puffing out a cloud of cigarette smoke as he talked.

"No, I don't," I responded, moving toward Eb's corral, holding Kery's hands more tightly.

"Ella, what's changed? Did you stop loving me because of Pete?"

"I don't want sex. You won't accept love without sex."

"You can love both of us, Ella."

I stopped walking and looked squarely at him. "Love *doesn't* have to include sex, Cal." Kery leaned over my shoulder for Cal to take her. But I shifted her back.

He put his hand on my breast. "Once sex happens between two people, it continues, especially for someone as oversexed as you," he said. "A woman like you can't live without it."

"Leave me alone," I said, stepping back. He put his arms around me and pulled me to kiss him. I stood rocklike.

Stopping, he said, "Be cold now. I can wait. You'll need me again. You can't live without it and we both know it. It's not *me* you're afraid of, it's *yourself.*" He walked away.

Crying as I stumbled toward Eb, I thought, *What kind of person am I? I can live without it, can't I? Haven't I been celibate since I went to school? Am I a phony, fooling myself? Maybe Cal knows me better than I know myself and one of these days I am going to break, like he says. Maybe no boy is safe with me, not even a minister like Pete. Is my life this way because I am different from other girls, oversexed?* I let Kery down my front and hugged her, my face buried in her neck. *It can't be. I won't let it. I'll prove I'm not oversexed. I'll never let sex with him happen ever again.*

Self-Assessment Guide

1. Do you catch the constant keeping of secrets in Ella's life? Look back over these chapters and list the ways Ella keeps secrets. Then next to hers, list the way you kept secrets.

2. Most abuse victims respond either by internalizing feelings such as responsibility, guilt, or pain, or by acting out their rage. Give examples of why you think Ella reacts one way or

the other. Which response is most characteristic of you? Do
you feel off balance in this area? How?

3. Isolation is characteristic of abusive families. It can be physical isolation, like Ella's family's move to the mountains;
   emotional isolation, like Cal's total withdrawal from Ella
   after Kery's birth and Myrna ignoring Ella's needs; or social
   isolation, like Cal discouraging Ella from seeing boys and
   Myrna disliking extending hospitality. Write about your
   own isolation. Be sure to include physical, emotional and
   social types.

4. As the chapter closes, Cal voices some common concepts
   that the world holds about sex. List them. Did you hear these
   or similar ones as a child? Using a concordance, search the
   Scripture for words like *man, adultery, marry, husband, wife,
   sexual.* You are looking for God's truth to expose the lies you
   were told.

5. Did fear for younger siblings keep you involved in abuse to
   "save" them? Talk about that.

6. Ella vacillates between being drawn to Pete's gentleness and
   offer of affection, and her concern for her effect on him,
   given Cal's assertion that she is oversexed. Describe Ella's
   ability to determine trustworthiness. Which of Ella's characteristics regarding trust/mistrust do you share?

7. What about Jesus? He says He is God and that we can go to
   heaven by trusting that He's telling the truth and giving Him
   our lives. Avoiding making a decision on His claims turns
   out to be a decision against what He offers. Write out any
   questions you may have. Find a church where people believe
   that Jesus came as God in the flesh to save us from sin, and
   get your questions answered, or write to us and we'll be glad
   to help.

Helper's Focus

The desperation to stop abuse or the euphoria of being free of abuse can make a person reckless in relationships, and thus vulnerable to further abuse. All human beings need love, acceptance and respect. The abused know better than most the pain of counterfeit relationships. Perhaps that explains why most of us strive to find someone who will meet our needs honestly without manipulation.

God intends for our legitimate emotional needs to be met abundantly. However, to find fulfillment in relationships, each of us needs to evaluate the people we meet in terms of their honesty, maturity and history. For the abused, great care needs to be exercised in choosing those to whom we will relate intimately. Unfortunately, many formerly abused people continue to choose friends, counselors and mates who are in turn abusive. Perhaps these people exhibit qualities we are used to, and we feel comfortable with them. Or perhaps it's something else that draws us to them, only to re-entrap us. But if we want to live healthy lives, we must learn how to determine with whom it is safe to develop a relationship.

Commonly accepted characteristics that do not realistically prove that someone won't prey upon our weaknesses are: professional credentials, an honest face, a position of authority, a direct look, self-proclaimed trustworthiness, an offer of marriage.

In any situation, time is the ally of the person who has been abused. Time allows us to check credentials and talk with those who have counseled with the person we are considering. Time allows us to see whether an honest face is accompanied by honest actions. An authority has the opportunity to exhibit his willingness to lay down his life for those he has responsibility for, when given time. If you take the time, you can ask people who are acquainted with someone who looks you right in the eye whether or not his direct look reflects an honest spirit. Generally, a person who asserts his own trustworthiness probably can't be trusted. But *time* will tell. Most important, time is our friend when someone is asking to spend his life with us. We should not run into someone's arms merely because he isn't our current abuser. We should spend at least a year getting to know someone we're considering marrying. We should vary the situations in which we participate in order to see how our intended spouse responds in good times and in bad, in peace and under pressure.

Someone helping an abused person who sees her rushing into dangerous relationships has no choice but to urge her to go slowly, back off and consider. However, once we've given our opinion, we have to be ready for the person we help to turn a deaf ear or even an angry face to us. She may interpret our advice as an attempt to keep her from the love, acceptance and respect she desires. It may even take going through another hurtful relationship for her to realize that your suggestion to take time is right. Be patient; recovering from abuse is a process, not a Polaroid photograph ready in six seconds. Continue to be there for the person. Time is your ally when the person you help makes mistakes too.

Chapter Four

Wake Me When It's Over

Setting my suitcase on a bench in the dorm lobby, I took my mail from its pigeonhole and riffled through it. The Associated Students had sent a flier about a dance, and Pete had written a note asking if I'd like to go to the movies Friday. Pete didn't have a car, so he bought gas for my Fiat when we went out, which kept me in fuel all week. Usually when I got back from trips home I had one of the guys call him, but today I wanted time to think.

My room was the fifth on the right. Its cinder-block walls were hidden here and there by posters and by photographs of Pete and me, and Sherrie and her boyfriend. It was much better than some dorm rooms I'd seen. It had two single beds, both on the floor, a big window and a separate place to study for each of us. We had our own sink and mirror and shared a shower and toilet with two other girls.

I dropped onto my bed, my mind doing double back flips. Cal had said a life of dirty sex was my destiny. He must know; he was practically an expert. He'd had three women that I *knew* of. Maybe he could see more about me than I would admit. I didn't want Pete to experience any part of what I'd experienced, much less the degradation that might loom ahead. A magazine article I'd read said that many girls who were abused as children became prostitutes, so maybe Cal was only saying what was true. I didn't want even to consider the possibility that I might become loose or a "working girl." But I had to consider it, if only to save Pete from the same future. If Cal was only accepting the reality that I was oversexed, how many times would I hurt Pete? Would God forgive me over and over? Women like me might be better off just accepting relationships with men like Cal.

On the other hand, I hadn't chased either one of them down, panting and slobbering or anything, so maybe Cal didn't know whether I would become a slut. Maybe he was lying again. I didn't *feel* like he was right. *Can I trust my feelings?* I wondered.

Pete never did anything but kiss me with those gentle kisses as if God had given him a flower. I loved him already. Only I couldn't imagine how a girl like me could fit into the life of a pastor, except disastrously. Even if I didn't turn into a slut, I had such a "past." I could just see me as a pastor's wife. "Now, Dearie, sex before marriage does us no good. Take it from me..." followed closely by the congregation running us out of town appropriately tarred and feathered aboard a rail. Would I tell Pete? I might have to spend my whole life hiding from Pete too. What if Cal told him? Would he know when he saw Kery? She looked more like Cal every day. I fell asleep in the midst of the confusion.

At breakfast I put my tray down at a table by myself. I wanted to ask Pete a question about God forgiving people for the same sin more than once. When he got there, I barely let him get settled before I started in. "Can I ask one more question, Pete? Then I promise I'll let you off the hook for a while," I said.

In a falsetto voice, he said, "Oh, good morning, Pete. I missed you over the weekend."

"Sorry."

He patted my arm and smiled. He always understood me and accepted me, even when I went right to the point, ignoring amenities. "Go ahead, I'm listening," he said.

"Okay. If a person prays to receive Christ the way you told me, can he ever stop being a Christian?"

"Nope. It's *God's* gift and He's the only one who can take it back. And He won't. I'll give you a list of verses where the Bible talks about that."

"Even if I sin again?"

"He took you in sin, didn't he?" Pete asked. I didn't answer. Did Pete think I was already a Christian? He continued. "He took everyone in sin. Now, will you take me to the movies on Friday?"

I hoped I could cool things between Pete and me, at least until I could decide what to do. He didn't need the problems in my life.

"I can't, Pete. I have to study," I said.

"*Friday night?*" he said in mock horror. "Nobody studies on Friday night, especially not you. Don't give me that. I want to go to the movies *real bad.*" He crossed his eyes and stuck out his tongue.

"Oh brother! All right, fool. You're buying and you're going to go to the poorhouse from purchasing my popcorn."

"You're so kind, m'lady." Pete pushed his chair back, stood and bowed a floor-scraper. A freckle-faced kid named Arnie, coming down the aisle to put his tray away, kicked his rear end.

Friday night arrived and we decided to see movies playing at the drive-in. During intermission Pete put his popcorn box down, made an exaggerated leer and scooted closer to me. What was it about Pete that kept penalty flags from going down all over the field of my brain? "How's about a leetle kiss?" he said in his best Italian accent. I kissed my little finger and put it on his nose.

"That little enough for you, mon sewer?" I asked. "I'm no cheap drive-in trick," I said, straightening my spine to its puritan best.

He "spidered" his hand over and jumped it on my hand.

Then his expression changed. "You know why I'm acting so stupid?" he asked, intently serious.

"Why?"

"Because I want to ask you to marry me and I'm scared," he said, his eyes searching mine.

Fiddling with the gear shift knob, I said, "I can't. Don't ask me now."

"Can I know why?" he asked. "I love you. I think you've known that. And I suspect you love me too. Is it because I'm going to be a minister? I would do something else, for you. Or did I misunderstand how you feel about me?"

My heart had started a rhythm in my ears. What should I tell him? Trying to hide my agitation, I spoke evenly. "I have to finish school. I think you're a wonderful person, Pete. It has nothing to do with you being a minister. If you stopped your ministry because of me it would only add to the problems I already have.

How could I live with God being angry with me for stealing one of His men? I thought.

I looked up at him so that he could see how I felt. "I can't waste Daddy's money by getting married now."

"Too soon, huh? I have a habit of jumping the gun in everything," he admitted, smiling ruefully. "Well, don't think you've heard the last of me. And don't think marrying me will keep you from graduating. I'd see that you graduated." He scooted back to his side of the car. "What did you say about problems you've got? Are they big problems?"

I smiled at him. But I said to myself, *He's getting too close. Looks like you'll be changing schools at the end of this year.*

"Oh, the normal, everyday, garden-variety problems," I lied, evading his question. The second movie started. I felt relieved to escape talking anymore about marriage, or worse, about myself.

Pete pulled me close to him and put his arm around me. I wondered if other girls let guys kiss them, take them to the drive-in and put their arms around them after they'd dated only a couple of months. I wished I knew the rules. Would he guess I had more experience than I should because I let him move too fast?

Jerry Lewis fell out a window and Pete pulled his arm away from me to slap his knee and howl with laughter. I took the opportunity to get back into my seat.

"Uncomfortable, huh?" Pete observed, rubbing the ridge of his bucket seat.

"Yeah," I responded.

He leaned over and put his hand at the back of my neck. His kiss lasted longer than it ever had before, and I could feel that old, weak warmth rising in me. With Pete it should feel sweet and safe, but I couldn't push back the fear that he planned to go too far. I felt myself beginning to slip behind the wall where I separated myself from sex. In a panic, I put what I hoped was gentle pressure on his hand to signal him to let me go. I couldn't let myself relate to Pete, in any aspect, the way I related to Cal.

"You're so beautiful," he said, releasing my head. "Do you love me, Ella?"

"Yes," I said without hesitating. "I love you." I did love Pete. Despite the ugliness in other areas of my life, whatever else was true, I had come to love Pete.

The next day I had to go home again to sign Kery's final adoption papers. I looked through Mom's plastic rose arrangement at the lady from the social services office who sat on the other side of our table shuffling papers. The skin under her arms swung as her hands moved. I tried not to stare at her hanging skin as I avoided looking into her eyes.

"Now, Ella, you understand, once you sign this paper, uh, your baby, uh, belongs to your parents," she said, sighing. The smell of onions drifted over the table.

*Her sigh means she is tired of feeding that line out to each of her
assigned natural mothers like a computer, I thought. Just part of the
job. But this moment is not routine to me. When I sign her paper, I
give away my own blood, my bone.*

I looked up at my grandfather's picture on the wall. He'd
been killed in an airplane crash when Mom was ten. Did he
know about what was happening to me where he was now? His
kind eyes stared down at me. Could he see me hiding the truth
from everyone? "My baby's name is Kery," I said to the lady.

"Have you explored the alternatives for Kery?" she asked.

So many thoughts careened through my head that I couldn't
catch one to answer with. I only looked at her.

Mom interjected, "She's only eighteen. She's away at school.
My husband and I have agreed to take the child. Please don't
make this harder for her."

The lady sighed again and pushed the papers across the table
to me. "Sign wherever there's an X," she said.

Elizabeth Wainwright. Elizabeth Wainwright. Elizabeth
Wainwright. Elizabeth Wainwright, I wrote. *What are you doing,
Elizabeth Wainwright?* I thought.

"Thank you," she said, pulling the papers back to her. "Good
luck in school." She gathered her things, and as soon as she
passed the door Mom shut it behind her.

Coming back to me, Mom put her hand on my shoulder. A
cold, freezing hand.

"I'm going to take Kery out to see Eb," I said and got up.

"Guess I'll pay some bills," she said.

*Have I considered the alternatives? I thought. Every day for the
last six months. I could give up resisting Cal, take Kery and run away
with him like he suggested, continuing to hide and keep secrets. If I
choose Cal's life of illegitimacy, whoever I really am will stay hidden
in the phony shell that coats me now.*

*Or, I could let strangers adopt Kery. But Mom said if I did that I
would look for Kery the rest of my life, and how did I know someone*

*kind would get her? Mom said somebody might get her who wants
free labor when she grows up, like in those newspaper stories, or
somebody resembling my cousin and her alcoholic husband, who just
adopted someone's baby girl.*

Or I could keep her myself. In my mind I saw myself in a white
uniform at the door of somebody else's home, handing Kery to
a lady in an apron; then dropping into a dilapidated armchair
in some dark apartment, exhausted, while Kery held up her
arms from her playpen. No choice I made could guarantee love
and security for Kery. Giving her to Mom and Cal would at least
provide her as much security as I'd had and assure me the
chance to know she was all right.

If someone held her hand, Kery could walk now, the way a
drunk does, looking like she would take a nose dive any
minute. She loved to go with me, especially to see Eb. I kept a
firm grip on her pudgy fist to keep her from falling when she
lost her balance. When I was home we went to visit Eb often;
our walks were an excuse to have Kery to myself. Today I
needed time alone with her more than I had any other day of
her life. She stopped at all her favorite places outside. In the
yard she chattered back at the squirrel who scolded angrily
when we walked under his tree. When we got to the bottom of
the hill, she liked to stand on the fence post. I hugged her tight
and said, "Wave hello to the meadow, Kery," and she did. We
piggybacked the rest of the way to Eb's corral, stopping so she
could pick him an apple. I liked this part of our walk best
because of the way the sun danced on the path under the pine
trees and in Kery's hair, and the way the air was filled with the
smell of pine needles crushed under our feet.

I bridled Eb and held Kery's hand as he moved around the
corral with her. "If only she wasn't a girl, Eb," I said. "What if,
though I've tried to pick the best life for her, I've put her in the
most dangerous place she could live?"

Eb turned his head to me and I scratched behind his ear. "Will Cal leave her alone, Eb? I couldn't let her, or Jessi, go through what I've gone through. I'd kill him first."

But would I really? It's one thing to *talk* about killing someone, but quite another to *do* it. Kery bounced on Eb's back as if she wanted him to run. I laughed at her little bottom going up and down and she giggled back at me.

"I realize now that Cal includes sex in attraction, even in friendship. Is there any guarantee that he won't pretend 'friendship' with Jessi or Kery?" Eb put his head down to check the ground for stray alfalfa, and then, hearing something, lifted it and looked up the hill.

"Ella," Cal called, striding down the path.

I turned Eb so I could see him. "Yeah?" I said.

"Your mother says you should come up for lunch. Here, I'll ride Kery back." He lifted her off Eb and onto his own back.

He waited for me while I pulled Eb's bridle off. Here was my opportunity to question him about Kery and Jessi.

"Cal, if we don't do it anymore, you wouldn't..." I couldn't think how to say what worried me without Cal getting mad, so I turned to hang the bridle on its nail. Then I wouldn't have to see his face. "You wouldn't switch to Jessi or someday to Kery, would you? I mean, I could trust you to leave them alone, couldn't I?"

Cal turned me around and looked right into my eyes. "You aren't like Jessi, Ella. I love you. I want you to love me again. You can trust me; I'd never touch anyone but you."

"I knew that," I said. "I just had to make sure." He'd already had a relationship with two women at once. I still couldn't be certain, even with compliments, pretty words and promises. I stood there in God's world wondering how my twisted life could exist alongside all this beauty.

"Are you okay after that old bureaucrat?" he asked.

I had pushed her and her papers out of my mind, determined to take the adoption like an adult. But something broke when he asked if I was okay. An unswallowable knot grew in my throat and I stood there, alone.

My baby belongs to my mother. My secrets distance me from everyone on earth, except this man I can't love because he takes too much, I thought. I desperately wanted to control myself, but my shoulders jerked and tears began to drench my face. Still I stood away from him.

He brought Kery down against one side of his chest and pulled my head against the other. "She's mine," I whimpered. "She'll always be mine."

"Ours," he said. But he didn't try to kiss me this time. After my shoulders stopped jerking he said gently, "Dry your eyes now and splash some of Eb's water on them. We've got to go up for lunch."

Sunday, as Jessi and I maneuvered the crooked road home from church, she said, "Ella, to become a Christian, do you just pray and tell Jesus you want Him to run your life?"

"According to all the Christians I've met, that's it," I said.

"Don't you have to stop doing bad stuff first?"

Twisting the steering wheel back and forth to follow the road, I answered, "I met this guy at school named Pete, Jessi. He's a preacher and he showed me verses in the Bible; I'll show you when we get home. You know the one the pastor read this morning about people who aren't sick not needing a doctor?"

"Yeah," Jessi said. She watched me closely, though I couldn't look back at her and drive too.

"Jesus meant sickness compares to sin. He's making the point that He has the strength to take care of our sin; we don't by ourselves. So it's silly to think that we could get rid of sin before we surrender our lives to Christ."

"Seems too easy," she remarked.

"I know," I agreed.

When we arrived at home, Kery lifted her arms for me to take her out of her car seat and said, "Eda."

Jessi beamed. "Did you hear that? She knows your name!"

"No, she's too little," I said. "It was a coincidence."

Life moved along pretty quietly until Christmas vacation. Pete and I said goodbye to each other in the dorm parking lot. He was going to Kansas with his family to visit his grandmother for Christmas. "I'll write you every day," he said as we parted. "Will you write me too?"

"Of course. Write down the address," I said. He looked blank.

A man in slacks and a blue sport shirt was walking across the parking lot toward us. He came up behind Pete and put his arm around Pete's shoulder.

"Oh, hi Dad. Dad, this is Ella. Ella, Dad."

I offered my hand. "Hi, Mr. Allen," I said. He was tall and bald. He wore glasses and had friendly eyes. I wondered if Pete would look like him when he got older.

Shaking my hand firmly, he replied, "Hello, Miss Ella. It's nice to meet you. Pete talks of you often."

Pete smiled. "Dad, do you have Grandma's address?" he asked.

I wrote down the address Mr. Allen gave me, and Pete and I said goodbye for the holidays with only a squeezed hand.

Each day of Christmas vacation the mail had brought a letter or postcard from Pete. One postcard pictured a horse with a long, wind-swept mane rearing on a bluff. It looked like Eb, but Pete wrote that it reminded him of me. I remembered feeling free with distant horizons like that, but not lately. Nevertheless, joy for life must still be in me somewhere because Pete had seen it.

The day after Christmas a box arrived with a pearl ring inside. The note said, "I'll settle for going steady until you'll say yes to marriage." It lay softly shining in my hand, but I couldn't let myself wear it.

I didn't think I could muster the courage, or maybe it should be called foolishness, to tell Pete the truth about me, and I wouldn't live a lie with a good man like Pete. I couldn't marry a *minister* either. The risk of ruining his reputation was too great, especially if Cal's assessment proved to be true and I *was* oversexed. A minister, with an oversexed wife whose scarlet past rivaled any pornography I'd ever happened upon? I decided I wouldn't tell him no in any of my letters; I'd wait until we were back at school. As I put the ring back in the box, I shuddered. Could I ever allow myself to be close enough to anyone to tell them the truth? I nested the ring box in my suitcase.

"Ella, I've got to go out of town for a few days," Mom said as I walked into the kitchen. "There's a client who wants to trade a house downstate for one up here. I have to go look at it. Can you take care of Jessi and Kery until the second?"

"Oh no, do you have to? You'll miss New Year's Eve. Don't real estate people believe in holidays?" I pouted, twirling a nutcracker soldier ornament on the Christmas tree. But I was really thinking, *Please don't leave me with Cal.*

"I have to go. If you can't watch them, I'll have to pay a sitter." Her underlying message was, your baby will cost me money and you won't help. Many times before, she had interpreted the real message of her words for me after somebody she'd been talking to had left. I had become a pro at reading between the lines.

"No, that's all right. I can watch them," I said. Cal had backed off some. Maybe I could manage.

Mom left New Year's Eve morning. She and Cal had fought before she left, and she stormed out of the house. I had heard her scream, "At least with George I didn't have to work all the time!" Sometimes when she got that mad, I wondered whether she would come home or leave forever. But she probably wouldn't go without Jessi.

To help us stop feeling deflated, I made pizza for dinner. Cal brought Pepsi and ice cream when he came home from work. We were going to have a real bash. We even had some blower whistles left over from a birthday party. Jessi kept tickling me with the feather at the end of hers while we were making pizza. Kery pulled herself up on the cabinet and put her pudgy hand out for pieces of cheese.

When Cal came in from feeding the animals, we took our pizza into the living room so we could eat and watch TV. Kery had pieces of hamburger, mushroom, cheese and the other toppings without the sauce. She wasn't old enough for spicy tomato sauces yet. When she finished eating, Jessi and I dressed her in her pajamas with feet, sang goodnight songs and tucked her in her crib. Jessi had been saying she would make it to midnight this year, but the later it got the sleepier she looked. I tried turning to all her favorite shows, but her eyes were still drooping. After a while I said, "Let's play Yahtzee, Jessi."

Cal said, "I want to play too. But I'm going to have a drink. Ella, would you like to try a light drink? You're getting old enough, and after all it *is* New Year's Eve."

"Okay," I said. I had been wondering for a long time what adults found so appealing about alcohol. Jessi and I got the Yahtzee game out.

Cal brought my drink in one of Mom's crystal glasses with a Maraschino cherry on top. "Pretty fancy," I said, tasting it. It tasted like I imagined liquid Scotch tape might taste. "Yuck! I'd rather have a Pepsi," I complained.

Cal laughed. "Well, here," he said. "Let me put Pepsi in it for you. It takes a while to acquire a taste, I guess."

He poured my glass as full of Pepsi as possible. I tasted it again. The Pepsi made it okay. I liked the way Cal made me feel like an adult. We were having a good time; maybe everything would be all right after all.

Jessi won the first game. Usually I had bad luck at Yahtzee; that's why I had chosen it. I figured if she won she might succeed at staying awake until midnight. "Want another drink?" Cal asked.

The first drink had made me feel a little bit warm. I wondered if my cheeks were pink. They felt hot. "I don't think so," I answered.

"Aw, come on, Ella. I don't want to drink by myself on New Year's."

"Well, okay. But less liquor this time."

"No problem," he said, taking our glasses to the kitchen.

"I've got to go to the bathroom, Jessi. Be right back," I said. When I came back to the table, Cal had replaced my glass, which started out a little darker brown this time.

"I changed to vodka," he said. "It doesn't taste so strong."

This drink seemed milder. I sipped it through the second game, which Jessi also won. It was 11:45 when we finished.

"Get the stuff, Ella," Jessi ordered. "I made it!" We got out all the pots and pans, the blower whistles and big spoons. The crowd in Time's Square began to count down: 10, 9, 8, ...

"Let's go outside, Ella," Jessi said, dropping her pans to open the door. We trooped outside banging away furiously, hollering and screaming.

"Happy New Year," Cal yelled, looking at his watch. He bent down and kissed Jessi. "Happy New Year," he said.

"Happy New Year!" she shouted, overjoyed that she had finally made it to midnight without having someone wake her up. I couldn't help grinning, remembering the first time I had done that. I felt incredibly happy, so much that I let myself whirl around the yard. Jessi followed me, and we whirled some more. Finally, Cal caught me.

"Happy New Year, Ella," he said and kissed me. Dizzily happy, I kissed him back. "Happy New Year!" I shouted. Finally Jessi wound down, and staggering, said, "I really am tired. I think I'll go to bed."

"Okay," I responded. "I'm right behind you." We gathered the pots and pans and returned to the house. I went to check on Kery. She was sleeping all rolled up in a little ball. Her face looked as if a dreamland for babies really existed. I tucked her in again and went to put our ice cream dishes in the sink.

Jessi had gone to bed. Cal was turning off the outside lights. "Want to watch the late movie with me?" he said, handing me another drink.

I gulped it down. "No," I said. "I'm pretty sleepy." I picked up the last ice cream bowl and put it and my glass in the sink. Cal put his arms around me as I turned.

"Ella, we're finally alone," he said. He kissed me. My head felt like a bee buzzed inside. I couldn't seem to tell whether he was kissing me too long. *I shouldn't have gulped down that drink,* I thought. He took my hand and guided me to the couch. "Just watch the movie with me," he said. "Don't leave me lonely on New Year's Eve."

"That's all you want, watching television, right?" I said. My words sounded mushy.

He sat me so that my head fit in the hollow between his shoulder and neck.

"Sure, babe, just a little television," he said. He was rubbing the side of my breast. I didn't want him to, but I couldn't make myself move fast enough. When my response to that came slowly, he began unbuttoning my blouse. I brushed his hand away a couple of times but he kept returning, and finally I let him. When I realized he was working at my pants, though, I forced myself out of the stupor I'd slid into.

"No!" I said, shoving him away. I sat up and began buttoning my blouse.

"Don't be such a tease," he said, ignoring my hands and undoing the buttons I had done.

I pushed off the sofa. "I hate you. You got me to drink so you could do this, didn't you?" He didn't answer. He just leisurely encircled my leg with one arm and resumed loosening my jeans.

I started to cry. When he noticed, he stopped. Turning away, he glared at the television.

I still felt dizzy, but I pulled my clothes around me and stumbled into the bathroom. Hating myself for drinking and losing control that way, I woodenly rearranged my clothes and got a drink of water. I felt like nobody, numb, dead. It didn't matter whether he did that to me again, I was nothing. Why did I care?

I slipped quietly into my bedroom, past Jessi's room. But there was no reason for silence, I could hear her breathing as she slept.

I don't know what I'm going to do. But I can't stand this anymore. I'd take the blame for starting it if only I could make it stop. I can't tell Mom. It would kill her. I can't tell Daddy. He'd kill Cal. I can't tell Pete. Even if he does want to marry me, it's not his problem. I can't stop it myself. I feel dirty. I'm guilty of adultery. My life amounts to ugliness. Things would improve for the rest of the family if I didn't exist.

I got out of bed and went back to the bathroom. I knew where to find Mom's sleeping pills. Taking the bottle from the medicine cabinet, I stood staring at myself in the mirror. My eyes looked like I wasn't really there. I couldn't make myself open the bottle. *You dumb, dirty slut, you can't even kill yourself right*, I said to myself. I began to sob.

But then Jesus slipped into my thoughts. I didn't know why, He just came into my mind. It occurred to me that He might have the only power strong enough to get me out of this mess. His love and understanding of people and all the things that the people at church and Pete had told me about Him filtered back through my mind. I put the pills back and returned to my bed. "Jesus," I said. "I'm not sure You can really listen to me, because I don't know whether You really exist. But I'm going to take a chance that You do, because there's no one else who can help me but You. I've done terrible things. I started this whole thing. I planned to make Cal like me better than Mom. But I guess You know that already. I can't stop it now. I got it started, but I can't stop it. And it appears that I'm not even strong enough to help everyone by taking myself out of the picture. If You can't stop it, nobody can. Please help me. If You'll stop my relationship with Cal I'll give You my whole life. You're not getting much, maybe nothing, but I need You real bad, Jesus, please." I was sobbing again.

Jesus heard me and slowly a feeling of peace came. I stopped crying and fell asleep.

The soft light shadings of early morning had already passed when I woke on the first day of the New Year. I lay in my bed, wondering how Jesus could manage to stop Cal. *I already stay out of Cal's way. I don't even come home very much. I promised myself it wouldn't happen again and still he thinks of new ways to get what he wants,* I thought bitterly. "God, what do I do now?" I said out loud.

I turned back and forth to tuck the quilt in around me like a cocoon. *Nothing I do myself will stop him. I need an adult, someone as old as he is, who can force him to leave me alone. Who?*

A family member would be best. Maybe we could work the problem out on our own without policemen or a trial.

Someone coughed in the kitchen. *Mom! She was home!* I realized then that the only person I could choose was Mom. Though knowing would devastate her, it also would, by keeping the incest private, help her. "Did you bring her home, Jesus?" I asked quietly. That feeling of peace came again. I got up and dressed.

"How come you're back so soon?" I asked coming into the kitchen.

"Deal fell through," she answered. She looked tired.

"When did you get in? I said, hoping she hadn't seen any of the scene with Cal and me the night before.

"About four," she answered. "I'm really beat, too tired to fall asleep."

I hated to tell her when she was tired, but I didn't want to lose my courage or to face Cal again. "Mom, I have to tell you something," I said with a shaky voice.

"What?" she asked.

"Kery is Cal's baby."

She didn't pass out or start screaming, she just looked at me. "I had an idea something was going on," she said. "Let's see what Cal has to say."

Cal lay in bed, his eyes open, his hands folded in back of his head, as if he'd been thinking when we came in.

Walking up to the bed, Mom said dully, "Cal, Ella says Kery is your child."

His eyes turned to me, burning. "What are you trying to do, kill me?" he asked.

"No. No, I just want it to stop," I whimpered.

Mom sank into the chair beside the bed. "Why, Cal?" she asked.

"I wanted to show you I'm not the only one who can raise bad girls," he replied.

He was talking about Spider Legs. He had deliberately turned me into his whore because Spider Legs's morals disgusted Mom. I couldn't believe he would do the things he'd done to me only to hurt Mom. I wanted to scream, "Do you really mean that? You never loved me? You let me love you and took things from me that didn't belong to you, and you never loved me?" During the six years he had manipulated me to trade love for sex, he had lied more than I had ever guessed. In reality

I had been worse than alone throughout those years. Suddenly I wanted a bath, a hard one with a scrub brush and lye soap. What had I done to myself in my anger at their marriage? Cal looked only at Mom.

"Do you two want each other, or am I still a part of this picture?" Mom snapped.

Cal looked at me as if for one last chance. He still thought, no matter what I did or said, that he could have a relationship with me even after what he had admitted to Mom. He had never loved me; he didn't have mixed-up thinking about love. His actions were totally consistent with those of a man who was manipulating a girl. "No, we don't," I said. "You are Cal's wife, and I'm very sorry for what I've done." Cal said nothing.

"Well, we'll work it out. I think, under the circumstances, that you should go back to school a little early, Ella. There's no point in your staying around. This is between Cal and me."

What did she think? Did she blame me? Did she still love me? I hurried to my room, packed my things and left before Jessi or Kery woke up. "God," I prayed as I drove blindly toward Morley, "please help them work it out. If I could still be part of the family after all I've done, please let that happen too." I didn't sleep much that night, wondering what was happening at home. I felt I had taken Jesus' hand and walked away from the mess I had started.

Pete got back the next day. I wanted to tell him about praying to receive Christ, but I felt so responsible and deflated about the rest of what had happened that it took me a while to get the words out. When no one else was around, I finally said, "Pete, I prayed to receive Christ. He *is* alive, just like you said." I knew my confession to Mom had come from Jesus, and I would never forget that. But after the scene with Cal, the initial cleansing I'd felt had given way to guilt.

"Welcome to the family, Ella," Pete said, and kissed my cheek. "Any excuse for a kiss, right?"

"The family?" I asked.

"Yeah, the family of God," Pete answered. "When you prayed that prayer you became an adopted daughter of God. He's your dad now, even more than your real dad. Now you have three dads: God, your real father and your stepfather. Boy, are you in trouble at Christmas time." He grinned at me.

God loves me like a father, I thought. Like Daddy does, not like Cal. I have three very different fathers. One of them is God. But Pete said, "More than your real dad." God has a huge, big father's kind of love that He loves me with in spite of the awful things I did. I know He does. Yesterday He showed me His father's kind of love. What I'm feeling must be joy. I don't remember ever feeling like this before. What's happening? Is it that I can see a dim point to life now? A perfect God, who never sins, runs the world I live in. Maybe He even had a reason for the incest. Could it be that I would have thought life was so good I didn't need God if it hadn't been for all that with Cal?

And yet underneath the joy and new understanding I was experiencing, I knew there still lurked that feeling of guilt. Pete was saying something. He was looking intently at me.

"Are you listening, Ella? I said, now will you marry me?"

There he stood again, asking me to become a minister's wife. *My life did take a 180-degree turn this week. I don't have to live the life of a hypocrite with two men in my life anymore. But I still hide so many ugly secrets. And what about school?* I thought.

"Pete, I love you," I said. "But school is important to me and I'm afraid to get married now. I don't think I'd finish. We already have trouble getting our homework done."

"Agree to an engagement, and we'll plan a wedding right after you graduate." Pete waited.

An engagement wasn't a final commitment. Maybe God planned to work out the problems of my past. How could I tell? It would be horrible to have run from Pete and then find out God was planning to work it all out the whole time. *I'll ask*

Daddy, I thought. *If he thinks it's okay, then I'll take the first step and see what happens next.*

"One thing first," I said. I ran to my room for a dime. Returning, I explained, "There's one person I have to talk to." I took Pete's hand and we went to the phones in the lobby. I was glad Pete had asked on a weekend or Daddy wouldn't have been home. When he answered, I said, "Daddy, it's me. Remember the boy you told me to pay attention to at Thanksgiving? He wants to marry me."

"Are you in trouble?" Daddy asked. I had been pretty abrupt, and he never played word games with me. I was used to his straightforward honesty.

"No, of course not. We won't get married until after I graduate, but we want to be engaged and I promised I'd ask you first."

"Well, find a chicken house and lock him in it. If he comes out okay, you can marry him." That was an old family joke. We all knew it meant yes!

I covered the receiver and turned to Pete. "Yes!" I whispered to him. He hugged me as I turned back to the phone. "Thanks, Daddy," I said.

"Ella, you may be planning to wait too long," Daddy observed. "I won't refuse if you decide to get married sooner."

"I love you, Daddy," I said.

"I love you too. Now get off the phone," he said. "It's my nickel."

"Bye, ya' old coot," I shot back and we hung up.

All my doubts still lurked about a girl like me married to a minister, but my heart wanted so desperately to forget what lay behind and answer yes. I wondered why God would make all the changes in my life, including Pete, if some good wasn't part of it.

Pete sprinted down the hall, then ran back to me, encircled me with his arms and whirled me around. "You're *mine*. We'll live together *forever.*" Then, as quickly as he went crazy he became sober. "There's one thing, though. I know your folks are divorced. With me, marriage is forever. You have to know that in the beginning."

Sure, I thought, *until it gets too tough, and then I'll let you go. I love you too much to spend our nights screaming at each other like Mom and Daddy, or Cal.*

"Well, my innocent," I said. "That's the plan anyway. But I want you to know that if life gets too hard or you ever feel stifled with me, you can get out. I love you too much to hold you."

Pete's face went to stone, and suddenly the door he'd closed behind his eyes disappeared and I saw that anger burned clear into his soul. "Love doesn't mean I wait around for you to please me. It means I nurture you, raise you up to the sun like a flower, encourage you to become everything you possibly can. If you don't please me, the fault will lie in my not doing my job, and I will work harder, not leave."

I was amazed. Did I have the commitment to say the same thing to him? I had never thought of love like that before. "Pete, there has always been a little door shut behind your eyes with me. Just now it opened. What happened?"

"I love you. You've never hurt me, only built me up. My whole world has been filled with people dying to criticize me and set standards for me that are impossible to keep. With you, I'll always be open, trusting you like I've never trusted anyone."

Oh no, I thought. *What have I done? I've brought him to the top of the mountain, only to throw him down when he finds out the truth about me.*

Self-Assessment Guide

1. Look through this chapter for what Ella thinks about and says to herself. List your findings in columns labeled "positive" and "negative." Put a star next to items you have thought or said regarding yourself.

2. Which people influence how Ella feels about herself? How? Which people in your life influence how you feel about yourself? How?

3. Why do you think Ella said she knew Cal was telling the truth about not bothering Jessi or Kery when she didn't really trust him? Have you ever reacted falsely in this way?

4. What did Ella do to determine Pete's trustworthiness? Which methods were reliable means of determining trustworthiness and which were not? Why?

5. Look up the following Scripture references. Each tells something about what you should think about yourself and who you should let influence the way you feel about yourself. Write each verse in your own words, and note beside it how it should affect your life.

   Proverbs 13:20, 15:22, 29:5, 30:5
   Ecclesiastes 12:13,14
   Romans 12:3
   2 Corinthians 12:7–10
   Philippians 4:8

6. Research on child abuse shows that the response of the victim's parent(s) will affect the victim's ability to recover. Look at how Myrna responded to Ella's admission of the incest. Write down your opinion on what is missing for healing to begin. Now pretend you are a neighbor looking at your own admission and the events surrounding it. Role-

play for yourself what did happen, and then what you would have liked to have happen.

7. Through her prayer on New Year's Eve, Ella takes the step of faith that makes her part of God's family. Think about or write down what you need to do about Jesus Christ. Why not do it?

Helper's Focus

When the victim reveals incest in a family, every family member is faced with a crisis. The victim generally already realizes that her life will change, because if nothing else the power structure in the family will be altered. The offender has the choice to admit or deny the truth of the accusation. Whether he denies or admits, he also faces a fork in the road: whether to continue the abuse or stop. The non-offending parent, usually the mother, faces a choice between her mate and her child. If her husband denies he has abused the child, her dilemma is whether to believe him or her child. If he admits he has sexually abused a child for whom he is responsible, the wife must decide what to do with his admission: whether to stay together, call the authorities, insist on counseling, or keep her child in the home. Many other crisis questions come up as well, a number of them financial. Siblings also have choices to make. Usually because they are children, they feel someone must be designated as the bad guy, and the only people to pick from are people they love. Often it is more comfortable for the sibling to choose the victim as the culpable one, because to choose an adult would undermine the authority structure in the family and threaten the sibling's security. This creates barriers between family members.

Coming into this morass of upheaval, the person who seeks to help may be overwhelmed. The capacity to take apart the situation, looking for what must be done first, is the need of the family. With the myriad of issues that must be faced, there may be no family member capable of rational thought. The helper should attempt to clarify these issues and encourage the adults in the family to take the necessary action, rather than taking the obvious actions herself. If the parents can be convinced to do what is right in this situation, they will improve their self images and advance the capacity of the victim to heal. However, if the abuse continues and the adults in the family will not call in the authorities, then it is your responsibility before God to do so. As you do this, you may find that everyone in the family sees you as the enemy. Nevertheless, we are more concerned for what God wants than what men want.

Initially, it may be best for you to work with only one family member. It might be too difficult for one helper to empathize with several people who are at odds with each other, especially when one is the abuser and another the victim. It is also important to avoid showing extreme emotion during discussions with any of the family members. If they feel you have difficulty personally dealing with what has happened in their lives, they may assume that you are incapable of helping them work through the issues they must face.

A program called Parents United was begun in Santa Clara, California, a couple of decades ago. This group works with victims, convicted offenders and other family members to create a healthy family environment in which each member's role is clarified and families are healed. Parents United has spread over much of California, and programs similar in aim are available throughout the United States. This means that the family facing the crisis of incest can be offered hope of healing. The helper can serve the family by finding out what process they will be exposed to when the incest is reported and what counseling is available in the community.

The involvement of the church should be part of crisis intervention. Incest happens in religious families as well as in non-religious families. But it never happens where the marriage has not been troubled previously. Therefore, the helper must assume that there are non-abuse issues to resolve for the family to function in a healthy manner. The spiritual state of each family member should be determined and the cleansing of salvation or rededication suggested. For a family not affiliated with any church, an active church should be sought where biblical principles for family life can be gathered and put to use. For a family with church affiliation, you may have to notify those in the church who can help. Or you may only have to connect the family with understanding church leaders. Many churches now have programs to help abused children and adults who were abused as children. In a later chapter, we will explain how we began a support group for adults abused as children at First Baptist Church in Modesto, California.

An attitude that sees incest as sin, separate from each individual, will assist the helper to talk with the people involved in a way that encourages each to accept the healing process necessary for them. It is also helpful to know who you are, and more important, who you aren't. If your training in the area of child abuse is limited, admit that and seek professional help for a family where abuse has recently been uncovered. If you are dealing with an adult who explains her past to you, it may only be necessary to listen and give feedback. Remember Paul's words as you do this work:

> Am I now trying to win the approval of men, or of God? Or am I trying to please men? If I were still trying to please men, I would not be a servant of Christ. (Galatians 1:10)

Chapter Five

It's Not a Secret Anymore

"I can hardly wait for you to meet Jessi and Kery," I said as we neared the farm. "You'll love everything: the meadow, the apple trees, Eb. I know you're going to love Eb," I chattered away. I always talked too much when I felt anxious. What might happen when we got home? When Pete asked Cal if he could marry me, what would Cal say?

Pete gripped the steering wheel and kept his eyes on the winding road as we climbed into the mountains.

"Are you mad at me?" I finally asked. He had hardly said five words all the way home.

"I can't drive and talk," he answered. "Aren't you used to me yet? I'm not mad. You talk."

In my anxiety I had forgotten Pete's total commitment to driving. "Are you scared about meeting my folks?" I asked. I could have added that he didn't need to be, but I wanted to tell the truth.

"I already met your stepfather," he answered. "Ella, I just don't talk much on long trips." He turned to look at me and I grabbed for the door handle when he nearly drove into the creek beside the road. "See?" he said pointedly.

Overlooking his object lesson, I said, "Turn left here." Little patches of snow peeked from the base of trees and shaded spots. The last few miles of the road climbed steeply. I knew the farm would be covered.

"There will be plenty of snow by the time we get to the farm," I observed. "Maybe Cal will hook the sleds to the back of the jeep for us. It's great to go roaring up and down the road. We always put Jessi on the last sled so she bumps along in the gutter. You'll love it," I assured him.

"Right here our property starts," I said, pointing to the railroad tie and barbed wire fence. *If this visit goes well, I thought, and Mom and Cal say Pete and I can get married, I'll tell Pete that Kery's my daughter. He probably wouldn't benefit from knowing who her father is. But at least a major part of keeping the secret will be over with.*

That was the old me, talking from fear. The new me understood that God wouldn't put up with half truth. But on that day I hadn't had enough experience with God; I didn't realize that He would control the time and place in which I revealed my ugly secret. I had already forgotten how powerfully He had answered my prayer on New Year's Eve. *Does committing myself to Pete in marriage mean God wants me to tell Pete everything?* I kept wondering.

Coming home to this place that I loved helped settle my nervousness. The beauty of God's creation nearly overcame the sad things that happened here. As we neared the farm, the road was covered with snow and the Fiat began to slip, but Pete held it on the road.

"Nice job, Barney Oilpan," I teased.

The pine boughs covered with snow contrasted with the leafless apple tree limbs that looked like tiny slices of chocolate cream pie. "Turn in here," I directed, pointing to our driveway. "And take a right up the hill."

It seemed like a dream having Pete come to the farm. If only Pete and I, married—instead of Cal and I, illegitimately—lived here together.

Walking up to the porch, our feet crunched up to our ankles in the snow. "What a great place to live," Pete said. He hesitated, so I opened the door.

Mom had turned toward the door and stood smiling at us. As keenly as if she were doing it to me, I felt her eyes sizing Pete up. Jessi's eyes were gigantic as she took her turn staring at Pete. She had been doing her homework at the table so she would be there the moment we came in. Kery stood by Cal's knee. She said, "Eda," and ducked under the table to come to me. Cal read the paper and didn't look up. Everybody except Kery seemed frozen for a second.

"Hi, everybody!" I said. "This is Pete." I picked Kery up and sat her on my hip.

Mom offered her hand. "Well, hello Pete," she said. "We've heard a lot about you."

"Hi," Jessi said shyly.

Pete shook Mom's hand. "I'm glad to meet you, Mrs. Phillips. Hi, Jessi. Hello, Cal."

Cal looked up from his paper as if he were startled. "Hi," he said. "Have a good trip up?"

"Yes, fine," Pete answered. Cal went back to reading the paper.

"You two get your things from the car," Mom said. "Ella, I fixed up your room for Pete and you can sleep with Jessi and Kery," she added.

"Can I show Pete the farm and then help with dinner?" I asked. "I want him to see it before the sun goes down."

"I guess, but don't get lost." Mom glanced sternly at me, which meant she had no intention of doing all the work when I brought someone home for the weekend.

When Pete and I had ended our tour and were closing Eb's gate, he said, "I think I'll try to catch Cal alone after dinner and ask him formally to let me marry you."

Panic rose inside me. But I managed to walk nonchalantly up the hill and respond, "I would much rather you asked him and Mom when they're together and let me be there too."

Slowing his step to match mine, he asked, "Why?"

"Just would," I answered, doing my best to sound calm. What if Cal told him about me to keep him from marrying me? Or what if Cal said no?

"Okay," Pete said. "They're *your* family, you ought to know how to approach them. This side of your family sure is different from your dad."

Little do you know, I thought. I love Mom; without her I wouldn't exist at all. And I don't hate Cal. We've both made mistakes. After all, sin is sin. People sin easily; I know from experience. Most of us fall into sin, we don't plan out how we'll hurt people. My intention to take Cal's love blew up into something I couldn't control. But I didn't get up one morning intending to do such awful things.

After dinner, while everyone lounged around the table, Pete said, "Mr. Phillips, Mrs. Phillips, Ella and I came up here for a reason. We want to marry when she graduates and we want your permission."

Mom glanced at Cal, who kept concentrating on lighting a cigarette. Finally he looked up, then feigned surprise when he saw everyone staring at him. "What's everybody looking at me for? She's not my daughter, I don't care if she gets married."

"I guess that's a yes," Mom said, and came around the table to hug me. Then she took Pete's hand and said, "Be good to this girl, she deserves it."

Her words flooded my mind. *She deserves it,* I thought. Mom must not be as angry as I had thought. She hadn't even mentioned Cal and me since I told her. Maybe this meant I misunderstood about her thinking it was my fault.

Jessi pushed her chair back with a jerk and ran out the front door.

"Uh oh," Mom said as the door slammed.

I smiled at Pete and said, "It's all right. I'll go after her. I know where she'll go, but don't expect us back right away." Jessi's footprints in the snow led up the hill to the well house, as I had known they would. She leaned against its rough boards, shivering and crying. *Winter is not a good time to need the comfort of the well house,* I thought. "Jessi, we'll always be sisters and I'll always love you," I soothed. I turned her around and hugged her.

"Ella, Mom makes me do all the housework, or most of it anyway. She's always at work. And when I try to talk to her about it she gets mad. She doesn't understand. Then later she yells at me about it all over again, over nothing. And I have to babysit Kery for free when I'd rather goof around with my friends." She stopped a moment, looking sheepish. "That wasn't a cut at you about Kery. I really don't mind, and how often I babysit isn't your fault."

I smiled.

She resumed, "Mom and Cal go square dancing every Friday night! When is it my turn?" She shrugged. "If I don't have you to talk to, how will I make it through high school?"

"I'm not getting married for a couple of years, Jessi. By then you'll be a sophomore, and I'm sure Pete won't move me far away. I'll still live close enough to talk."

Jessi began to sob into her hands. "Oh, Ella," she said, her voice muffled, "I'm sorry I'm acting like such a baby. I felt so deserted when you went away to school. Now I'll get to see you even less."

She might be right. I probably won't come home on weekends, at least not as often as I have so far, I thought. I patted her hair and smiled at her. "It makes me feel good that we love each other so much," I said.

Later everybody watched television. A little after nine Pete excused himself and headed for bed. I admired Pete for trying so hard to anticipate the needs of other people. He had assumed

my folks might want to talk with me. Cal said he needed sleep
too, so Mom and I turned off the TV and went into the kitchen
to not disturb anybody.

Mom poured a cup of coffee. "What are your wedding
plans?" she asked.

It was getting cold, so I picked the chair near the fireplace.
"I haven't thought about the wedding too much," I replied. "But
I don't want a big wedding. In fact, I'd like to have it at the little
church."

"Oh no, Ella. You can't get enough people in there, and it's
not pretty enough. Your pictures won't look nice," Mom protested.

"I know, Mom. But the little church means a lot to me, and
I don't need a lot of people."

She stirred saccharin into her coffee. "What about your
dress?" she asked.

I fiddled with a spoon left from dinner. "It's a long way off,"
I said. "I still have two and a half years to go."

"I'd like to make it if you'd let me," she said from behind her
coffee cup. I felt amazed. Mom could sew, but not well. "And I
have my wedding hat that you could wear for something old,"
she added.

"Sure, Mom. Just let's not get too fancy, okay?" *A mother who
hates you doesn't offer to make you a wedding dress, does she?* I
asked myself.

"You only get married once," she said. Then a shadow
crossed her face, and I suspected her thoughts had turned to
Cal and Kery and sadness at her daughter's ineligibility for
virgin white at her wedding.

"Mom," I said, "Are you ever going to talk with me about
what happened with Cal?"

She hesitated. "Well," she faltered, "I have been wondering
about a few things."

"What?"

"I knew you and Cal liked to do things together outside, but I had no idea what was happening. How..." She stopped. "You mean how could we live in the same house and you not know?" I asked.

"Yes," she whispered, exhaling her breath gratefully.

I looked down at my hands. "Most often it happened outside. Before New Year's I had promised myself that I would make it stop. Then he nearly managed again, on New Year's Eve when you were gone. I considered killing myself with your sleeping pills. But the neatest thing happened, Mom. I don't know if you'll believe this, but I'd like to tell you." I paused and looked at her.

"Go ahead."

"I've been listening to Pearl at Sunday school and Pete has answered a lot of questions about Jesus for me. When I stood there with your sleeping pills in my hand, all the things I've learned about Jesus came into my head. Instead of taking the pills, I prayed to ask Jesus to become my personal Savior. The next morning I told you about Cal and me. For years I had thought I couldn't tell you. I think Jesus gave me the strength to do it. I didn't want to hurt you, Mom; I wanted it to stop. That's all." I had said it so fast, and now I started to cry.

"I'm glad you've become a Christian, Ella," Mom said.

"Mom, have you ever prayed to receive Jesus as your Savior?" She looked out the window. "Yes, when I was a teenager. We had a youth pastor who was wonderful. We used to do all kinds of fun things. He'd fill up his whole car with kids, one on top of another, and off we'd go. I prayed then." For a moment her face looked young, but then it was as if a tattered curtain fell over it.

After a moment she said, "Was it all Cal's idea?"

My heart squeezed. "No, not exactly," I confessed. Rubbing my thumbnail with my first finger nervously, I continued. "I'm very sorry for all this and would do it differently if I knew then what I know now. But it's too late. Remember when you said if Cal and I didn't stop fighting you'd lose another marriage?"

"No, I don't. But go ahead."

"I felt angry then. I wanted Daddy back and I hated Cal for taking his place. I guess at first I tried hard to get rid of him. I felt like a leftover from a life that didn't exist anymore, and I blamed you for pushing me aside. So when you sounded like your marriage meant more to you than I did, I decided to make Cal like me better than you. I thought I could take a person you loved away from you the way you had taken Daddy from me. I had no idea sex would be part of it, but I guess it was my fault." Under lowered lashes, I looked to see her reaction.

Her face expressionless, she said, "I see. Well, that's about enough questions for tonight. Let's get some sleep, okay?"

"Do you still love me?" I pressed.

"Yes," she said dully. "You are my daughter, and I will always love you. But one thing, Ella. This should stay in the family. You shouldn't talk to anyone else about it, ever. Okay?"

"Okay," I agreed. She sounded as if she had made herself say she loved me. As if it was written somewhere that mothers must love their children, that she couldn't hate her own child, no matter what the child did.

"By the way, Ella, I've started telling Kery she's adopted so she'll get used to the idea. I know she doesn't know what it means yet, but I want her to feel comfortable with being adopted as she grows up. No surprises, like we said," Mom added over her shoulder on the way to her bedroom.

I wondered if that were her way of hurting me back for the hurt she felt while we were talking. But it really didn't make any difference. Giving up Kery hurt more than anything I could have imagined. A little more was barely noticeable. What really hurt was that though I should have been used to never knowing for sure where I stood with Mom, I never got used to her "I love you, no I don't" messages. I longed for her to accept me, all the time, no matter what.

In the morning I asked Cal if he would hitch the sleds to the back of the Jeep and give us a ride in the snow. Mom stood at the sink working on breakfast and said, "Make sure Jessi doesn't have to ride in the gutter. And Kery's old enough to go now."

Cal poured orange juice from a crockery pitcher. "Yeah, Kery will love it," he agreed. "Ella," he added, "I need to talk to you about something. Eb isn't getting ridden and he eats all the time. I can't afford to keep him anymore and I need to know if your dad will pay to board him near school, or whether you'd rather I sell him."

"I...I don't know," I stammered. "How soon do I have to decide?"

"As soon as possible. Every day is more hay and oats."

It's because I told, and because I'm getting married, I thought. *You're hurting me on purpose.*

Pete had come in and heard the part of the conversation about Eb. Now he said, "Ella, you don't have much time for him anymore. Maybe you *should* sell him."

"What do you know about it?" I snapped. I wanted to scream, "He was all I had through this. My friend, my only friend! I could talk to him. And now I know why you're doing this!" to Cal as I ran out the door, but I didn't. Why rub everyone else's face in his manipulations?

I tore down the hill to Eb's corral and threw myself through the gate. Eb stood inside the barn, looking out at his world. He didn't know why it turned white every winter. He didn't know lots of things, but he loved me. Rubbing my hand over his cold side, I muttered, "He doesn't care about the hay and oats. He wants to hurt me, Eb. I told Mom, and he's getting rid of you to punish me. Eb. Oh, Eb." I burst into tears that ran down Eb's side like millions of tears had before. He nuzzled my hair with his hairy old lips. It was his habit. I cried and cried. I wanted to go on crying, so I'd never have to make the decision Cal demanded of me.

Realistically, I couldn't ask Daddy to board Eb. He already spent a great deal of money on school. If Cal wouldn't feed Eb anymore the only thing to do was sell my horse. But this was Eb. Eb, who had gone through every minute of pain and manipulation with me. If only he was a poodle or a little calico cat. But he wasn't. He was a sixteen-hand horse, and I couldn't hide him away in a dorm room. I was about to desert my best friend. What kind of person does that? I wished Pete understood so I wouldn't appear a raving maniac.

I took Eb's bridle down and put it on him. If we rode higher into the mountains maybe we could find a deserted miner's cabin and claim squatter's rights. *Grow up*, I thought. *People don't do that. You would starve to death, and so would Eb.*

"Eb," I choked, pulling his bridle off and wiping the bit before I hung it back on the wall, "I'm going...I'm telling...This is the last...I love you." I buried my face in his mane and wept again. Then I got his curry comb and brushed him until he shone. "I hope someone who deserves you buys you," I whispered in his ear as it flickered forward and backward as if my breath tickled.

I stumbled up the hill, blind from tears, whispering goodbye.

Cal caught me without my realizing he was there. He began to talk while I desperately wiped at my tears. "Ella, your mother knowing about us and you getting married doesn't mean we can't still love each other," he said.

I couldn't stand it. After the scene on New Year's Eve, me telling Mom, and him asking me if I was trying to kill him, he still didn't believe I meant to end it.

"I probably don't have to sell Eb, really. I could find the money to keep feeding him if you were planning to come home and ride him pretty often," he suggested.

"Sell him. And leave me alone. It's over," I said. I started to stride up the hill. He grabbed me around the waist and pressed me against him. I went stiff and said, "If you don't let me go immediately, and if you ever touch me again, I will not come here anymore."

He let me go.

I walked around the farm, patting my face with snow now and then to decrease the puffiness I could feel in my eyes. As I walked I rehearsed possible excuses I would make to Pete at the house. I had acted in a way I imagined looked at best like the antics of a two-year-old. And now I would rather go back to school, but Pete wouldn't understand. I had to keep up the facade until Sunday. Besides, I would feel proud to show him off at the little church.

We rode the sleds after breakfast. Mom was mad that I hadn't helped and the waffles all got cold. In the afternoon Pete and I went for a walk. When we got to my favorite spot on Digger's Ridge, with the entire mountain range displayed before us, he kissed me.

Everyone at the little church loved Pete. He sang for the service. He had a rich bass voice, which vibrated through the little sanctuary.

Driving back to school in silence, I couldn't help myself. I asked again if he was mad at me. I had a difficult time getting used to not having my family jabbering away in the car. He seemed even more pensive than on the way up. But he said, "I don't talk when I drive very far." This time he said it a little more sternly.

Once we had put our things away at the dorm, I said, "After my temper tantrum, do you still want to marry me?"

He shrugged his shoulders. "No, I guess not." But there was a twinkle in his eye.

"Then I have to tell you something," I said. "Let's go for a walk."

He gave me a puzzled look, but took my hand to go with me. When we were out of earshot of the dorm, I said, "I told you once I have problems. You asked what they were, but I kind of lied. Now I want you to know. I can't live my whole life lying to you." I looked up at him to see how he had received me so far.

His face appeared to say he still loved me. "Go on," he said.

There went my finger on my thumbnail again. "Kery is my adopted sister." I hesitated to gulp down a huge lump in my throat. "But she's my natural daughter." I looked up at him again.

He was poker faced. "I see," was all he said.

I rushed on. "I had her last summer before school started, and Mom and Cal adopted her." There it was; the next step Pete had to take.

He took hold of my shoulders and turned me to face him. "But that's not all, is it?" he probed.

I looked down at the grass. "What do you mean?"

He tilted my chin up so I looked him in the eye. Gently he stated more than asked, "Cal is her father, isn't he?"

Pulling my chin from his grasp, I whispered, "I can't tell you that; don't ask me."

He allowed me to look away, but said, "I already know, but I want you to tell me. You shouldn't allow anything to stand between us, Ella. Cal is Kery's father, isn't he?"

Mom's caution not to tell anyone rang in my ears. "No!" I shouted. "Leave me alone." I turned and ran toward the dorm. I didn't need marriage, I didn't need people. I didn't need Eb. Maybe I didn't need Jesus, either. He sure hadn't taken the pain out of my life.

Pete caught up with me and spun me around. "Tell me!" he shouted, trying to hold my eyes with his. "I'm not angry with you, Ella. Tell me. You've got to tell me. I *love* you."

I struggled in his grasp, but he was stronger than me. *I can't hurt you by telling you about Cal,* I thought. *Please, it's ugly and it hurts. Just because God helped me end it doesn't make up for the fact that He also allowed it to happen. I'll leave here and my family and start a different life.* "I won't tell you who Kery's father is, ever. I promised my mother. It's enough for you to know that she's my child."

He dropped my arms and looked into my eyes as if he was searching my soul. His eyes held deep sadness. "Then you don't love me enough to marry me. I want you to talk to me. If it's Cal, and I think it is, you need to talk to someone. I want to be that someone. I want to be more than that someone."

I didn't answer him, I just looked back down at the ground, using the old passive resistance method that worked with Mom. I had promised, and she was hurt enough. Happiness with Pete didn't justify more pain for Mom.

Pete shook my shoulders hard. "Ella!" he shouted. "Don't throw us away. Tell me. I want you to be my wife."

"I can't."

"I won't hurt your family, Ella. But I can't live a lie any easier than you can." He grabbed my chin again and turned my eyes to his. His eyes, open to me, where sincere love shone now like a beacon.

I twisted my head from his grasp and looked away. *What do I do, what do I say?* I pleaded inwardly. *God, you allowed incest because of my sin. I know You are just, and I'm not really angry with You. I was weak and I chose wrong. Am I a fool to run from this good man You've brought me to? Are you offering me love and protection in Pete?*

I looked back at Pete. "Cal is Kery's father," I said woodenly. I trembled and began to shiver uncontrollably.

Putting his arms around me, he gently guided me onto a
bench, holding me tightly. When I stopped shaking, he said,
"Tell me what happened."

I told him everything I could remember, beginning to end.
I finished far into the night. "And now, I'm here. Do you still
love me?" I asked.

He pulled me up from the bench. "I love you, I'll always love
you. You are incredible." We began to walk toward the dorm.
"It wasn't your fault," he said.

Oh, Pete, I thought. *How I love you. The way you support me is
incredible. You goose, it* was *my fault.*

"Now I want you to go get some sleep," he continued.
"You've told me, and everything will be all right."

"But you haven't told me what you think," I protested.

"I'll talk to you in the morning," he answered. "I'm not sure
what I think altogether. Except that I love you more than ever."

At the dorm I went toward my room, but at my door I
looked to see if he was still there. He had gone. I ran back down
the hall and made it to the door to look out just in time to see
him disappear back up the path. *Where is he going?* I wondered.
Fear squeezed my heart.

I learned years later that Pete had considered everything he
knew about me that night. My love for my family, the way I
acted with the kids at school, laughing and having good times,
my newfound faith and my acceptance of him. He had made up
his mind that when he married me, he would never criticize me
for my past, even when he was angry, no matter what. He made
that covenant with God.

I don't know why that wasn't part of what he said to me the
next morning. Maybe he wasn't positive he could keep his
commitment or maybe he thought I'd take him as boasting.
Anyway, when my French class ended, Pete was waiting for me.

I didn't look into his eyes, so that if scorn or pity showed in them, I wouldn't see it. And I didn't say anything because I had said it all the night before.

He reached for my hand as we walked down the hall. "If what happened to you had happened to me, I would never go there again. Personally, I'd like to kill your stepfather."

"My baby is there, and my sister. And killing Cal wouldn't change what happened. It would only put you in jail."

He pushed the button for the elevator. "Well, if you need to talk, I'll listen, but after today I won't bring it up."

"So you still want me, even though I'm 'used'?"

"I said last night that it wasn't your fault. And I don't want to hear any more of that 'used' garbage."

"A lot of guys wouldn't feel like that."

"I'm not a lot of guys. And you are wounded, not used."

Then I dared a look at his eyes, and saw tender concern.

He hugged me gently. "You are a victim of the irresponsibility of several adults, and I'm going to spend my life making up to you for what's been taken from you," he murmured.

The elevator door opened and several students hurried out. Pete and I were the only ones on the ride down. "But you don't understand, Pete. I acted in anger at Mom and then was too weak when it got out of control," I explained.

"What makes you think you could have controlled an adult man who had authority over you?" he countered.

"I don't know. Mom says the girl decides how far things will go."

We left the elevator and shielded our eyes from the bright sunshine outside the building. Pete controlled the rising irritation in his voice. "In normal situations, she's probably right. But your situation wasn't normal. And it really ought to be up to the guy as well as the girl to control himself in all relationships."

We were coming to the dorm and a group of kids burst from the door laughing, the guys punching each other. They surged past us and were gone in a moment.

"Pete, it wasn't just Cal's fault. I told you how Mom treats people. She's responsible too. In fact, you may think this is nuts, but I think if Cal knew Jesus, he'd be a kinder person than Mom, even though she claims to be a Christian. His values are messed up. But if what you told me about sin is true, it could be that he's caught and really wants a way out. I used to love the part of him that treated me kindly. Maybe somebody hurt him and it's like one of those trickle-down effects you hear about, of one person after another hurting, a sin cycle that only Jesus can stop."

"Possible. Why don't you tell him that?"

I shook my head emphatically. "No. Not me. It took too long getting out. I want *you* to explain Jesus to him. You do it right. And besides, I don't want to do anything that will make him think it isn't over."

"Is he still bothering you? I'll have him arrested!"

"Not really. I just don't want to be mistaken."

Pete hugged me. "I'll explain Jesus to him where you can't. We'll sit together. That'll keep you safe and it could help heal your relationship if you do the explaining."

🍒 🍒 🍒

We sat at the table with Cal for hours explaining, between the two of us, the answers to all his questions. Finally he said with regret, "I've gone too far for God to want me."

Pete put his hand on Cal's arm and said, "Cal, I know what you've done. And I forgive you. If I can, don't you think God's big enough to?"

Cal glanced at me and then shrugged.

I thought he probably wouldn't climb out of wherever he lived, so I excused myself and went to bed.

But Pete kept talking. In the morning Pete told me that Cal had prayed to receive Christ at about 3 A.M. Though I was glad and hoped his life would change, I carried a lot of brokenness he had planted. So I vowed not to be alone with him, even if he did know Jesus now—not unless he went to counseling, or we all went. And so far it wasn't a possibility. No one was brave enough to tell the secret.

But as the months went by, it was Cal who distanced himself from me. Cordial backed off to reserved. By the time Pete and I were married, Cal had become a nearly noncommunicative stepfather. Of all our family members, he showed the most avoidance of facing our relationships honestly. But a strange keeping of secrets hung over each of us. We went through all the motions of a wedding, looking perfectly normal. Underneath, none of us could be comfortable with the others because we had crossed too many barriers, acted out of self-interest too many times, and kept so many secrets that we had no bridges between us anymore.

Self-Assessment Guide

1. Find examples of Ella accepting the irrational actions of the adults she lives with and accommodating her actions to them. List first the irrational belief or action of the adult, next Ella's reaction, then any similar actions/reactions from your life, and finally a possible correction that would have changed the example to a rational, rather than irrational, situation.

2. Ella obviously cares for her mother and stepfather in spite of their abusiveness. This is common in victims. Can you identify reasons you have had for loving the person who hurt you?

3. Ella is adamant about the responsibility for the abuse being hers. Having gone this far with her, would you agree or not? Why? Who is responsible for your abuse: the victim or the abuser?

4. A boundary is a personal barrier we set that we determine others will not cross as we serve God as He directs. Ella says, "We had crossed too many barriers, acted out of self-interest too many times, and kept so many secrets that we had no bridges between us anymore." Can you identify places where you should have or could now set healthy boundaries for yourself? An example might be, "I will not allow anyone to convince me to pursue any activity other than worshiping God with His church on Sunday."

5. In the face of Pete's pressure to reveal her past, Ella dares to question where God was during Cal's abuse of her. Ella is not alone; most abuse victims legitimately wonder about God allowing abuse in their lives. Have you ever asked yourself, another person or God why He allowed abuse to happen in your life? What answer did you receive? Read Judges 6. Gideon, too, had the temerity to question God. He found answers. What are they? God deals gently with us, even when in pain and fear we test Him. If you take time to study the life of Gideon, you'll find it similar to the life of an abuse victim. Be sure to look at the plans God fulfilled in Gideon. There's hope for you too.

Helper's Focus

The healing process begins when the victim shares the secret of her abuse. James 5:16 says, "Therefore confess your sins to each other and pray for each other so that you may be healed." It is possible that you are not the first person with whom the victim has shared. Perhaps she is coming to you after being let down by a parent or a professional person. Hopefully, the victim has chosen to share with you because you are an adult who has a growing relationship with Jesus Christ, knows the victim relatively well and whom she trusts in this initial step to recovery. You need not be an expert on the subject of child abuse to help her. But you do need to pray consistently for her, listen a great deal and make biblical suggestions. It certainly wouldn't hurt to research the subject, but the fact that you are reading this book means you already know that. You need to show acceptance of her and refuse to show shock at whatever she shares. As we've said before, assure her that she is not responsible for the abuse.

She may face years of bitterness, anger and broken relationships. Her abuse is similar to a third-degree burn. A first-degree burn can be cooled off with ice and covered to keep it clean; the sufferer may go on with life. Sad advice we've heard given to abuse victims is, "Give it to God and get on with your life." This would work if abuse were like a first-degree burn. On the other hand, a third-degree burn requires stripping away of burned skin, a germ-free environment, nearly constant skilled medical attention, antibiotics, and lots of pain and time to heal. Abuse is like that.

If the victim rebels aggressively, she probably will display hostility to all authority, an independent spirit, and the "love me—no, don't" syndrome common to abuse victims. The victim who uses passive rebellion may turn inside herself and create an inner world in which to hide. Aloofness, passivity, inattention and social isolation can be employed as passive tools of response to past emotional suffering.

With either type of person, the ministry environment must be one of total love and acceptance. Even with this nurturing, recovery may proceed at a snail's pace. Then again, it could take off like a rocket, or perhaps vary between giant strides and regression.

In our experience, what leads the victim up out of the abyss is sharing with others that she has been abused. Move the victim toward viewing her experience from an objective adult position; this helps to avoid the trap of guilt from any natural sexual responses that were aroused in the child by the irresponsible actions of the responsible adult. A child would not feel guilty for feeling pain and jerking if an adult stimulated her with an electric cattle prod, and so should not when the stimulation is sexual.

You can be instrumental in helping the victim decide which people to share her abuse with. A support group may be the most logical beginning. But support groups, too, must be chosen carefully. If you feel God would have you do so, you may want to begin a support group in your church. Chapter Ten explains how Ella and Jane and Art Baker began Stepping Stones, the support group for adults abused as children at First Baptist Church of Modesto, California.

Chapter Six

The Truth Shall Set You Free

Pete and I sat across a modest desk from Pastor Samuels, whose weathered face made him look more like the plumber he used to be than the minister he was. But his intelligent brown eyes reflected the Spirit that had brought him here.

We had begun attending Morley Baptist Church right after we were married, on the advice of a friend who knew Pete was headed for the ministry. Before that we had wandered about to different churches in Morley feeling like icebergs. Our friend told us that the people of this church put Jesus first in their lives. He had gone on and on about Pastor Samuels being a unique minister. Our friend said Pastor was an administrator with a heart tuned to God's vision for His church, who also treated people with sincere compassion.

"Where are you going to seminary, Pete?" Pastor asked.

Pete was holding my hand, and he began to pull at my thumbnail the way he did when he felt nervous. "My folks wanted me to go to a seminary in Texas," Pete answered. "But I don't agree with all the teachings of the school they like. I guess I don't know where I'm going to seminary."

Pastor smiled. "It's difficult to disagree with your parents, especially when you've only been out of their home a short time." He looked at me. "How do you feel about being a pastor's wife, Ella?" he asked.

"I don't know how to be a pastor's wife. But I love Pete, and where he goes, I go," I answered. *Bag and baggage,* I thought.

Pastor leaned back in his big, black executive chair and put his finger on his bottom lip while he gazed at us. Finally he said, "Let's do this. Stay here and serve with us for about a year. We'll show you how things run. Then I think you would do best at Western Conservative Baptist Seminary in Portland, Oregon. Earl Radmacher is in charge up there, and he's a good man." He grinned at Pete.

I glanced at Pete. He didn't seem to feel put down.

"First thing we'll do is enroll you in a home Bible study. They're the backbone of the church. And it sounds like Ella could use all the help she can get to learn the Word. Yes?"

"Yes," I agreed quickly.

"Do you have a place to live?" he asked.

"We're working on it," Pete answered.

"Would you like to rent an apartment from the church? They're right across the street and inexpensive," Pastor offered.

"That's more than we could have hoped for," Pete replied. "Yes, of course we would."

Pete found work in a cannery. Morley is located in a heavy vegetable and fruit growing area, and canneries are spread all over town. His job sounded like something I would hate. He did the same thing over and over for an eight-hour shift, sometimes with peaches, sometimes with tomatoes. At night he told me stories about the pecking order at the cannery.

I, on the other hand, became a waitress. My work was varied by the variety of customers' personalities. Some were kind and talked a little with me; others were busy and probably couldn't have picked me out of a line-up. Still others were rude and demanding. It made for good after-work conversation, and counting the tips was fun too.

The next person we met at church was our Bible study leader, a gentle, soft-spoken farmer who could quote Scripture verses from memory. Important ones like, "Trust in the Lord with all your heart and lean not on your own understanding; in all your ways acknowledge Him, and He will make your paths straight" (Proverbs 3:5). Straight paths. That appealed to me. I'd had enough of crooked paths. And letting God figure out where my life would go sounded secure.

The study group met in his middle-class house, stucco like in most American towns, though people said he was very rich. His living room comfortably held the fifteen or so people who came every Tuesday night; the members were all different ages and types, men and women, no children. Children couldn't come so that the adults could pay attention. Members couldn't miss meetings without a good excuse, either. But then, Pete and I wouldn't have wanted to miss one anyway. They were a haven between Sundays, where we plugged back into God after struggling through Monday and Tuesday. The people in our study group showed me a new kind of love. It was love without fear but with understanding, and camaraderie through common frailty. Our leader called it *agape*, Greek for the love that flows to us and through us from God.

One night we talked about how hard it is to avoid sin. One couple in the group usually asked the best questions. The wife, a stout, smiling woman, had been a Christian awhile; the man, a thin, wiry type, wasn't yet. After about a half-hour discussion, he finally blurted, "I can't live up to all the expectations people have of Christians. I mean, no dancing, no drinking, no smoking, no nothing."

I wondered what the answer to that was, glad I didn't have to figure it out.

The leader said, "Any of you feel you can give Mel an answer?" He was neat that way. He didn't assume that he had all the answers, or try to show off how learned he was. And he had plenty to boast about if he had wanted to.

A man named Len, a handsome professor with a pretty wife, said, "Mel, none of us can live up to God's standards if we're depending on our own strength. But if we let Jesus work in us, we can do anything."

I didn't recall any Christians I'd met, either here or in Maplewood Springs, nailing people about the issues Mel had mentioned. But Pastor had said to Pete and me the day we met with him that if he gave up a little Schnapps to convince someone who didn't know Jesus that He really does change lives, it was no big sacrifice. I thought that made sense, and since Daddy's drinking hadn't helped our family, I wasn't planning to drink anyway. It must be the people watching Christians' lives, not the Christians themselves, who were so demanding. Or else I hadn't gone to church long enough for someone to mention this stuff.

What Len said about living better by depending upon Jesus got my attention. He went on to say that there was something called "spiritual breathing." When we sinned, we should stop immediately and apologize to God. An important verse, 1 John 1:9, says, "If we confess our sins, He is faithful and just and will forgive us our sins and purify us from all unrighteousness." Boy, did that give me a free feeling. Len continued that when we asked for forgiveness, we also requested to be filled with the Holy Spirit so that what we did next would be through God's power. I glimpsed a bright life, where many good things happened, when Len talked about spiritual breathing. What a contrast to my old life. I felt washed.

At home I hesitated before I turned off the light. Cuddling up to Pete's back, I said, "Honey, give me some input on what Len said about depending on Jesus for the strength to do right."

"I think he's right on. It takes a willing heart and prayer on our part, and God does the rest," Pete answered over his shoulder and then turned onto his back.

I propped myself up on my elbow. "My mom said that I've personally been responsible for what I did since I was twelve. She said the Bible said so." I didn't say it as a question, but it was one.

Pete motioned for me to rest my head on his shoulder. "If you find that anywhere, let me know," he teased. He was big on checking the Bible yourself for what is true.

"Prayer is important," I observed. "Much more important than I ever realized before."

"Whole new world, huh?" Pete murmured.

"Yeah," I agreed, and turned out the light.

The next morning I got up at 5:30 to do my Bible study. I had read in Psalms that it was good to talk to God first thing, so I planned extra time before I had to go to work and before Pete was up, when things were quiet. This morning I was working on Romans 12:1–2 where it says, "Therefore, I urge you, brothers, in view of God's mercy, to offer your bodies as living sacrifices, holy and pleasing to God—this is your spiritual act of worship. Do not conform any longer to the pattern of this world, but be transformed by the renewing of your mind. Then you will be able to test and approve what God's will is—His good, pleasing and perfect will."

Our Bible study leader expected more from us than just reading Scripture. We also had to ask ourselves questions about what it meant and then ask ourselves, "So what? What's this got to do with my life?" The first thing that caught my eye in the Scripture this morning was that God considers my offering of myself to Him a holy sacrifice, even with how dirty and useless I'd felt. I had seen a T-shirt somewhere that said, "God made me and He don't make no junk." This verse was a formal version of that T-shirt.

The verse also said that by renewing my mind—I guessed that meant filling my head with what God says in the Bible and praying every time I think about it—one day I would be able to figure out the will of God. Amazing! Me. Old Ella Wainwright Allen, who'd teetered on the edge of suicide only about two years ago.

Every time I found something good like this early in the morning, I would wake Pete up to tell him about it. Poor Pete. He already knew all this stuff, so I wasn't sharing anything he needed. But each time, after he cleared his head of sleep, he patiently listened to me, and usually had something to add that opened my eyes even more. This time he commented, "The 'do not conform to the world' includes falling for your mother's extra-biblical legalism."

"What?"

He propped himself up on his pillow, "When your mom says something came from the Bible, don't swallow it until you read it for yourself. Otherwise you're conforming to the pattern of the world. What's not of God is of the world. If it's not in the Bible, God didn't say it. That's true, no matter who's talking— your mother or anyone else. And the longer you practice doing this, the quicker you'll be able to recognize when someone is off base."

I propped my chin on my knee. "Seems like I'd need to spend a lot of time reading the Bible in order to get all of what God thinks. And not just skimming through without picking out what's going on, but digging around in what's being said to get the 'so what.' "

Pete stroked my hair. "It's a life-long process, but I have books to help. I'll show you how to use them. Ella, I think there's nothing more important than following God. He knows the answers to everything and He knows what direction He plans for you and me. That's why I think studying the Bible and prayer are so important. Before, you depended on me to tell you about God. But you shouldn't continue to do that. You know that minister named Jim Jones who took all those people to Guyana and had them commit suicide there? Those people depended on him to tell them about God, but he lied and manipulated them. We need to study for ourselves. You even heard Pastor say to double-check from the Bible what he says when he preaches on Sunday." He took a big breath. "End of sermon."

"That's okay, " I said. "Input. I need input."

Pete was still caressing me. "Want to fool around?" he asked with a wink.

"No, I've got to get ready for work."

He ran his fingers through my hair. "How about after work?" I flashed angry eyes at him. "How about a little romance?" I wished I didn't react that way. But when he made blunt suggestions about the sexual side of our marriage, even with caresses, I felt taken advantage of like in the old days.

"I'm only starting early, honey," he said, sounding wounded.

I had told him it bugged me when bedtime came and he suddenly had an agenda other than sleep.

"I'm sorry, Pete. You didn't do anything wrong." I stood to start getting dressed.

"I'm not him, Ella. I love you. I'd love you if we never had sex again."

"I don't want to never have sex again, Pete. I want softness, gentleness, lots of talking, so I know it's the inside of me, my heart and soul, that you love. I know I'm touchy and demanding. And you don't act like him. I'm not comparing, honest." I started to cry.

He held out his arms and I sat within them on the edge of the bed. "I don't want to be like this. But I don't know how to be different. I can't even make love without slipping away in my mind. It's an old thing I used to do to keep from wanting to die. Didn't help, though. I still wanted to die."

Pete smoothed my hair again and again. "We'll overcome it, together. Remember, one of those verses you read said that through Jesus we can do anything."

"Do you think God cares about sex, Pete?"

"He cares about everything, all the parts of our lives, even the things that seem insignificant to us."

Bouncing up purposefully, I declared, "Well, if I can make my sex life better by depending on Jesus, then I can get to work on time the same way."

Pete got laid off at the cannery shortly after that. He started looking for work the next day. But in November, unemployment in an agriculturally-based economy is high. He came home every day for a couple of weeks discouraged that no one would even let him explain what he could do. Then he heard that the church was sending people to Mexico to help a mission there. "I think being laid off might have been God's way of getting me to go to Mexico, Ella. What do you think?"

I didn't know much of anything about how God did things. But I remembered Mom sitting in the dining room the morning I needed to tell her about Cal. So I agreed, "You could be right. We can make it on what I earn for a while."

The first Sunday Pete was gone Pastor said during his sermon, "When you've prayed to ask God to forgive you, it's a sin to continue to wallow in guilt. He forgives us when we ask. When we're forgiven, there is no more guilt. By continuing to worry over the past, we're saying that God hasn't the power to forgive, and we're allowing Satan to defeat us."

I deflated. Guilt was my roommate. Guilt over my relationship with Cal, how much I resented Mom for divorcing Daddy, Kery being illegitimate, leaving her with Mom and Cal, and being so weak in all this. And I had prayed for forgiveness. So here I was, *still* in sin. Pete wasn't home so I had no one to talk with. Maybe I could wait for him. But they were supposed to be gone a month. After a few days I couldn't stand it anymore, so I made an appointment with Pastor.

I slithered into the chair on the other side of his desk, hoping he could help me work this out without my having to tell him who I really was.

He sat in his big chair, just as he had before. "It's good to see you, Ella," he said. "How's everything going?"

"Fine. I really like the Bible study, " I answered. I thought about telling him how funny Pete looked in our short, little apartment bathtub with his knees nearly under his chin. But I wasn't sure if he would think that was funny.

"Pete's in Mexico, huh?" he observed.

I nodded.

"You doing okay without him?"

"It's pretty lonely. Funny the annoying things he does that I plan not to nag him about anymore. Having him gone makes me wish he were here to do them," I replied honestly.

"Good for you," Pastor said. "What have you come to see me about?"

The Moment of Truth, I thought. "Remember last Sunday when you talked about guilt?"

"I think so."

Looking at a wonderful painting of a long table that stretched clear out of the picture and was obviously set for a big banquet, I said, "I need to know what to do about guilt. I don't want to sin, but I feel a lot of guilt even though I already asked for forgiveness." That was good—no details, question on the table.

Seeing my gaze, he said, "I'm looking forward to attending that banquet. What are we talking about here? What did you do?"

Fear. Pain. Panic. I started to cry, hard.

He opened his drawer and passed me a box of tissues. I gulped and wiped my nose.

"Ella, wounds have to be cleaned out to heal. Start anywhere you want and just tell me as you can."

"Pastor, my mother told me to keep what happened to myself."

"Talking about sin is the same as cleaning a wound, Ella. 'If we confess our sins, He is faithful and just to forgive our sins and cleanse us from all unrighteousness.' It's no accident the way that verse is written. The confession and the cleansing go hand-in-glove."

"You can't tell somebody else what I say to you. You're bound to keep my confidence, right?"

"That's right. And Ella, I carry so many people's secrets it's a wonder I don't weigh more than I do."

Relieved, I laughed. Pastor had such a way of making life seem less impossible. "Well, I...I..." It still didn't make it any easier to tell him. "I have this stepfather. Initially I hated him because my mom replaced my dad with him. But then I was so angry with my mom that I decided to make him like me better than her. He thought I wanted sex to be part of that. I didn't, but throughout my teen years... When I was eighteen, I had his baby." I said the rest quickly. "I've gone off and left her with my mom and stepdad. Just walked off and left her, and when I go to visit she cries and wants to come with me. I married a minister with all this in my past because he said it wouldn't matter. I have a younger sister who is still there and I don't know whether either she or my daughter is safe. My mother didn't know at first; I lied, saying I was raped. But when she did know, she didn't do much. I don't know if she'll protect Jessi and Kery. Pete is wonderful about it. He keeps telling me it wasn't my fault. But..." I dissolved into tears again.

"You're carrying quite a load," Pastor said when he could be heard above my blubbering. "Your stepfather isn't abusing you now?"

I looked up at him and his blue eyes were *smiling* at me. He wasn't disgusted or embarrassed. "No," I answered.

"Tell me what you did that caused this trouble."

"I was mad at my mom for making my dad go away. She said she'd lose her marriage to Cal—that's my stepfather—if he and I didn't quit fighting. So I decided I'd make him love me more than her. She's not very nice to him. It was easy. But I didn't mean to have the kind of love he gave."

"Who said no in your family?"

I only looked at him. He didn't seem angry, maybe exasperated was a good description.

"Ella, sin that involves people, as yours does, is hard to walk away from. You are accepting responsibility that isn't yours, though. Your mother, father and stepfather were adults. You were a child. Adults should take responsibility to do the things they are supposed to do, and not do the things they shouldn't. Maybe you had a small part in the sin, but very small, influenced greatly by irresponsible adults around you. Your father, what's he like?"

"He's great! He loves me and he's fun. When I was a kid, he took me with him when he traveled. At home he showed me how to do all kinds of things on the farm. I painted a whole fence when I was nine. He did drink a lot though, and he and Mom fought about that. She would go over to Cal's house to dance because Daddy was always tired when he got home, or drunk. And he hasn't much use for God. I think my marrying Pete put a distance between my dad and me."

"And your mom?"

"Mom thinks of herself first. After the divorce she had to work and she expected me to do the housework and take care of Jessi, my sister, and then Kery, my sister/daughter. Pete says Mom is a phony. She quotes the Bible as saying things it doesn't say and acts like she cares, but she smokes and cusses. When I lived at home, she screamed to make things go her way."

Pastor looked me in the eye and said, "Do you hear what you're telling me?"

I thought I might be in trouble for saying what I really thought.

"No one in your family was willing to take responsibility. Much of it was dumped on you. Your father drank and didn't control his wife, your mother didn't control herself and thrust her responsibilities on you, and your stepfather succumbed to temptation and took advantage of you when you were off limits. So now you feel guilty because you, in childishness—which was only natural since you *were* a child—couldn't be a wife and mother for people who had no right to demand that of you."

He wasn't mad at me for saying what I thought. He believed me, and he said the same thing Pete did. Maybe it wasn't all my fault.

Pastor continued, "From now on, when you hear me talk about guilt in sermons, you remember that I said this to you. Don't expect to give your past to God and leave it, because it's a someone, not a something. You have to deal with these people on a continuing basis. And by the way, I wouldn't spend any more time around them than you absolutely must. Each time you feel bitterness or rage, or one of them does something to hurt you, refuse to respond in anger or fear or any other emotion that isn't godly. Instead, back away from the situation and look for what God wants to happen. If you can help, do so. If it's up to them, leave it to them."

He rested his elbows on the desk. "Ella, concentrate on your marriage. Your past will only make you more useful to Pete in his ministry because you understand things many people have never experienced. But you have to spend your mental energy on being the best wife and mother you can.

"Your sister still lives at home. You need to go home and tell her what happened to you—right away. Your stepfather is likely to make her a substitute for you if you don't. Your daughter, on the other hand, is probably safe; men are less likely to molest their natural children."

I groaned. What he said was so logical. Why hadn't I admitted that Cal could turn to Jessi? Why hadn't I told her before in order to protect her? I had been so busy hoping for a miracle. How would I get home? We had barely enough money to pay our bills.

"I know you and Pete are strapped. How long will it take you to do this?"

"I guess I could do it Thursday and Friday on my days off."

"Then find out what it will cost to get there and let Bonnie know. She'll have a check written for you. Go now; don't wait for Pete to get back from Mexico. It may not be an emergency, but the sooner the better."

"Thank you, Pastor."

He smiled. "Ella, when you feel guilty, here's what to do. Tell God how you feel and then tell Him you know He has forgiven you and that this territory has already been covered. Acknowledge that your guilty feeling is sin and ask Him to take it away. You probably will need to do this often at first. But you will find, if you do it faithfully, that as time goes by you feel guilty less and less often. If you need to see me again, you know where I am. May I pray for you before you go?"

"Sure."

"Father, You have brought Ella out of one of the hardest situations people can face. Though her abuse is over, she still struggles with guilt. We know You understand how easy it is to fall into guilt over things that have happened in relationships. Ella knows You have forgiven her. We pray that You will help her forgive herself and make her strong in You. We also pray that You would show Ella what Your will is in her life. In Jesus' name, amen."

Pastor shook my hand. "You'll be a great minister's wife," he said, "because you understand the weakness of people."

I left wondering what God would do with me, and actually anticipating the future. *Looking forward to the future probably isn't a big deal for most people*, I thought, *but it's a giant step for me.* That night I wrote in my journal, but I told about other things that happened that day. I couldn't chance the possibility that someone would read the truth about my family, not even to record what Pastor said and how I knew God was leading me up from the pit.

The next Thursday I was in Maplewood Springs waiting for Jessi to get home from school. I had felt like a traitor smiling at Mom before she went to work and talking as if I weren't about to blow the whistle on Cal. But something inside told me that my feeling was illegitimate and shouldn't be trusted. I sat on the living room floor absently playing with Kery, and praying like Pastor told me to, when Jessi opened the back door.

"Boy! It's freezing outside. You want to crack these icicles off my nose?" she said, throwing her coat on the table. She dropped her books beside her coat and went to the refrigerator for milk while she talked. "There's this football player in my fourth-period class, one of those guys where the lights are on but nobody's home. I think he's cheating off me when we take tests because he twists around and leans forward a lot. He's going to get both of us in trouble, and I don't know how to stop him."

"Maybe you could ask the teacher to change your seat. If he asks why, tell him," I offered.

Coming to sit next to me, she exclaimed "That's perfect!" as if I had delivered the wisdom of Solomon.

I couldn't manage much small talk, so I began, "Jessi, our pastor said I need to talk to you about something serious."

"Oh? What?"

"I wish I didn't have to tell you this. Because I love you and I know you love me. And I want you always to love me. Maybe you won't after I tell you this, but I have to tell you anyway. I don't know how knowing it will affect you, but I want you to know before I say it that if you need me to do anything now, or ever in the future, I will." I sounded a little loony tunes to myself and wished I had said what I rehearsed. But when I started talking, I had forgotten it all.

Jessi was staring at me with eyes that said, "For crying out loud, put it on the table."

I rushed on. "I don't know if you ever realized why Cal and I always did things together outside or why he never took you when we went someplace."

Her face darkened. "Bugged me. Seemed unfair."

"It was unfair. I'm sorry about it. I need to tell you something about Cal." I swallowed hard. The truth could change everything. But when your sister's in danger, you risk the loss of her acceptance, companionship and support. "Jessi, you know how I told you before that Cal could misunderstand you if you were very friendly to him?"

"Yeah."

"I told you that because he adds sex to affection, at least he did with me." That was all I could say—I was crying uncontrollably and hid my head in my hands. Shame overwhelmed me. Finally I added, "I wasn't raped on the way home from town. I lied. Cal..."

I felt her hand on my head. "Ella, you didn't want to do that."

I lowered my hands to try to see her through my tears. Her eyes looked sad. "I only wanted a friend. Nobody loved me. I mean, you did, but I was supposed to take care of *you*. I needed a grownup to look out for me. I got badly mixed up. Daddy was gone and Mom..." I trailed off, not wanting to blame Mom, especially when Jessi would be left to deal with the confusion of that. She still had to live here.

Jessi looked down at the floor and said, "I hate Cal. I didn't like him much before, but now I hate him." She looked up with anger. "How could he take advantage of you that way?" she demanded.

Dully I answered, "I thought he loved me. But he told Mom he wanted to prove that she could raise as bad a daughter as he did." My heart started a U-turn back into the person I used to be. Old tapes of accusing voices began to play in my head. "If you don't lose some weight, no boy is ever going to look at you." "You dumb, dirty slut, why don't you kill yourself?"

I struggled to remind myself that I belonged to God and He had great plans for me. Wordlessly I said, "Father, help me." To Jessi I said, "But it doesn't matter whether Cal had a reason, Jessi. I belong to God now and I don't live here. Cal won't hurt me anymore. But you have to live here and he could decide to bother you since I'm not available. I told you so that he couldn't trap you the way he did me. If he so much as touches you in a way you feel uncomfortable with, tell Mom. She knows what happened with me. And tell me too, please. Mom responded pretty weird when I told her, and you may need more help than she can give. Has he bothered you?"

"No," Jessi responded with a shudder. She picked Kery up and played with her fingers.

"I'll tell Mom that I've told you so you can talk to her if you want."

"Okay," Jessi said and began to cry. "Ella, I love you. I love you more than ever. I'm so sorry all this happened to you." We hugged and cried.

We came out of it when Kery pulled herself up on my back and whispered gibberish in a sad tone. When we turned to look at her, her face was as crestfallen as a baby's face could be. She went right on sadly whispering something that she understood but we didn't. Jessi and I both exploded in laughter. When Kery saw she had caused it, her face turned from sadness to delight and she laughed with us. Barely able to talk for laughing, I said,

"Mom will be home soon. We'd better get dinner on." I stood, took Kery from Jessi and pulled Jessi up from the floor.

Late that night when Cal and Jessi each had given up and gone to bed, I explained to Mom that I'd told Jessi.

"I don't see how that was necessary!" she exploded. "Ella, you've got to get control of yourself. This is not everyone's problem. Now I'm going to have to deal with Jessi too."

"My pastor disagrees with you," was all I could say.

She slapped the table. "Your pastor! You told your pastor? Don't you realize you could endanger our whole family?"

"He can't tell anyone, Mom. He's sworn to keep confidences. I needed someone to talk to. And he thinks Jessi could be in danger living with Cal after I don't live here anymore."

"Sounds to me like you needed a whole lot of 'someones.' Who else have you told?"

"Pete."

"Oh, Pete too. So now Cal can feel as uncomfortable as possible when you come to visit."

"Pete is my husband. I didn't think it was right to marry him without telling him."

She adopted her teaching tone. "Even Ann Landers says that your husband doesn't benefit from knowing everything about you. You've made a mistake, Ella. I tried to tell you to keep this to yourself, and you assured me you would. But I guess your word is not as good as I thought."

What's the use? I thought. I stopped talking and silently wished I could move to the other side of the world from this woman. She never would care about me, so I wouldn't let her hurt me. I would do what Pastor said and concentrate on Pete and building a family for him.

Self-Assessment Guide

1. Look at the subjects that Ella mentally addresses throughout the chapter. Write suggestions on how you would make what she says to herself positive rather than negative. Can you relate to her negative self-talk? What suggestions for Ella could you take and apply to yourself?

2. Identify the principles Ella learns at Morley Baptist that influence her recovery. Replacing the lies of abuse with truth is important. How do these truths affect you? Did you already know them? How can you allow them to sink in and influence your behavior?

3. There are stages of recovery. List in paragraph form the details of the stages Ella has gone through up to this point. List the details of yours.

4. Ella struggles with her attitude toward sex with Pete. Compare what she feels with what you feel. What does she do wrong? What does she do right? How does Pete help?

5. Ella's courageous revealing of the abuse to Jessi was seen as weak and unnecessary by her mother. Since you revealed your abuse, have there been events that were seen by the people involved as the opposite of how you saw the events? How do you determine what to do?

6. Truth must begin somewhere. God says He is truth. Is it time to accept what He offers and commit your life to Jesus Christ?

Helper's Focus

Pastors, counselors and others who are confronted with abuse in someone's life hold a key that either unlocks the door to recovery or seals it more tightly. The victim desperately needs answers to issues she deals with, but her shame, desire to keep promises of secrecy, and fear of exposing herself to someone who wouldn't understand nearly paralyze her. Often she will try to get the answers she needs without disclosing the abuse. Since that generally doesn't work very well and definitely doesn't lead to full recovery, she is forced to show herself for a moment—"Peek-a-boo, I've been abused"—to see what reaction she gets. When the reaction is help and understanding, she draws closer. When the reaction is disgust, anger or disapproval, she withdraws into her ready-made shell.

Those who want to help must control whatever feelings are aroused by her disclosure of abuse, and offer a friendly, helping hand to the victim. They must recognize that intrafamilial abuse involves people she loves, if in ever-so-crooked ways. Therefore, the acceptance and willingness to help that you offer must extend to the abuser and to other members of the family as well. Outbursts of anger, vows to do harm to the abuser, or scorn for the weakness of the non-offending parent do not help. They are not constructive and they may send the victim into hiding for years to come.

The helper must be careful throughout the relationship with the victim to delineate what work the helper will do and what work the victim will do. She must not take over the victim's decision-making processes or insert herself into the victim's relationships unless the abuse is continuing and the victim hasn't the courage to report it. Assuming the abuse is over, the helper provides truth, a listening ear and encouragement to do what is right.

Since even controlled involvement with the victim can be time-consuming, this is an excellent point in a victim's life to encourage attendance in a Bible study/support group for adults abused as children. In the group the victim will find many people whose experiences are similar to hers and who, simply because there are more of them, have more hours to listen and offer feedback. Biblically developed material—on issues such as what abuse is, setting boundaries, anger, forgiveness and where life goes from here—can be taught in a setting where the victim has the opportunity to talk out her feelings while she works through the issues.

One prerequisite of the support group must be that confidentiality is strict. As confidentiality has been important to the victim's freedom to disclose, it continues to be an issue if she is to consider attending a support group. We must not forget, because of the progress the victim has made, that she has been badly wounded and needs special care.

Stepping Stones, the Bible study/support group we started at First Baptist Church in Modesto, California, both promises the victim, and binds her to, confidentiality. She also is allowed up to an hour a week talking with her small group leader if she needs to, and can speak with Jane or her husband, Art, or a pastor by appointment. Specific advice is not given by one member of the group to another. Only a listening ear is provided.

The guiding verse in this stage of recovery is Ephesians 5:15:

> Be very careful, then, how you live—not as unwise but as wise, making the most of every opportunity, because the days are evil.

Chapter Seven

A Silk Purse Out of a Sow's Ear

Varied shades of the green of Oregon caressed our eyes as we crossed the border. The farther north we traveled, the more lush the vegetation, until in Portland it looked as if the people constantly beat back the forest to maintain their hold on a place to live. With our belongings in the back of a truck and a new little "package" that I carried almost ready to make his or her appearance, we drove up to the barn-red house that we would call home during seminary.

The house was tiny, two bedrooms, but it had a huge basement. It reminded me of Daddy's mother's house. My favorite thing about our new home was the vacant lot with blackberry vines in the back where we could plant a garden. Compared to apartment living, this was paradise. And it was far away from Mom and Cal, which suited me fine. Pete and I took the bedroom closest to the street and put the crib, given to us by a family in our Morley Bible study, in the smaller room that we would use as a nursery. We put the kitchen table in a wonderful nook with huge windows on all sides where we could view the backyard while we ate. The house had hardwood floors and a generally old-fashioned style. I loved it immediately.

We had only a week to move in before Pete's classes started. He converted a corner of the basement into his study by enclosing it in muslin "walls," and we christened it his tabernacle. Thursday I was grocery shopping when I began to feel labor starting. By the time I made it to the checkout stand, I was having to stop and breathe through each pain. We took the groceries with us to the hospital, and Pete Jr. was born shortly after we arrived.

I held him, revelling in the fact that I did not have to give him up, that he belonged to Pete and me. Pete gazed down at him tenderly, and I felt protected, cherished and safe. Petey had long fingers and huge feet and he was wonderful, a gift from God. I kissed his pudgy soft cheek, smoothed what little hair he had and cooed motherly sweetnesses to him. He seemed an expression of God's forgiveness. I never wanted to let him go.

When Pete called Mom to let her know that the baby had arrived, she said I now had a baby of my own. Didn't she realize that Kery was my baby, no matter what? I wished the telephone had never been invented. It allowed her to shower me with her never-ending distortions in the midst of my joy. It brought her close enough to wound me again if I'd let her, which I determined not to. Seeing my struggle, Pete apologized for telling me what Mom had said and suggested that I not call home more than once a month, and then try to talk to Jessi.

Right after Pete's classes started, mine did too. Mine were classes for wives of seminary students at Western. I'd heard that some seminaries didn't have classes like these and I was grateful that Western did. Input, I needed input. This first semester I took a class on Bible study methods and one on mothering a Christian family.

In the Bible study methods class, I learned that to competently study the Bible for myself, I have to read the passage I'm working on several times until what it says becomes firmly rooted in my head. I write questions about difficult-to-understand content as well as who is doing what to whom. Next, I study the cross reference passages to find whether they shed light on my questions or create more questions. Then I look at commentaries for the answers I couldn't find on my own, always comparing with other Scripture to make sure the commentator didn't go off chasing rabbits. Finally I ask, "What does this mean to me and what should I do about it?" The process is time-consuming, but I am immersed in what God says, completely assured that I understand and am equipped with more knowledge of God with which to live my life.

The professor of the Bible study class and the teacher of the other class were husband and wife. One of the first nights of class she said, "If you think your husband is wrong about something, tell him gently once. If that doesn't change anything, pray about it. Don't be a nag. God is in control, talk with Him."

The next week in the Bible study class, her husband was telling a story about their marriage to illustrate what he was trying to teach us. In the story he changed his mind about what he was going to do. Leaving the story for a moment, he said to us, "God wouldn't let me rest on that issue. I guess my wife must have been praying about it. That's what she does when she can't get my attention." All the women who attended both classes started laughing, and he said, "Oh, she's already told you how to do that, huh?" The couple's attitude stood in marvelous contrast to the marital field of war in which I had grown up. I wondered whether Pete and I could put into effect the example of the professor and his wife.

We had decided that I would babysit while Pete attended seminary so I could stay home with Petey, and Pete would only have to work part-time. About a month after Petey was born I got my first children to babysit: a girl, Susan, who was four, and her ten-month-old brother, Adam. Their mother was a nervous woman who worked downtown. Her demeanor evidenced itself in her children. Susan and Adam became agitated whenever an adult spoke to them, whether in anger or not. I began reading stories to them while they sat on my lap, and that helped them to calm down around me. Nevertheless, every day for the first hour or so after they arrived, they quivered when I spoke to them. That's how reading stories first thing in the morning became a ritual at our house. Petey liked it too, when he was awake.

The next child we cared for was April. She was two weeks old when she first came, a little angel. Her impoverished mother worked hard for the money she earned, and she loved April dearly. When she had to get into her car and leave, tears ran down her cheeks. I didn't blame her—it was hard enough to have to leave her baby each day, but April cooed and enjoyed life. Susan loved to sit and hold April while she drank a bottle. I was beginning to feel the strain of caring for four children, but since we needed one more to balance the budget I persevered.

I turned down several families with more than one child, hoping to add only one more to our troops. But two weeks went by and I couldn't wait any longer, so I agreed to talk with the next mother who called even though she had two children. I thought when I met her that Dee's children might be a challenge, but I was in for a surprise at how much of a trial they turned out to be. Actually, Angela, the older sister, wasn't a problem. But Dee had decided that Tony, who was just at a year old, must be potty trained. He wasn't ready, and he wet and soiled everything stationary for two weeks. After worrying a whole day over how I would speak to her, I told Dee in exasperation that for me to continue to sit for her, she would have to send diapers. She did the next day—well-timed since I was starting into the part of my cycle when I experienced PMS. I could hear my internal voice saying, "Your life is too hard.

Why does God expect this of you? Why do other people get to be rich and have no worries?" These unreasonable thoughts about my life warned us that my husband, "family" and I were in for another bout when I wished I could be someone else and made them wish I were some*where* else. Lately this pressure took all but about two weeks of my existence every month and a half.

The following day Dee sent training pants again. Tony had diarrhea and filled his pants before his mother made it down the block. I screamed at Angela to bring his Kaopectate. Hurrying to open the bottle, she tripped over the rug and threw it, more than spilled it, across the living room floor. My head swelled with rage. Even though it was their mother that I should have dealt with—and only after I calmed down—the children were there and became the target of my rage. I grabbed Angela by the shoulders and shook her fiercely. "Look what you've done!" I yelled. "You go get something and clean this up. Every last drop!" Turning on Tony, I jerked him off the sofa and marched off to the bathroom where I scrubbed him angrily.

Susan looked in timidly and said, "Can I help?"

"No!" I yelled. "Just stay out of my way." My yelling woke Petey up and he started to cry. I roughly sat Tony down on the cold edge of the bath tub and said, "Don't move. You better be here when I get back." His little face was terror-stricken. Coming into the nursery, I said bitterly, "Petey, I don't need this right now. Can't you be quiet?" He kept crying. I plucked him from his bed, grabbed Tony by the hand and screamed at Angela and Susan to come to the sofa. Adam was playing with a toy on the floor and I threw his toy down and plopped him next to Tony. Lining them all up—except Petey, who I had silenced with a pacifier—I scowled at them angrily and said, "The next one of you who says or does anything wrong is going to get it! You better all behave or I'm going to spank somebody, and you're not going to like it! Now you all sit here while I change Petey.

I don't want to hear a peep out of you, and when I get back I don't want to see any of you in any position except the one you're in right now."

I left the light off in Petey's room, hoping the twilight would help to calm me down. The children all looked so frightened. I knew they thought they had caused it; children always think adults are right. But I also knew that though it had been a tough morning, I had caused the explosion. I reminded me of Mom, and I hated myself. Where did all this anger come from when I was dealing with PMS? Why didn't being a Christian keep me from doing things like this? I stood crying as I automatically found baby powder and a fresh diaper. Petey looked at me from behind his pacifier with a bewildered frown. I scooped him up and walked past the frozen children on the sofa, threw our jackets on and escaped into the backyard. Pacing the perimeter I prayed, "Father, those children need me to act like a sane, normal, friendly, kind adult. They might even like to do something fun instead of listen to me rant. I don't know what's wrong with me, so I don't know how to fix it. Please help me." As I prayed, calm came back at least enough for me to go back into the house.

I knelt in front of them, sitting there like little stones on the sofa. "I'm sorry," I said. "You weren't really bad. I shouldn't have gotten so mad at you. Will you forgive me?" Susan slipped off the sofa and laid her little head on my shoulder. "Sure we will," she said. Angela nodded her head and Tony jumped down to run over and grab the toy Adam had left laying on the floor. All forgiven. Children are so resilient, and thank the Lord for that.

After Pete and I had dinner that night, I told him what had happened and how impossible it seemed to me that I would ever become what God wanted me to be. "I see the other wives at school. They're so together. They walk calmly through life, dealing with everything in peace the way God means us to," I said. "But I'm not like them—I get angry and I hold grudges and I don't even brush my teeth some days."

Pete took my hand as we settled on the sofa. "Ella, you see only the public side of the wives at school. They face many of the same problems you do, and most of them probably don't do as good a job of handling themselves as you do. Since you don't see them at home, you assume they always act like they do at school, but that's not how it is—trust me. I've been over to a few of their houses."

I had started decorating for Christmas and I sat watching the colored lights at the window blink on and off while I listened to Pete. "This is my third Christmas as a Christian, Pete. But I feel like I'm hardly different than I was before I became a Christian."

Pete put his finger under my chin and turned my head to look at him. "Ella, you don't cuss anymore, ever. And you know how to study the Bible better than some deacons do. Not only that, you make time to study. I think you are trying to fight on too many fronts. Why don't you ask God to show you one thing He wants you to deal with? Then work on only that one issue. Put all the other subjects that bother you about yourself on hold until you have this first weakness mastered. They say that will take about three months."

I laughed inwardly at his three-month comment. Pete was very specific about everything. He contrasted with me, who got the drift and forged mightily ahead. We made a good combination. I considered myself, wondering which of my weaknesses God would like me to work on first. "Do you think self-discipline could be it?" I asked Pete. I thought about my angry outburst today, my refusal to do dishes right after a meal, my struggle with weighing too much.

"Self-discipline is a pretty broad subject," Pete answered. "Can you narrow it down some?"

"Well, my teacher says it will make life much simpler if I wash dishes right after meals and get our Sunday clothes ready on Saturday night."

"Good. Do that."

I started practicing with dinner dishes. The first night I was motivated to get the dishes done right after dinner because we had talked just the night before. Sure enough, the next day I had more fun with the children because I didn't have to hold them off while I got the dishes done. That night we had to work with the youth group at the church we were attending, so I left the dishes in the sink "to soak." True to form, the next day was the pits—until after the dinner dishes were done and we went to get the Christmas tree.

When Saturday night came it was dishes - 3, misery - 2. But I had noticed, in the midst of refilling the sink and adding more soap for the third time because the stopper didn't fit right, that Pete enjoyed helping dry the dishes, and we had a good time talking. It was the night before Christmas Sunday and I wanted to wrap presents. But the teacher's words rang in my ear, so instead I began to choose clothes for us to wear and find missing socks.

Sunday morning we drove into the church parking lot smiling, roast in the oven, table set. Light snow fell and I thought the church steeple and the falling snowflakes looked like a Christmas card.

May, an older woman who had taught Sunday school since Moses, always sat in the back pew in the sanctuary "in case she was needed." But today May looked haggard. Even in the tinted light from the stained glass windows, her face appeared pale.

"How are you doing, May?" I asked.

"A little poorly, Ella," she replied. She rubbed her shoulder. "Guess old Arthur's come for Christmas."

Thinking of how Dr. Radmacher had told us that regardless of how plain the hospitality we could offer, we should open our homes to each other and to those to whom God led us, I said, "May, would you like to not have to cook today? We have a roast in the oven that I hear calling your name." She cooked wonderfully. We had enjoyed dinner at her house many times, devouring biscuits that would float if you let them go.

May reached for Petey and said, "My goodness, does that mean I get to hug this little fella all afternoon?"

Pete smiled down at May and said, "Absolutely." He excused himself to teach his high school kids as I took the place next to May.

Class hadn't started yet, and she began to talk. "Christmas has changed since I was a youngster," she remarked.

"Tell me about Christmas a long time ago, May," I pleaded. I loved to hear gray-haired people tell stories about the old days.

May let Petey suck on her knuckle. He waved his feet and held onto her hand as if she were a candy bar. "Well, we didn't have much money, so to us an apple or an orange in our stocking was a treasure. And our stockings came right off our feet, much better than today. Ours stretched." She giggled girlishly. "Most of our presents were homemade. I remember one Christmas my mama fixed me a doll out of flour sacks. I named her Hannah and she was the softest thing. She had yellow yarn hair and Mama stuffed her with duck down she had saved all year." May's eyes saw a time long since passed. I was quiet, enjoying her memories.

In my mind's eye I could see her mother rocking and with a needle and thread painstakingly sewing together the little doll. I envisioned their Christmas tree decorated with popcorn and cranberries. Then I thought about how I had to teach myself to sew, cook, can, everything a girl is supposed to learn from her mother. *Here we go again*, I thought. *Right in church I'm mentally putting down Mom, and the Bible says thinking things is as bad as saying them out loud.* Mom had become harder for me to deal with emotionally than Cal. She talked of herself as a martyr to the decisions of people around her, totally ignoring her part in her circumstances. Because she didn't admit the effect her self-centeredness had on her life and the lives of people close to her, according to her there was nothing to forgive. Yet my soul cried out that she hurt me. It frustrated me to continually have to go through this mental wrestling match with myself. Since May didn't need me to get depressed, I stuffed my thoughts in the furthest closet of my mind and set about enjoying having May over for the day.

I had worried that the holidays without our families would be lonely, but Pete, Petey and I had a warm and cozy celebration of Jesus' birthday. The lack of noisy conversation and bustle gave the Lord a chance to come very close to each of us and all of us as a family. I decided that I liked both ways of celebrating. But soon the holidays were over.

Pete was learning homiletics and hermeneutics and every other *ics* I had never heard of. I took a class on the Old Testament from Ron Allen, not realizing how privileged I was to learn from him. And I took another class on the Christian woman taught by Anne Sandoval, a tiny, white-headed, pastor's wife whose eyes sparkled when she taught. She taught us a thousand things, from how to tell our children about Jesus, to a relaxing technique where you lie on the floor and loosen and tighten all your muscles one set at a time, starting with your feet and ending with your face. The thing I remember best changed my life.

The night she talked to us about marital sex, she said, "Girls," which didn't seem demeaning coming from her, "you have only a little time to make the man God gave you happy. Be his shining helpmate when you're at church, make him proud of how you look and how you act, be his empathetic wife for the women of the church. But when you come to your home and you are alone in your bed, be his comfort, his listening ear and his excited lover. In Genesis, God says the marriage relationship is 'very good.' Whatever a husband and wife agree they feel comfortable to do in the privacy of the marriage bed is blessed by God. Loosen up with him, let your hair down. The two of you should know each other intimately, better than anyone else except God knows you. Do you realize that your husband would treasure it if you would suggest having sex?"

I marveled. Apparently I couldn't blame abuse for my difficulty in abandoning myself during sex with Pete. Other women must struggle with this, or Mrs. Sandoval wouldn't have brought up the subject in class. And she said God thinks sex is very good. I had given Pete such static about how often he wanted to have sex. But our teacher said I *could take the initiative to suggest it.* That night I put Petey to bed and coaxed Pete from his tabernacle. He was amazed, as Mrs. Sandoval had suggested he would be, and we talked long into the night about how things had gone thus far and changes we would both like to make. I even had the courage to tell him that I liked him to run his fingers through my hair.

Seminary went by quickly, with Pete taking various assistant pastorates to garner practical experience and with me helping in a program that welcomed new women to the seminary. Finally we started our last year. Late in October, Petey and I were outside picking apples to make mint jelly, him in a jacket and a little stocking cap pulled down around his ears against the cold. He culled the apples that had fallen on the ground, checking each with me before placing it in the paper sack. I picked from the branches I could reach. The phone rang and we grabbed our sack and ran for the house.

"It's Aunt Jessi, Petey," I said, answering his question so he would stop asking it and I could hear.

"How would it be if I come up for Christmas?" she asked, sounding a long way off.

"Absolutely magnificent," I squealed.

"Okay, I'll let you know what bus to meet. I need to talk with you, Ella."

"Something wrong?"

"Nothing that won't wait until I get there."

Christmas finally came and we met Jessi at the bus station, with Petey almost bouncing he was so excited. He didn't know Jessi, but I had told him so much about her that he could hardly wait. Her appearance when she came down the bus steps didn't seem to throw Petey off, but the Jessi we were meeting was not the Jessi I had said goodbye to nearly three years ago.

Her skirt was short, her hair frizzy and huge gold rings hung from her ears. Her eyes had deep shadows under them. What had happened to my Jessi? I hugged and kissed her, and we bundled her into the car. She fell asleep on the way home, which was her pattern throughout the two weeks she stayed. And though she had said she wanted to talk with me, she didn't mention anything more than whether I could take her to the store for another present for Petey. Petey loved her because, when she was awake, she read him story after story.

Finally, the day before Jessi left, while Petey was taking his nap, she looked at me and said, "It's been tough at home without you." She had rented an apartment with a friend from Maplewood Springs in a college town about fifty miles away.

"What do you mean?"

Leaning against the kitchen cabinets while I chopped celery for dinner she said, "College is hard, and my social life keeps me almost too busy to study."

"What kind of grades are you getting?" I asked.

"I'll tell you if you don't say anything," she answered.

"Okay."

"Mostly C's and D's."

"Um," I said. "Do you feel okay, Jessi? Your eyes look really tired."

"Yeah, I'm okay," she answered. "Cal tried with me after you left, Ella. I told him to stuff it, and he stopped. But I still hate him!" She smiled ruefully and picked up a stalk of celery to munch. Between bites, she added, "I get headaches when I think about it."

"I'm glad I warned you," I said, feeling sad that Cal had validated Pastor's warning, but glad that Jessi didn't have to live there anymore. Apparently Cal praying to receive Christ wasn't enough to stop his addiction to dysfunctional sexual practices. "Do you think you should go to the doctor about the headaches?"

"I went. But Mom said not to tell him about Cal, so it didn't help. Something else is wrong too," Jessi continued. "I keep looking for a boy at school to love. You know there's no love at home. But most of the boys I've dated interpret my attraction to them as a request for sex. Maybe I'm giving the wrong signals because of all the crazy stuff that's happened to us. Have you ever noticed that after you give in to a guy, he doesn't want you anymore?"

I stopped cutting celery and with the hand that held the knife, ticked off the thoughts I was thinking. "I know you couldn't learn dating habits from my life," I said. "But like you said, our situation is weird. I think normal girls, who feel good about themselves, handpick the guys who respect girls and date only them. They also take responsibility to keep making-out from going too far."

"But look at you, Ella, you did a lot of wrong things and you've come out all right," Jessi said, her eyes averted. "I figure if you can survive, I can too. You're happy, have a good husband and a terrific little boy."

Her logic jerked me into realizing that I had to fill her in on what was going on inside me—the truth, maybe not everything, but enough for her to see reality. I couldn't let her continue for one more minute to think that sin has no consequences. *God's blessings in my life have blurred the truth about sin for Jessi*, I thought. I slapped the counter. "If you think what happened between Cal and me didn't hurt anybody, you're very wrong," I exclaimed. Changing to counting fingers instead of swinging the knife, I continued more quietly. "First, Mom and I don't have a mother/daughter relationship. How could we, with the pictures of Cal and me that must be in her mind? Two, I'm afraid even to talk to Cal or be alone with him. Three, Pete has to put up with the nightmares I have that the whole thing has begun again. If Pete weren't patient, didn't listen to my fears and assure me almost every day that I'm a worthwhile person, I would have committed suicide a long time ago. I tried once while we were at seminary, when Pete and I had only a *little* fight. You know why? Because without Pete, I would have a choice of Cal, Mom, or Daddy: a child molester, a self-centered mother, or a man who lets alcohol get in front of people. Jessi, if I seem all right, it is because Jesus brought love and acceptance into my life just in time."

Jessi picked up a bell pepper and started slicing it to smithereens. Finally she said, "If you commit a big sin, does God ever want you anymore? I mean, what I've done while you've been gone you wouldn't want to hear about. I think I may have committed the unforgivable sin that Mom talks about and gone too far away from God to come back. And besides, some of what I do is fun."

Too long, I thought. *We have been gone too long and I didn't keep good enough track of Jessi.* I'd grown to believe that I ought to fix every scrape Jessi got into, probably a leftover from feeling responsible for my folks' divorce. "Jessi, I have learned a lot at seminary. I want to show you my two all-time favorite verses." I found my Bible and looked up Luke 22:31,32 and read them out loud to her.

"Simon, Simon, Satan has asked to sift you as wheat," I read.

"But I have prayed for you, Simon, that your faith may not fail. And when you have turned back, strengthen your brothers.'"

Laying my hand over her madly slicing hand, I said, "Jesus knew Peter would deny ever knowing Him, in a moment of danger and death. Nevertheless, even before it happened, Jesus forgave Peter, and even gave him an inkling of the purpose He planned in Peter's life. God is planning for when *you* come back to Him before you even decide to go away."

I put my hand on her shoulder. "Confessing your sin to God, and to me if you think it might help, will bring instant forgiveness from God and a fresh start for you."

She shrugged.

"Are you going to church?" I asked.

"When I went to church with you on Sunday, I looked around at all those clean-cut looking guys and thought, 'None of these guys would even consider me because I'm a slut.' I sleep around. I take drugs. I don't belong at church, Ella."

"Jessi, don't do that to yourself. You may have made mistakes, but God would never throw you out like you're doing to yourself, calling yourself a slut. You can change. I'll help you clear it up with God right now if you want."

"How?"

"Prayer. Do you need words?"

"I can do it." She bowed her head.

"Say 'amen' so I'll know when you're done," I said after a second. I heard her begin to sob and hugged her while she prayed.

"In Jesus' name, amen," she finished. Her eyes were red, but there was a glimmer in them.

"I'm sorry life has thrown you such a curve, but you can change now," I assured her. "For me, being in church makes a lot of difference. Our church people are more family than Mom and Cal, much more. They act to meet our needs, which is the real meaning of love. You need that kind of brothers and sisters, that kind of love. There's great joy in giving that kind of love, too."

"I'm scared to look for a church. How do I know which ones go by the Bible?" Jessi asked.

"I'll ask at the seminary. They know which churches are good in most places. Remember Jessi, people can't be strong without God, and communicating with Him and His people is the way to receive His strength."

I began to suspect that I sounded like "Seminary Sam" and decided to add a little humor. "Besides, you're part of the body; without you at church the belly button's missing." I paused for the laugh I deserved, and she gave me a weak smile.

Finally, she said, "Okay, I'll get back into church."

"Good. Now finish that bell pepper. You've got to earn your keep," I ordered. Jessi went home in better shape, but I still worried about her. I wished Mom were reliable, and felt angry with her almost daily because she wasn't.

One day that spring I was out in the garden planting green onions and radishes, since they were the only thing that would come up fast enough to harvest before Pete graduated. Pete drove into the driveway and, hurrying out of the car, nearly dropped a pile of books under his arm. "Ella," he said excitedly, "a pastor named Bill Yaeger preached at the seminary today. He's wonderful. His priorities are evangelism and discipleship, *and* he offered to let us intern at his church in California. It's huge, has 3,000 people. Can you imagine? I told him yes. We'll leave right after graduation. Ella, I'm so excited. What do you suppose God's doing with us?"

I had many questions, but I had promised Pete that where he went, I would go, and it looked like we were on our way.

Self-Assessment Guide

1. Pete moves Ella to Oregon and encourages her to distance herself, even by phone, from her mother and stepfather. What benefits can you see for abuse victims who are beginning recovery to give themselves space away from their abusers in order to heal?

2. Do you see times when Ella tells herself she's not hurt when she actually is? What would lead her to do this? Have you struggled with refusing to acknowledge pain in your life? How does that affect your recovery?

3. What principles for healthy family living do you discover in this chapter? How would you apply any that are new to you?

4. What do you think caused Ella's blowup with the children she cared for? What could she have done to avoid it? Can you use any of these insights in your own life?

5. Have you ever struggled with wanting to "fix" everyone else's life, or have you desperately desired to be perfect? Can you identify events during your childhood that may have contributed to your dealing with life this way? Pete told Ella to deal with one thing she wanted to correct in herself at a time. What could you do to balance yourself better?

6. Abuse victims suffer from the "imposter syndrome" because of poor self-image. Ella evidenced some of it when she compared herself with the other wives at the seminary and judged herself insufficient. How did Ella deal with her feelings? When you feel you aren't good enough to be where you are, what do you do to clear your vision?

7. Ella picks Jesus' encouragement of Peter before he denied Christ as one of her favorite passages. Have you found a passage where God speaks to you of His love and purpose

for you? Try Isaiah 40:31, Isaiah 41:10, Psalm 40:1–3 or 1 John 3:1–3.

Helper's Focus

Counselors, pastors and support group leaders should acknowledge that abuse does not happen in a vacuum. All family members are involved and affected. That is not to say that all are culpable, but all feel the effects. Thus, all family members must be involved in the healing process.

Non-abusive parents have to deal with feelings of failure and weakness. Self-accusation is common, based on a feeling of ignorance at not realizing abuse was going on. There is probably a measure of truth in these feelings as well as a measure of overreaction. Helpers can assist in sorting the truth from the overloaded emotions.

It is also common to rationalize that lack of action and castigation of the victim are for the good of the family. It is best if parents can be convinced to take action to stop the abuse themselves and get counseling. However, if the family members don't have the strength to do these necessary things, then the helper must take action to end abuse in the family.

An odd relationship between non-abusive parent and abuser may develop from stress added to previous dysfunction. Current research indicates that all parental sexual abuse stems from a faltering marriage. The faulty roles played by the parents before the abuse will generally twist further following disclosure. For instance, if the wife had been leading the family due to the husband's abdication of responsibility prior to the abuse, it is likely that following disclosure the wife will hold the abuse above the husband's head as a weapon to further subjugate him. Without counseling, these dysfunctional parents may behave in an ever-widening spiral of anger and bitterness toward each other.

Siblings may react in aggressive or passive ways. The attention given to the victim, whether positive or negative, leaves the siblings unattended. Some children will do their best to be good to lessen any further stress on the family. Others may run away, take drugs, or join a gang to regain the attention they need. Most children will confuse the irresponsibility around them for reality, and thus will need counseling to help restore normality to their lives.

It is important for all family members, victim to abuser, to understand that healing and maturing are processes, so that they won't expect overnight recovery. The abuse didn't progress overnight and the learning process that leads to godly living is not instant either. If the helper explains at the beginning that a long, difficult recovery process lies ahead, a measure of trust is created. The guiding passage to motivate the whole family is Exodus 20:5b–6:

> For I, the Lord your God, am a jealous God, punishing the children for the sin of the fathers to the third and fourth generation of those who hate me, but showing love to a thousand generations of those who love me and keep my commandments.

Chapter Eight

Not to Have What It Takes

I wondered as I ferried boxes from the truck to the house how much more God could bless us. Pastor Yaeger had found us a farm! The family who owned it had been called to South America as missionaries. Instead of selling their farm, they wanted a Christian family to live here and take care of it. The farm was only ten minutes from church, but far enough into the country for a horse, feeder calves, chickens, a pig, a duck pond, and a couple of turkeys. The latter, I was told, graciously produced offspring for Thanksgiving and Christmas. Flowers bloomed everywhere and the huge garden was already planted in rows across half of it and harrowed in the rest.

When Pastor had discovered I was raised on a farm, he assumed I would be perfect because I knew how to care for the animals. He also said we might be able to take in a boarder or two, since we couldn't use all five bedrooms. "That way," he concluded, "you won't have to leave Petey to go to work. We'll bring the work to you."

The house was a two-story Victorian. We were storing most of our furniture in the barn. Who would choose to live with estate-sale tables instead of these beautiful antiques? The mahogany dining room table would require Pete and me to shout to be heard from either end.

Not only that, Pastor had enrolled us in a Bible study before
we arrived, and ten members were energetically helping us
move in on a Saturday afternoon. I hadn't met the huge man
who worked in the back of the truck throwing our furniture to
Pete on the ground. The lady who helped me with the large box
I was carrying was Phoebe.

"Ella, we'd be more than happy to have the Bible study meet
at your house," she offered facetiously. "It would be a sacrifice
to drive out here, but we probably could arrange it if we get to
curl up in those overstuffed sofas."

We both laughed. "Give me a week or two to unload these
boxes and you're invited," I replied.

Phoebe jerked to a stop and I nearly dropped my side of the
box. "Forget that, we plan to have everything put away today."

I thought she was kidding. "Sure," I laughed.

"No, really." Phoebe hesitated. "Unless you don't want us to.
We think there will be a ton of work out here for you two, and
it starts first thing in the morning. Pete will be running nonstop
keeping up with his job and an internship too. I advise you to
grab the help while it's available."

I was dumbfounded. I'd had help moving before, but it
usually stopped short of putting things away. This woman was
saying they had considered what we would need and planned
to provide the extra hands before we realized what we faced. By
now, I should have been used to how God shows His love
through people, but each time something like this happened I
felt surprised.

"But of course," I answered with the sarcasm I customarily
used when I wanted to hide my emotions. Their willingness to
help embarrassed me; I wondered why I felt embarrassed but I
was too busy to think it through. After we unloaded boxes,
Phoebe checked with me before they put things anywhere.
Twilight darkened the farm before I knew it, but it found us
completely moved in. These wonderful people who had spent

their entire Saturday helping us wouldn't even let us buy them a pizza. They all waved goodbye, calling that they would see us Tuesday night for Bible study at our house. Ted, the big guy, had been feeding the animals before we arrived, and he'd assured us he would come first thing in the morning to show me how to find everything.

Bone tired, Pete and I climbed the stairs to our second-floor bedroom. I looked in on Petey in his new child-size bed. We had replaced his crib with the bed today. He was so exhausted that he hadn't even tried to get out; he simply turned over and went to sleep. Now he slumbered peacefully with his Raggedy Andy doll tucked under his arm.

Our room looked like a wonderland. A canopy like I had coveted in old movies graced the bed. On the nightstand stood a white washbowl and pitcher with tiny blue flowers. The carpet was deep enough to lose a cat in, and the whole scene beckoned me to sleep. Slipping my shoes off, I padded across to the bed and turned down the comforter and satin sheets. "Have we died and gone to heaven?" I asked Pete, who had headed for the bathroom.

The lady of the house had filled the bath with antique water closet-type fixtures. The handles on the faucets were fat white X's with "H" or "C" stenciled on top. The toilet flushed using a chain hanging from the ceiling. The lion-foot bathtub was completely enclosed by a shower curtain that fell from a rectangular rod attached to the ceiling. The ivory wallpaper felt fuzzy.

"I could sleep until the Fourth of July," Pete said, sloshing water on his face.

Pulling my nightgown over my head, I asked, "Did all the help we got embarrass you?"

"No, we needed it. Why?"

"I felt embarrassed, as if a weakness were showing," I mused.

Pete meandered back into the bedroom, drying his face. "Not surprising. You hate to appear weak," he observed.

"I do?"

"Sure. You are as independent as a hog on ice, and you know it."

Slipping between the satin sheets, I responded, "Independent, okay, but what's that got to do with weak?"

"You tell me."

Independent to avoid weakness, I thought. I remembered how I had intended never to love anyone after Daddy, but been unable to avoid it. I had felt out of control, so weak, with Cal. And now, anything that made me feel weak was repugnant. I wanted control of my life more than I wanted most anything else. "Maybe independence that covers weakness is a natural response after abuse," I offered.

"Bingo," Pete said.

"Is it wrong?" I asked.

He sat on the bed and pulled his jeans off. "Yes and no. Identifying that you tend to insist on controlling your life is definitely a step toward center. I never told you this before, but my mom abused me when I was a kid. There were reasons, one of them that she married and became a mother too young. One day she beat me with a belt buckle until my back bled. I couldn't go to school because my folks were afraid someone would see. So I can relate to you hating to feel weak."

"Oh, Pete," I sighed.

"She has never mentioned it since then. Maybe she doesn't remember. I don't know." He wiped at his left eye with the shirt he had taken off.

Sensing that Pete didn't enjoy the emotions his memory had uncovered, I said, "Okay, Reverend, begin sermon."

He slid into bed next to me and said, "Man, I'm not crazy about satin sheets. These feel weird. I could slide out of here before morning."

"Yeah, I'll change to ours tomorrow. The comforter is nice. Maybe we ought to use our own linens and not wear theirs out, though. You were going to explain about weakness and independence."

"Right." He lifted his arm so I could rest my head on his shoulder. "I believe if we want to honor God, neither weakness nor independence should be carried to extremes. There's nothing wrong with weakness; 2 Corinthians 12:10 says, 'That is why, for Christ's sake, I delight in weaknesses, in insults, in hardships, in persecutions, in difficulties. For when I am weak, then I am strong.' Paul is saying that weakness uncovered in doing what God wants us to do only gives God an opportunity to display His strength through us. In other places, God has said to be strong in Him, bold and courageous. The idea is that our weakness shows our need for Him and when we are strong it's because we are depending on Him.

"On the issue of independence, there are also two sides. Most people who choose to be independent of others do it because someone has hurt them. They want to avoid pain. But in Philippians, at the end of the first chapter and beginning of the second, you'll find where God said that along with believing in Christ goes suffering for Him. He wants us to let the suffering draw us together, not push us apart. He goes so far as to say it should create thinking alike, loving equally and pursuing the same purpose.

"On the other hand, we have to be independent enough to take care of ourselves. For instance, there's a verse that says if a man won't work to support himself he also shouldn't eat."

"Mind boggling," I remarked, fighting to understand what Pete had said as sleep dragged me under. I drifted off to face a huge man who chased me unendingly through the night, towering over me. Sometimes he was Cal and sometimes he was a stranger. One time I awoke, his rancid breath roaring just behind me, to find that Pete was snoring. I pushed his shoulder and he rolled over and was quiet. I was used to these nightmares, and since they upset Pete, I didn't awaken him. I woke him up often enough crying out in my sleep. But as I drifted back, the nightmare continued, the huge man awaited. I could hear the zipper open on his pants and I began to run again.

In the morning, we were awakened by Ted banging on the door. "Been a while since you were a farm girl, huh?" he said as I stumbled down the stairs, bleary eyed, trying to get my other tennis shoe on.

Pete laughed and said, "Usually she's up with the chickens. I think we wore her out yesterday." Pete knew, without my asking, that I would want him to go with us to see how Ted fed the animals. I couldn't deal with being alone with any man, Christian or otherwise. Besides, Pete needed to know how to feed the animals, in case I got hit by a truck or something.

Ted pointed out the quirks in individual animals and how to secure the different gates. The horse had been curried recently and the chicken house had only a few eggs. Ted had done an excellent job of looking after the farm. As we walked back to the barn, Pete asked, "Did you plant the garden?"

"Yeah," Ted answered. "Things that need an early start, like corn and melons and stuff."

"Nice of you. Thanks."

Ted shrugged. "You would have done it for me."

I bent and picked an oat stem to chew. This was definitely *home*. "Where's the nearest feed store?" I asked.

"Down at Seventh and G is close, or in Turlock at the corner of West Main and Central is a good one," Ted answered. "If there's anything else I can do for you, call me anytime. I'm in the book." He slammed the door of his pickup.

"Wait—what time is church?" Pete asked.

"Either 9 or 10:45," Ted answered. "See you there."

"Foof, we'd better get moving," Pete said, striding toward the house.

Pete stopped on the porch to kick off some stuff he had picked up on his boots. When I came through the front door I could hear Petey calling me. "Mommy, Mommy, where are you?" he cried, with the beginning of panic in his voice. He had gotten out of his bed and I found him in the third bedroom upstairs.

"It's okay, Petey, I'm right here. Do you remember we moved to a new house yesterday?"

"I can't find Andy. And things look funny," Petey complained.

"Well, I'll help you find Andy and then we'll have waffles for breakfast. That ought to make you feel at home."

"Blackberry syrup?"

"Sure."

"Let's go, Mom."

Andy had fallen underneath the bed. We had to knock some dust bunnies off him, but he was restored. At the stairs we sat and bumped down on our rears, laughing as we dropped. The waffle iron was right where I had directed that it be placed, along with the flour canister and the salad oil, and Ted had even left brown eggs he'd collected yesterday in the refrigerator door.

"Look at this, Pete," I marveled. "Brown eggs, can you believe it? We get brown eggs just by feeding the chickens. I love it." I hadn't had brown eggs since I was a kid. We gobbled up breakfast, threw on our clothes and made the 9 A.M. service.

The sanctuary was a huge cement building with a blue roof. A couple shook our hands and welcomed us at the door. Inside, the first thing I noticed was that the pews were blue and hot pink. Pastor Yaeger was preaching in the Middle East, and Pastor Ron Blanc talked about how people who believe in Jesus Christ inherit with Him everything that comes from God. Since God is love and truth, this sermon opened new vistas for me. It meant that love and truth were mine; all I had to do was follow Jesus.

Our Sunday school class had as many people in it as the entire membership of most of the churches Pete had served during seminary. Some of these people were the ones who had helped us yesterday, and they began introducing us to what seemed like the entire world. We chose a small class that was studying Philippians. When it was over and we picked up Petey, his teacher introduced herself to us while helping him unpin his name tag. She was pretty and kind and Petey's eyes sparkled as he handed her the paper tag and pin. "See you next Sunday, Petey," she said.

After supper Petey and I explored the farm. I explained that roosters, the pig and calves were dangerous—and sometimes boy ducks and turkeys, or girl animals who had babies were too—so he should stay out of their pens. I introduced him to the horse, Sam, and promised him a ride on Monday. We found a willow tree with branches that cascaded clear to the ground where he could make a secret hideout. But I didn't mention the hiding place; he'd have to think of that himself or it wouldn't be secret. Finally, I showed him how to dump peelings and leftovers into the pig's trough and mix them with corn from the feed store, and how to give her water. "This will be your job, in addition to keeping your room clean and helping me dry the dishes, and you'll get an allowance if you do it right everyday," I explained. *Farm kids learn more than city kids about responsibility and all sorts of things, because their help is needed,* I thought. I was glad Petey had become a farm kid. "You can count on me, Mom" he said, sounding like a grownup. He was so proud to have a job that he marched like a soldier straight back to the house and told Pete all about how to feed a pig.

It was about a week later that I saw the television show about incest. I realized that day that God had brought me a long way, but that using what I had learned at seminary as bricks, I had built our family on top of a shaky foundation. Pete's underpinnings stood firm, but I had shoved so much of my abuse into the back of my mind without dealing with it that I knew I wasn't as steady or reliable a person as I should be, or that my family needed. The woman on television had quoted research, so I went to the public library to see whether they had any, hoping that I could glean a better understanding of what had happened in my family. I borrowed a couple of books and devoured them overnight. They confirmed what the woman on television had said. Average people—not slithery fiends and a stray girl every century or so—became enmeshed in childhood sexual abuse. And if I looked at four girls, one of them was likely to have been abused. I felt a little less weird and alone. Then I tried the college library in Turlock, a school people laughingly called Turkey Tech because it had been built among turkey ranches. I took home every book they had on the shelf about sexual abuse. Among this set of books, the authors who dealt with incest most comprehensively were Jerome A. Kroth, Sandra Butler, and Rita and Justice Blair.

Kroth did a computer study of the Child Sexual Abuse Treatment Program (CSATP) in Santa Clara County, California. His research, from the end of the '70s, was getting old but noted the same things the incest victim on television had said. One thing I noticed was that Henry Ghiaretto, founder of CSATP, had convinced the authorities in Santa Clara County that prosecution and jail sentences for incestuous perpetrators do not serve the best interests of the families. I remembered how I had been drawn into more lies and secrecy by Cal's explanation that he'd become a prisoner if I told the truth. What a gift Ghiaretto had given to children unable to defend themselves. If his approach had been available, I could have assured my family of the intervention necessary to break the patterns of our relationships. Not only that, but a non-existent or at least very short time of incarceration for Cal would have been followed by mandatory counseling for Cal, Mom, Jessi and me.

Where before I was so intent upon hiding the fact that I had been abused that I never wrote anything where someone might find it, now I began to write in my journal the principles from the books I had read and how their content affected me. On New Year's Eve fourteen years after my abuse began, I noted, "I need to write that on Christmas, Cal told 'Dolly Parton' jokes about big breasts. It reminded me of how he used to compliment mine, and I wanted to cross my arms over my chest. We were at their house, so I figured he had the right to do whatever he wanted and I didn't say anything. I didn't leave the room either. I could have done that. I felt uncomfortable, but my perspective on my involvement is balancing out, and he didn't totally blow me away.

"Kery visited us this week. She has just gone home and I feel relieved, because loving her drains me and I feel vulnerable."

I wished Cal couldn't affect me simply by telling off-color jokes. But the books said it would be a process to throw off his old psychological chains. I was beginning the process just by writing how I felt.

Every one of those books, except one written by some guy in a society that promoted sex with children, repeated what Pete and Pastor Samuels had said: that a child is not responsible for a sexual relationship with an adult. Reading Butler's book one night I came upon this paragraph:

> In cases where an adult male has, for whatever reason, chosen to eroticize his relationship with a girl child, the socialization process for females has taught the child to deny the angry, aggressive and rebellious feelings his behavior generates in her. Female incest victims suppress such feelings about the inappropriateness of the adult male's behavior and are thus doubly victimized. They are not only victims of parents who are unable to provide genuine and supportive models of adult behavior, but also are victims of a society that holds them

responsible for the actions of adults and will not permit them to be angry and insist on their right to their own bodies. They are expected to internalize their angry feelings and accept the fate adult males hand to them. (p. 36)

Had I suppressed anger? Was that why I so easily became angry about nothing? I began to search my memory for how the abuse started. As pictures formed in my mind, suddenly I was shaking. Still holding the book open at the page I'd been reading, I walked into the bedroom where Pete lay propped on pillows preparing his Sunday school lesson.

He glanced at me and exclaimed in concern, "What is it, Ella?"

I trembled uncontrollably, unable to speak, glaring at him.

"Ella!" He shook my shoulders. "Tell me what's the matter."

I found my voice, a terrible hissing growl that grew into a raging scream. "He used me!" I screamed. "I didn't make the decision for sex, he did!" I roared. "How could he tell me he'd go to jail and I had to treat him with love after he'd treated me so shabbily? How could he touch me, treat me that way? I was a child. He was an adult. He was responsible. He tricked me into loving him when I should have hated him—and now I do. I hate him, Pete. He's black and ugly on the inside, where you can't see it." I dropped onto the bed.

Pete sat next to me and gathered me into his arms. Wisely, he made no attempt to observe or correct. He only held me at first, until my body stopped shaking and I began to weep. "How long you've needed this," he finally said, his eyes full of tears.

I cried until I was empty. My characterization of Cal might no longer be true, but it definitely had been once, and I needed to begin from that point. Though my raging emotions frightened me, I knew Pete was right and I was on the road to freedom.

My healing process became a series of losses followed by gains. I lost the illusion that the incest was my fault, and shortly after that I met Jane Baker. Pete and I had gone to Stockton, about thirty miles from Modesto, to attend a meeting of alumni from Western. We found out that Jane and her husband, Art, who had graduated about ten years before Pete did, also attended First Baptist Church. Jane is impulsive, friendly and has one of those rolling-up-from-the-pit-of-your-stomach laughs that only a statue couldn't respond to. Art is steadier, thinks his conversation through and takes care to encourage others. When we met them, Art was praying about where God would have him serve and working in a furniture factory in the meantime. Jane looks like one of those well-endowed women in the paintings by Rubens and Rembrandt. Art looks like a cowboy psychologist with a heart-warming smile.

We met to discuss the possibility of opening a seminary in the San Joaquin Valley. Art said, "I'd even enroll if it offered a master's degree in biblical counseling."

Jane set her glass on the coffee table and said, "We're interested in working with adult victims of childhood sexual abuse."

I nearly swallowed my tongue.

Jane continued, "I am asked, every now and then, to speak with a woman struggling with issues that stem from abuse, which she feels powerless to overcome or at least stalled in the process. I have studied the research on abuse and have applied biblical principles to my own situation, but I still worry and stutter when I am called upon to help these women. Art has helped me and he needs legitimate credentials to help others."

Pete was fidgeting, and I hoped he wouldn't elbow me or do something to draw the others' attention. Mercifully, the conversation turned to other subjects, and I could breathe again.

When the host invited us to sample the snacks we had all contributed, I slowly moved through the couples until I stood next to Jane. "I'd like an opportunity to talk with you back in Modesto," I said.

"How about next Tuesday?" she suggested.

"Terrific, about 10 o'clock Tuesday morning?" I asked.

"Fine. Your house or mine?"

I looked at her eyes. Her soul seemed open for inspection and best of all, I couldn't see the slightest hint of suspicion in her eyes. "If mine will work, that's best. I have a little boy," I said.

"My kids are older and I work for myself, so it's not a problem to come to your house," Jane said. "I'll need your address."

I told her how to find our farm on Carpenter Road, and shortly after that Pete and I drove back to Modesto. I was filled with anticipation of Tuesday, and yet apprehensive about revealing my secret to someone else. Would she truly understand? What did I want to talk about?

We met our first boarder that weekend. Cheryl was a petite redhead with acne scars. She attended Modesto Junior College and First Baptist Church. We helped her move into the bedroom to the left of the front door, close to the street, and watched her fill it with posters that said things like, "Success in your journey is not what you find at the end of the road, but how you make the trip." She wore jeans and T-shirts and drove a white VW bug. Her tinkling laughter at meals was a welcome addition to our family.

I made sure all the chores were done early on Tuesday. Sam, the horse, an Arabian palomino, was becoming my favorite. Maybe I liked him because he was a horse or because of his friendliness. Each day he stuck his head over the fence and whiskered mine as I filled his grain box and gave him his hay. When I had let Petey ride him the day before, Sam went ever so carefully around the farm as if he knew Petey was a little fellow.

Jane drove into the drive right at 10 o'clock. It turned out to be unnecessary for her to come to my house because our Bible study leader was watching Petey, but I didn't have Jane's number to let her know. Cheryl was at school. We had privacy and plenty of time to talk uninterrupted.

Jane wore jeans and a shirt and didn't offer to shake my hand. She walked up and hugged my shoulders. "I've been out here before. You and Pete lucked out big time," she said. Her casual appearance and familiar greeting made me feel as if I had known her forever, and I was instantly comfortable. If she treated the other women she had talked with like this, then I thought she suffered more from self doubt than from lack of ability to help abused women.

"Come in," I said. "Would you like a cup of coffee?" I led her into the kitchen where we sat with the table between us; even though I liked her, I was so uptight that I needed the distancing the table provided. I hadn't talked to anyone about being abused since Pastor Samuels and I had sneaked into the libraries anonymously to find the books I'd read. Jesus had healed many things over the last years, but having talked only with Pete, I wasn't sure where I stood. I wasn't sure I could proclaim myself recovered. *Am I finished? How can I tell?* I thought.

"Sure, I'd love a cup. But I need milk and sugar too; Art says I pollute coffee. The doctor warned him to quit drinking it because it makes his heart race. I think if he had put a little flavoring in it over the years, he'd still be allowed to drink it. I win, he loses, game over."

I laughed, and then Jane did too. I don't think she realized at first that she'd said something funny.

"Ella, I don't know whether we're getting acquainted today or you had something specific you wanted to talk about, or both," Jane queried.

No beating around the bush here, I thought.

Jane continued, "Just in case, I'll say right off the bat that as a child I was sexually abused for several years. I didn't know the Lord at first, but He rescued me. I've worked through denial, anger, bitterness, unclear boundaries, difficulty trusting, forgiveness and a bunch of other issues that are the results of abuse. It is my belief that abused people never finish healing. But we can serve God long before we understand all of our malfunctions. I also think that everyone in the world has been abused to some extent, because we live in a sinful world. Therefore everyone is involved in a healing process. Well, everyone who knows the Lord. So, if we all waited to be fully healed, none of us would ever serve each other."

If I had worried that she wouldn't understand, I could forget that. She had even taken the initiative to tell me about herself so I wouldn't feel uncomfortable. The things she said she'd worked through were the things I couldn't find answers for in the books I had read. The books said they existed, but not what to do about them. I imagined the Bible said what to do about them, but I must not be handling it as well as I should because I still felt uneasy about whether I was fully recovered or not. Excitedly I said, "I was abused too. I invited you because I was hoping you would have the answers I need."

"I'm not a counselor," Jane said. "But I'm willing to share what God has taught me. Art has talked with me at least a million hours and I imagine you have that kind of help in Pete. But they *have* to love us, they're married to us. Something in me needed to talk to someone who could look at me objectively, and that's why I talk to other women. You must understand that I may not do this exactly right. I'm only willing."

"Fine with me. You're doing great so far." *Man, her self confidence is flying pretty low*, I thought.

"Start with telling me what happened that led into the abuse. Describe your family members and add whatever else you want," Jane prompted.

I repeated the facts I had told Pete, Pastor Samuels and later Jessi. This time I said them with less emotion, in fact I thought I sounded like an automaton.

"You are beginning to realize how much all this hurt you, aren't you?" Jane asked.

"Yes. And now I'm beginning to dislike going home. Nevertheless, my daughter and my sister are there, and I can't stay away forever."

"I can tell that you are beginning to face the realities in your life from your tone of voice." She sipped her coffee. "Terrific coffee. We may put you on the coffee-making team at church," she said.

Clasping her hands on the table, she said, "Okay. Now think yourself into the place of a neighbor of your first family. You are the neighbor, not yourself anymore. You know about all the ugliness of this family, the mother's reaction to the incest, so calm and cool and yet claiming to know nothing about what was going on. When her daughter tells her about the incest, she reacts as if her daughter had just told her, 'Mom, I brought home a stray cat.' Remember, you're the neighbor now: Would you call your mother disturbed?"

I thought several moments and then answered, "I would call her a product of her society."

Raising her eyebrows, Jane said, "Is that the answer to the question I asked? What do you mean, 'a product of her society'?"

"I think she was taught to depend on men too much. I think she believed the family was inviolable and when her husband did violate her family structure she couldn't believe it or protect me."

"I see what you're saying," Jane said. "I want you to look again. Your mother defended her husband over you, her child, by keeping him in the home without counseling. She had your stepfather's confession that he'd molested you and proof in your baby daughter. She said she would lie if you told the authorities of the incest. If you weren't related to her, would you say her behavior was disturbed?"

The word "disturbed" seemed such a finger-pointing word. Reluctantly, I said "Maybe." Calling my mother disturbed was so unthinkable that instead I had believed myself hard to love, not worth protecting.

Jane smiled. "Yes," she said. "Yes, you would. Anyone would." She paused a moment, then said, "Would you treat your own children like that?"

I thought how ridiculous it was to imagine Pete molesting Petey. Perhaps, though, Mom had had the same thought about Cal. And yet, if presented with evidence, as Mom was, I would protect Petey. My heart would ache at the choice, but Petey was a child. I would need counseling then because I would be an emotional wreck. "No," I said, feeling a huge sadness in my chest for Mom's lack of courage. She had let her pride deprive her, and us, of the help we needed to get our family back. But at the same time, I felt a new idea of myself appearing inside me. If Mom had failed to take a mother's responsibility by not protecting me, then I must be worth more than I thought.

"I want you to say, yourself, 'My mother is disturbed,' " Jane said.

"You want *me* to say she's disturbed?" I parroted, wishing to avoid the words.

"Yes."

Very slowly, one word at a time, I repeated, "My mother is disturbed."

"Now that you know she behaves in a disturbed manner, you will never see her quite the same way again. And she will never have the power to make you grope for her love the way you have always done. It won't be instant, but now when she says those things designed to push your button, you will mentally step back and look at her. You will be free to act as you feel you should, rather than as you feel she wants you to."

"I never considered her free to choose her actions. I thought circumstances overruled what she might have wanted to do. But I was wrong; she did have the choice," I said, feeling like an infant in a world where everything waited to be recognized.

"Good," Jane said. "I had to go through this process myself. You have some interesting days ahead of you."

For a moment I sat there like a wooden Indian, marveling that I could have viewed the world through so skewed a glass, like those old panes in the armoire upstairs. Finally, I came to myself and grinned sheepishly at Jane. "Would you like to meet the animals?" I asked. We wandered around while I explained the personalities of ducks, the pig and Sam. Jane enjoyed meeting them because she'd spent time on a farm as a young girl too. Just as she opened her car door, I said, "You know, Jane, you help more than you think."

She slid into the seat. "Oh, I was in rare form today, Ella. God must have wanted you to know that stuff. There have been times when a woman would share her past with me and all I could do was sit there and say, 'Uh huh, uh huh.' No help, no understanding. It was the pits. Maybe I'm overwhelmed by the horrible things people do to each other. Maybe I haven't learned enough answers. I don't know."

I shut her door. "Maybe God's developing your ability to help, just like the healing process keeps on going. You understand because you've been there, Jane. I hope you will keep trying to help. You helped me today."

She turned the key. "Never can tell about God," she said. "Let's get together another time."

"You're on," I said over Paul Overstreet singing *Sowing Love* from her car radio.

Self-Assessment Guide

1. How would you describe the stage of recovery Ella has reached in this chapter? What actions characterize her now that are different from the way she used to behave? What effect do you expect her feelings about weakness and control to have on her life? Draw comparisons and contrasts between Ella's recovery and your own.

2. Look at how Pete has dealt with Ella throughout the book. What is his attitude? Where does he get his counseling material? What makes him effective or ineffective?

3. What reasons does Jane give for feeling incompetent to counsel? What do you believe would be required of someone who was able to help you recover? Which of your requirements does Jane fulfill and which is she lacking? In light of that do you think it is possible that Jane suffers at least mildly from the imposter syndrome mentioned at the end of the last chapter?

4. Is there anyone in your life who affects you as Ella's mother affected her? Who? Why? Put yourself through the process of asking whether that person is disturbed and write out your reactions.

5. What motivated Ella to talk to each of the people with whom she has shared her abuse? How would her recovery have been affected had she avoided disclosing her abuse to these people?

Helper's Focus

Praise be to the God and Father of our Lord Jesus Christ, the Father of compassion and the God of all comfort, who comforts us in all our troubles, so that we can comfort those in any trouble with the comfort

we ourselves have received from God. For just as the
sufferings of Christ flow over into our lives, so also
through Christ our comfort overflows. (2 Corinthians
1:3–5)

As well as explaining that Jesus also experienced the suffering we experience, 2 Corinthians 1:3–5 is the biblical basis for
the abused to comfort the abused. The qualification necessary
to be a comforter is that we have been comforted by Jesus. That
means we are Christians who are working through our own
recovery issues with the Lord, and we have experienced His
comfort to the point where we are able to empathize with other
abuse victims and want to comfort them. Noticeably absent
from this list are psychological training, research or credentials.

That is not to say that psychological training, research and
credentials would not be helpful. We should take advantage of
whatever resources are available in order to do our best in
whatever we attempt for the Lord. However, we don't have to
wait until we have become experts in the field to comfort the
abused. A pastor who has graduated from seminary can, with
prayer, use the counseling methods he has learned to help the
abuse victim through recovery. An abuse victim who is honestly
working with the Lord through the issues resulting from her
abuse can share what she is learning. A relative who knows
nothing about abuse can at least help the victim understand
that a child abused by an adult is not at fault, and assure her
that God also holds that opinion.

A great many victims go through a period, long or short,
during which their need is so great that all they can do is *receive*
comfort. These people are marked by chronic procrastination,
rambling and self-centered conversation, self-pity, negative
points of view and/or chronic depression. Anyone willing to
listen and be there for them is qualified to help during this
period. The precaution is that the comforter needs to structure

the relationship so that she doesn't invest so much time that her own priorities get out of balance.

In contrast to these "receivers," there are many abuse victims who do not malfunction seriously, and who live well-rounded, fulfilling, successful lives. Their need is to deal with unresolved issues and dysfunctional relationships, and for that they simply need someone to walk with them who understands and cares.

There are times when a professional counselor is necessary to the recovery process. Some of these instances are: when the victim is a minor and the abuse has recently been disclosed; when the victim is so wounded that she will not take responsibility for her recovery; or when multiple personalities or serious personality disorder have come into play.

Our experience is that because so many individuals in America today have been abused, at some point one-on-one work will transition to a group setting. In the next chapter we will discuss the birth of Stepping Stones. This is the support group/Bible study that Ella, Jane, Pete and Art began at First Baptist Church of Modesto.

Chapter Nine

Names Changed to Protect the Innocent

The next time I asked to visit with Jane, she invited me to her home because she needed to finish a newsletter for a hospital. It was one of those summer afternoons when huge thunderclouds roll high across the sky and collect at the Sierra Nevada. The soft breeze beckoned me to lie on my back in the grass and find faces and shapes in the clouds.

By connecting finding faces in clouds to fantasizing, I managed to bring up my question. All afternoon Jane and I had talked about my habit, that grew from the abuse, of fantasizing during sex. Jane understood the fear I felt about bringing it up, and she answered my questions matter-of-factly. She assured me that my inability to mentally stay in the room during intercourse resulted from my early association of sex with sin and hiding. She explained that it is common for abuse victims to use fantasies to short-circuit panic during sexual activity. She suggested that I mentally return to reality by small steps, and she helped me feel that I had reacted normally and was capable of breaking the habit.

Now we sipped mint ice tea in her living room as we finished sticking labels on the newsletters. Her son, John, and daughters, Maryann and Laura, rode John's skate board with the neighbor kids out in their cul de sac. From where I sat on the sofa, I glanced past the low-hanging boughs of Jane's pine trees to see them doing 360s and occasionally a crash and burn. I loved the happy noise of children playing.

"They're a bunch of barbarians," Jane said. "But I'm crazy about them. John was born before seminary and the girls came after. Pretty funny, huh?"

"Yeah," I agreed.

Jane went to the front door and called her children. Coming back to sit next to me, she said, "Ella, God has been tapping me on the shoulder about something. You have experienced emotional and sexual abuse, pregnancy, giving up your baby— many things common to abuse victims. All the while God has walked with you, steadily working to effect your recovery. I keep thinking that the things God has taught you would help other women if you wrote them for publication. If you agree, I'd help you any way you want."

I remembered the straight paths Jesus had brought me down all these years—the one that led out of abuse to the one that led me to confide in Jane. I considered the record of my recovery that I had written in my journal, since that day I finally allowed myself to write about the abuse. Her idea sounded possible, though from my point of view, frighteningly transparent. I also was hesitant because I couldn't hurt Mom or Cal by writing their names in a book. Besides, the only other things I'd written since I got out of school, other than my journal, were letters. I looked out Jane's sliding glass door into a backyard that was large for a house in town. Among fruit and nut trees she had a garden with about ten tomato plants right down the middle. Pointing, I exclaimed, "Look, the sprinkler's making a rainbow over your garden!"

She laughed and said, "God's giving you a sign that He thinks I'm right."

"Yeah, Mom?" John said, sticking his head in the front door.

"It's time to start dinner. You can clean off the table and set it," Jane said.

"No sweat," he replied, and dropped his skateboard next to the fireplace. He was about thirteen, and his voice wavered with approaching manhood.

Maryann and Laura shoved each other and nearly fell through the door. "Creep!" Laura yelled.

"Bakers don't act like that," Jane corrected.

Both girls straightened up and stood glaring at each other. They were almost the same height and could have been twins, about seven or eight years old. Maryann had straight, blond hair that fell halfway down her back. Her jeans and T-shirt looked as if she'd just put them on instead of having played in them all afternoon. Laura's strawberry blond hair curled at the ends and she had a dirt smudge on her pug nose.

"It's time to get dinner. Maryann Spaghetti, you empty the dishwasher. Laura Noodle, you open two cans of beans and put them in a pot to simmer."

"Why can't Laura empty the dishwasher?" Maryann complained.

Jane held up her index finger and calmly said, "One."

Both girls scooted off to do as they'd been told.

"One?" I asked.

"We used to give them until the count of three to obey. Now they're old enough that all they need is 'one.' "

Great idea, I thought.

I pulled the last label off my fingers, which felt in danger of losing their skin with the label. Jane said, "Thanks a lot for helping me. What do you think about writing something?"

"You were abused. Why don't you write your own story?"

"Mine's not as comprehensive as yours. Your story would give God the opportunity to explain almost all the dynamics of abuse."

"I couldn't write Mom and Cal's names where other people would know," I said. "That wouldn't be forgiving. And I really don't know anything about this kind of writing."

"You could give each member of your family a pseudonym. I don't want to push you, but I would write it, if you agree God wants you to do it."

Art came in from work. He looked different than he did at church. He wore a plaid shirt with blue suspenders and jeans. On his head was a Greek fisherman's hat, brown and sweat stained. Growing down his face from under the hat, his beard— which normally just looked like shredded wheat on his chin— made him look like a stevedore. "What about writing?" he asked as he dropped his lunch box on the kitchen floor.

"We're discussing whether to publish some of Ella's life," Jane answered.

"Do it," he said to me. "Jane's told me how much you've grown, and it would help people."

Picking up my purse, I said, "Maybe we will. But I better get home now."

ૐ   ૐ   ૐ

Gently rolling hills filled the windshield and then disappeared as Jane and I drove with the first chapter of *My Father's Love* to a critique group. The group was meeting in the home of a friend of Jane's, who lived in a town two hours away from Modesto. I had prayed about it, and God had confirmed that Jane was right about Him wanting my life in print to help other women. He took me to verses that said, "Plans fail for lack of counsel, but with many advisors they succeed." I reasoned that meant I should pay attention to Art and Jane, and Jessi and Pete when I asked them about it and they were vociferously in favor. "Anyone, then, who knows the good he ought to do and doesn't do it, sins," came up right after that and hit me pretty hard. Writing the book meant that I had to go back into my past and dig up memories I had buried somewhere in the convolutions of my brain. I wasn't extremely excited about doing that. Actually, when I gave it some thought, I didn't want to do it at all.

But God did. Pouring all over me was the peaceful assurance that He seemed to flow into my brain when I looked to Him for an answer. And once I began to look at my childhood through my adult eyes, I began to see truth that I had never recognized before. As we wrote, I envisioned a woman reading the book who was like I once was. She stands in a dark closet, hiding a secret, but hating the dark loneliness. Finally, she notices a light through the keyhole and with a very tiny courage, she gropes for the knob and turns it. With the barest crack between door and jamb, she whispers, "I was abused," and waits, trembling, for the response.

Jane and I had developed a way of working together where I told her what happened and answered her questions, then she wrote and I read and corrected where she hadn't quite caught what had happened or what I felt. When my thinking became twisted, she wrote it the way I told her and then we discussed why I had constructed the world incorrectly and how I should reconstruct.

She also had been encouraging me for two weeks about coming to this critique group. I felt apprehensive about reading the chapter aloud to a group of women writers. I had talked to one person at a time about abuse, but never a whole group.

"You're sure they will understand?" I asked for the nine zillionth time.

"I'm sure. And I'm certain their reactions will help make you believe you were not responsible," Jane answered. She steered onto a freeway exit.

"I'm petrified," I mumbled. "I feel as if I'm going to walk in there and say, 'Here, let me rip my guts out in front of you and see how you react.'"

Jane patted me on the shoulder, and in her low, soothing voice said, "Settle down. You need this. I'm seeing to it that you get it." She turned onto a five-lane street and continued, "Besides, the book will be better. Life is life, and these women may not have experienced what you or I have, but I'll bet every one of them has suffered. They all know the Lord. If they can't, for some reason, handle your story on their own, He'll supply what's needed. Trust Him."

We parked at the curb and I clutched the manuscript as we rang the doorbell. Jane's friend, Ann, answered the door wearing a full skirt with a pretty woven vest over her blouse. She's a Christian whose eyes give away her love for God and for people, before she even speaks. I liked her house because she had rejected the usual American color-coordinated decorating pattern in favor of coziness and hospitality. Nothing matched and I assumed she had put together her furnishings the same way Pete and I had: through yard sales and gifts. I was to spend a lot of time in this friendly room.

After we went through all the introductions, one woman read her work before us. She prefaced her reading with how awful her work was, no editor would ever look at it, and on and on. Then she read us humor so funny that I developed a stomach ache from laughing. Next Ann asked Jane to read. Jane had agreed to read the chapter only because I said I thought I would cry and be unable to get through it. But she had warned me that she would be totally silent afterward. As she read the last words, I looked down at my hands.

"This is Ella," Jane said, inclining her head toward me. I had been introduced with my real name.

I inhaled deeply. What they said now would determine something of my opinion of myself from this point forward.

There was a collective sigh. At first they glanced at each other, as if trying to give one another the first opportunity to speak. Finally one woman, a tiny lady about grandmother age, said, "I wish a book like this had been available when I was growing up, so my sister and I would have known we weren't the only ones having this kind of trouble."

Another said, "God has given you a ministry in this book."

I could barely hear the comments afterward through the exulting of my mind. *They don't blame me. They believe it is the way I remember it. They aren't asking me if I was seductive or advising me to leave it in the past. Oh, thank You, Lord.*

Finally the women got down to critiquing the manuscript. "What's your theme?" the humor writer asked.

I had worried that my theme was too simple, and at that time it was. I blurted it out anyway. "That Jesus can heal anything, and my family can be normal again if I let Him lead me through healing them."

"Why do you think it's up to you to heal your family?" another asked.

Speaking in a tone that must have sounded like a condescending parent, I said, "Remember the verse from Philippians that says, 'For I am confident of this very thing, that He Who began a good work in you will perfect it until the day of Christ Jesus'? Well, except for Jessi, who's not directly involved in the problem, I'm the only one in my family who tries to walk with God, so it must be up to me to work things out."

"No - it - isn't!" a big woman said with loud determination. She made me think of the impulsive side of me, swift with an answer. "You've been fixing situations your whole life. It's time to quit."

Ann, who had simply listened until now, said quietly, "You need to read the verse again, Ella. It says *Jesus* will perfect what He started, not you. Have you forgiven your parents?"

"Yes," I answered. "You'll come to that in a later chapter."

Ann continued, "Then I believe it's your parents' turn to mend relationships. You have forgiven them and that is right. One day you may need to speak with each of them about their responsibility for what happened in your home. You should do that only when you understand who was responsible for what. You should wait until your only motive is to stand up as an adult and tell the truth about what happened and who was responsible. You shouldn't expect anything from them that day, not an apology or reconciliation."

"After all, who do you think you are, God?" the lady with swift answers said.

I wondered how Ann had become so wise. I shot a questioning look at Jane, and she nodded that Ann was right. But I cringed at the thought of telling Mom that I considered her responsible for setting the stage for incest in our family. Though I had learned to back up and look at reality when she pushed my button, I had never stopped defending myself from her through silence. Not only that, but speaking to Cal about the abuse, face to face after all these years, was a nightmare too.

"The only thing is, there's another side of me too," I said. "With my mom I don't try to fix anything. I gave up on her changing long ago, and any expression of love from her now strikes me as phony."

Tears began to flow, but I managed to explain. "It's not only untrue to insist that your daughter does no wrong, as my mother always has, but it's bad for your daughter. My mom tells me how good I am one minute, and the next points out that because I weigh too much I'll never be taken seriously and Pete will probably look for another woman. Once she said I needed to discipline Petey more and as proof blamed him for something she says happened two months before. What am I supposed to do when two months have passed? I couldn't even determine whether he actually did what she claimed he did when that much time had passed. I don't trust her enough to let her know who I am. She hurts me enough as things are. What would she do if she knew my weak places any better?"

"Being a Christian means being courageous enough to allow yourself to be hurt," the funny lady said sadly. "If you want God to heal your family, you have to face hurt in the process. Maybe you are not strong enough right now. That could mean you need to stay away from your family while you think this through with God. Then, when you are strong enough... "

"Transparency of spirit is important, otherwise how can we share Christ through ourselves?" Ann asked. "All of us could hide to avoid being hurt. You are more severely wounded than many people could ever understand, and you should give yourself time to recuperate. But the other side is, Ella, you were important enough to Jesus that He allowed Himself to be abused and die for you, before you loved Him. Loving someone can mean telling them the truth, even though they may respond in a way that brings you pain. Is your mother important enough to you to suffer for?"

Of course, I thought. *No matter what her weaknesses, she gave me life.*

I knew God had taken me another giant step as Jane and I drove home from the critique group. "You know, Jane, a lot of people think the worst of someone who has had something bad happen to them, even when it wasn't that person's fault. The reason, I guess, is that if bad things can happen to people who don't deserve them, then they could happen to anyone. That thought is too frightening for most people to cope with, so we think that people who experience evil must have deserved it somehow. I didn't see the slightest hint of that attitude today," I observed.

"Told you," she teased.

She pulled into a fast-food drive-up and when the kid said, "May I take your order please?" she put her hand over her mouth and mumbled loud but unintelligible syllables.

"Excuse me?" the speaker said.

Jane mumbled louder with a noticeable touch of anger in her voice. I convulsed with laughter.

"I'm sorry, our machine must be malfunctioning," the speaker said. "Could you repeat that one more time, please?"

"Two medium Diet Pepsis," Jane said clearly. She turned to me and said, "Isn't life fun?"

❧ ❧ ❧

I could hear the phone ringing and finished the last few yards to the house at a run because Pete had been in the shower when I went out to collect eggs. "Hello," I panted.

"Oh, I caught you at a bad time," Mom said.

"No, I was on my way to the house. I ran."

The whole kitchen was filled with the smell of the gardenias that bloomed around the kitchen door. It was intoxicating.

"Well, catch your breath. I have some good news," Mom said. "I called to tell you that Cal has said I can go home at the end of the summer."

By that she meant her childhood home in Tennessee; a bunch of her aunts, uncles and cousins still lived there. She loved to visit them. The "Cal has said" part was a smoke screen. Mom still did what she pleased despite what Cal thought.

She continued, "I'll be gone for a couple of months. He thought it would be a good idea to go now, what with the new Trans Am and all."

They had recently purchased a cherry red Trans Am that, according to Mom, could really tear up their mountain roads. She had always wanted a fast car.

"Kery will get a kick out of seeing the country," I said.

"Oh, Kery can't go. I won't be back until after school starts."

"Who's going to watch her?"

"Cal, of course. He's not dead, you know."

I couldn't believe it. She would play the game of "nothing ever happened" forever, even if her denial put Kery at risk. "Kery could come down here and stay with us while you're gone if you'd like," I offered. "Petey would like having her around." "Ella, Kery will be fine with Cal."

In the old days I would have left it at that. But it wasn't the old days anymore, and I was used to the bad-guy role, though I was tired of it. It was time to tell the truth, if I really loved Mom. "Mom, the books I've read say that most men who molest children continue unless there is intervention by the authorities. Our family has had no counseling. I think chancing whether Cal would do what he did to me again, leaving open the possibility that he will molest Kery, is too big a risk. We could even enroll her in school here, and she could transfer back when you come home."

"Don't be ridiculous. She'll be fine," Mom snapped. Topic no longer open for discussion. "By the way, she's been bugging me almost constantly about who her mother is, so I finally told her about you the other day."

So nonchalant, so "the weatherman says it's going to rain." I sighed. "I thought you were going to let me be there when you told her."

"Oh, did I say that?"

Yes, you said that, I thought. *In fact, when you said I could never take her back, that was my only request.*

When I was silent, she said, "Well, she took it well. There's no harm done."

Easy for you to say. You're not ten years old. You sure are good at messing up preadolescent girls.

"Well, are you going to say anything?" Mom said loudly.

"Maybe we'll come for a visit before you leave on your trip," I said.

"That would be super. Let me know when, so I can have extra food ready."

"Okay."

"Tell everybody we love them," she said, and hung up.

I felt like I was disappearing down a muddy whirlpool. I sat at the kitchen table, suddenly exhausted. "Father," I called out, "I'm trying to do what You want me to do. But I feel like I'm drowning."

Pete came into the kitchen and said, "Where's that omelet?" Then he saw my face. "What happened? Fox get in the hen house?"

"Sort of."

"What do you mean?"

"I just hung up from talking to Mom. She told Kery a couple of days ago that I'm her mother."

He sat next to me and gently stilled my nervous finger, which was madly doing circuits of my thumbnail. "She promised she would let you be there if she told her."

Feeling a good cry coming on, I turned and looked into his eyes. "So much for that. But what's worse is, she's going to Tennessee in a few weeks and leaving Kery with Cal for the rest of the summer and into the fall."

Pete pounded the table with his fist. "That woman will never learn. What are we going to do?"

"I offered to keep Kery while Mom was gone, but she told me I was being ridiculous. I'm going to talk to Jane. Remember when Mom told me Kery had shoplifted a blouse?"

He nodded.

"The books on intrafamilial sexual abuse say that kind of acting out is one of the symptoms of a child who is being molested. Add this trip to that fact, and I feel very shaky about the whole situation. Whatever Jane says, I'm going to follow her advice."

"Talk it over with me before you decide," Pete said.

"Absolutely," I answered. Then the tears spilled. Though he wanted to stay to comfort me, Pete had to leave, without his omelet. *How can I concentrate on this little family, when the other one keeps behaving in irresponsible ways that I have to do something about?* I wondered.

I called Jane. We asked God to show Pete and me what to do about Cal staying alone with Kery for two months.

"Ella, I'm not sure what God wants you to do," Jane admitted. "I know that most molesters continue molesting until they are arrested. If that's the case with Cal, you may be the only one to help Kery. But you said Kery is very close to Cal. It could be that something else is wrong, and he's no danger to her. On the other hand, to onlookers, it must have looked like *you* were very close to Cal. That leaves me unsure what to do. Because Kery's self-image is tied up in this, if it isn't absolutely necessary to tell her Cal is her father, I wouldn't do it. I'm just not sure whether it is or isn't absolutely necessary."

I wished I could be someone else, or that my job on earth was done and God would take me to heaven before I had to decide what to do. I wished Mom were someone else, and Cal too. I wished I could sleep long enough for Kery to grow into a mom with a family of her own when I woke up. But it was all silly dreaming.

Jane continued, "I think I would go talk to Pastor Yaeger if I were you, and maybe call the county incest treatment team."

I smiled weakly and said, "Okay."

"I'll pray for you. Call me when you decide what to do."

"I will."

It didn't work very well to ask Pastor Yaeger and the woman at the incest treatment team. Pastor said he thought Cal wouldn't molest Kery because she was his natural daughter. The woman said that wouldn't make any difference and I should go tell Kery that Cal was her father, otherwise I couldn't be certain that she wouldn't face what I had lived through. She urged me to do it immediately. I couldn't tell whether I should listen to Pastor, who knew God, or the woman, who was trained

in incest treatment. I couldn't tell whether I was seeking revenge under the guise of protecting Kery. I couldn't tell whether
it was talking or being silent that would be a courageous act of
following God.

Pete listened to all the different discussions I'd had and said,
"I wish I could tell you exactly what to do. But this is definitely
a judgment call, and I think you'll have to do what your
conscience says is right."

I prayed about it every time I thought about it for several
days, vacillating about what God thought. I searched the Scrip-
tures, finding first the verse that says to forgive seventy times
seven, and then the one indicating that God thinks a person
who makes a child stumble should be drowned. With each
Scripture, I changed my mind again about what God thought I
should do.

Friday morning I was once again weighing what to do when
I finally realized that forgiveness wasn't the issue. Trustworthiness was. Since I could not be one hundred percent certain that
Cal would not molest Kery, even if I asked him directly, my only
choice was to make sure that she was not deceived as I had
been. The knowledge that he had hurt me and had the capacity
to hurt her would give her the freedom to share the secret or
say no if it was necessary. Pete and I agreed that whatever we
could do to save her self-image we would sacrifice to accomplish, including shedding the best light on Cal's abuses that we
could under the circumstances. She had to know the truth that
might protect her. I was headed home again, except that it
didn't feel like home. I called Jane to let her know and asked
her to pray for me. As Pete and I traveled, I could almost feel
her talking to the Lord.

Mom and Kery were yelling at each other as we walked up
to the front door. When we knocked, the yelling stopped and
Mom opened the door. Kery looked at me strangely. I won-

dered what Mom had told her about me being her mother. Regardless of that, or the scrutiny I felt, I went instantly to hug her and whispered in her ear, "I have always loved you."

"Maybe you can talk some sense into her," Mom said. Her comment reminded me of her parting shots to arguments when I was still living there.

"I'd definitely like to talk," I said, looking at Kery, who looked back with a poker face. We'd been home very little since moving to California and Kery probably wasn't sure what kind of person I was. I felt deeply sorry for her being pushed into this intimate relationship with me, a woman she could only dimly remember from her childhood. I wished I didn't have to tell her about Cal. "Could we go into your room?" I asked.

"Okay," she said.

We sat on the bed facing each other. "Mom said she told you I'm your mother," I started.

She nodded, circling the flowers on the bedspread with her index finger.

I lifted her head and her eyes searched mine. "I love you," I said, tears breaking out in my voice and my eyes. "I always have, and I always will."

For a moment I had to show my love for her in my eyes because I couldn't swallow the lump in my throat. When it receded I said, "There's nothing wrong with you that made me decide to give you to Mom and Cal. I know that lots of girls keep their babies now, but when you were born I would have stigmatized you and Jessi and everybody if I had kept you. I believed I couldn't keep you. And I didn't think I'd be the mother you needed. I gave you up hoping you'd have a better life, knowing Mom would love you and I could keep track of you. I love you, very much."

"Oh, Ella," she said, and threw her arms around me. "I love you too." We hugged and cried.

Finally, I said, "Kery, there's something else I need to tell you. I wish I didn't, but with Mom going away and leaving you alone here with Cal, I have no choice."

She waited. All my carefully rehearsed words seemed inappropriate in the face of her watchful silence.

"Kery, our family was having a tough time before you were born. Mom and I didn't relate to each other very well. I liked Cal better than Mom."

"I do too," Kery said.

"I know," I responded. "And I know you're having trouble. Mom told me about the blouse you shoplifted."

She shrugged her shoulders and just looked at me.

I clasped my hands in my lap. "Cal didn't understand me. The outcome of him liking me better than Mom was not what I planned." I stopped and took hold of both her hands. "Well, Kery, I think you need to know what I'm going to tell you. I could be wrong, but I can't take the chance should I be right. Cal is your adoptive father. But he's also your natural father, not just adopted."

Her mouth dropped open. She looked toward the door as if she would like to escape.

I moved to hug her, but she felt like a board.

Letting go and settling for putting my hand over hers, I said, "Mom knows, and you can talk with her about it if you want. I'll tell her and Cal that I've told you." I paused and finally asked, "Has he ever tried to be sexual with you, Kery?"

"No," she answered distractedly. "No, he hasn't."

Relief flooded me, along with guilt. It appeared that Pastor Yaeger was right—I hadn't needed to tell her. Unless she was hiding it like I did.

"Jessi knows too," I said. "You could talk to her if you can't talk to me."

"Everybody knows but me," she said woodenly.

"I hoped never to have to tell you. But I couldn't be positive you would be safe."

"I'd like to be alone," she said.

"Kery." I put my arm on her shoulder and she inclined her head toward me.

"Please, I don't blame you. But I need to be alone," she begged.

I wanted to encircle her and protect her. But I had just shattered her world. What was protective in that? Besides, I was only her sister. She had asked me to go away. Though I'd had help, I had confused her life enough, and I opened the door and went into the kitchen. Cal had apparently gone outside. Pete sat listening to Mom gossip about people in town.

I dropped into the chair next to Pete and said to Mom, "I've told Kery Cal is her father. I did it because if you are going to leave her alone with him, she needs to know his weakness so that she has the capacity to protect herself if necessary."

Mom looked from me to Pete and said, "You don't understand... "

Pete said, "Myrna, you're the one who doesn't understand. You let two of your daughters be molested, and looked the other way. You were responsible for protecting them and you didn't. Ella did what had to be done."

Mom's face became rigid. "Pete, you haven't been a member of our family very long," she began.

"And that's just as well," he countered, "because this family functions in a very sick way when it comes to this problem."

Oh, Pete, please don't hurt her this way, I thought, my emotions at war with my sense of justice.

She stared at him in angry silence. "I don't know," she finally said. "I've had to take care of myself ever since I was twelve, after Daddy died. I didn't cause any of this, but everyone's expecting me to fix it." She looked at me.

Mom always mentions her dad when she feels threatened, I thought. When I didn't say anything, she added, "I'm not sure what is right."

Pete looked with great gentleness at Mom, and said, "I understand how hard the decisions were for you, Myrna. You had daughters to raise, and I'm sure even the thought of what had happened in your house made you want to disappear. I know you had to decide whether to trust Cal, how you could afford to raise the girls if you didn't. I know you did the best you could. But you have to understand Ella too. Kery is her daughter, even though you have been Kery's mother. Ella had to make a decision, and I think she made a very courageous one."

"Well, you can't tell Cal what you are thinking," Mom said. "He can't believe you still don't trust him. He says that every time he thinks it's going to sink into the past you bring it up again."

"We've never talked," I said. "He said he did that to me to show you I was bad. I have nothing to trust him with."

"Well, go talk to him then," Mom said, flipping her hand toward where Cal worked outside.

"It's all right?" I asked.

"Well, of course," she said impatiently.

"I never tried to talk to him before," I sobbed, "because I thought you would think I wanted to start something again." My words came between gulps.

"Oh, Ella. I don't blame you for what happened," Mom said, putting her arms around my shaking shoulders.

"She has felt that you blamed her for it all, for many years," Pete said.

"I didn't. Oh, I never did," Mom said, beginning to cry herself.

"It took a lot of reassurance that she was innocent to talk her out of the guilt she felt," Pete said.

"I know how hard it's been for her, but I didn't know what to do," Mom said.

"It's all right now, Mom," I said. I didn't want her to have to explain herself. It was obvious anyway. She had thought talking about it would hurt me. She didn't realize the truth was that it would have helped tremendously. "Could I go out and talk to Cal now?" This time I looked at Pete.

He nodded approval.

I felt as if, with each step I took down the hill, I regressed through time to the thirteen-year-old girl I had once been. So I stopped at the bottom and said to myself, "God expects you to act like the adult you are and to face the adult Cal is. You aren't looking for an apology. It is time to plant responsibility where it belongs, expecting nothing. If it comes out well, so much the better. But for now, get hold of yourself." I made myself stride purposefully toward the barn, looking for him.

He was mending a halter, and looked up startled when I opened the door. "How are you doing?" he asked.

I took a big breath because I was going to say my piece before my courage ran out. "I'm okay. I need to talk with you, though."

"Go ahead."

"Mom told me that my struggle through these last years with what happened between you and me made you think I was going to keep bringing it up forever. I'm not. But I've never talked directly to you and I need to. Cal, you were the adult in the relationship, and you took what didn't belong to you by manipulation. I have struggled with my view of myself and fear of authority and all kinds of things because of that. Nevertheless, I forgave you. I can't say that I trust you now, because you haven't gotten help. But I don't plan to try to hurt you because you hurt me. And after today I will not bring it up again." I just stood there.

"Ella, I'm sorry if I hurt you. If I were you, I would try to forget it and concentrate on raising your family. I think you are a good mother. If I can ever do anything for you and Pete, I want to."

My heart moved, and torn between wanting the relationship mended and being unsure whether he could ever be trusted, I reached out and twisted a button on his shirt. "Cal, I told Kery you're her father," I said.

"I knew you would tell her someday," he replied.

"How did you know?"

"I don't know, just knew. Let's go up to the house," he said. He didn't reach for me like in the old days. In fact, he was careful to walk with space between us, a space filled with pain.

When Mom called dinner, Kery came out appearing composed. She showed no sign that anything was different than before. Knowing that she was cut from my cloth, I guessed that this was a coverup. But until she asked me to help her, I was handcuffed. *Oh God*, I prayed, *did I do the right thing? How could I know? Please watch over Kery. I would like to help, Lord. If I can, please show me how.*

In the morning Mom and I were sitting alone at the table drinking coffee. I hesitated to ask her—she had given and withdrawn love and approval from me in nearly the same breath so many times—but I guess hope reigned eternal. "Mom, has something changed between you and me?" I asked. "Yesterday when you said you didn't blame me, I felt like you were saying something more."

"Ella, I decided if Jesus can forgive you, I can too."

After a minute I said, "Well, I'm glad."

Is she trying to say, with the wrong words again, that she has figured out how small my part was in the incest and dealt with all of it between herself and God? I wondered. Or is she blaming me and forgiving me for what Cal did, as her words appear to mean? I want to be forgiven for letting my anger at her for divorcing Daddy turn to rebellion, and yet I also want her to say that I was a manipulated child. Double meanings—I can't stand them. I wish she would apologize for her part, that's what I wish.

I decided I would be transparent. It was risky because I couldn't determine what she would do. But what God wanted me to do was to put my best effort into clearing the obstacles from my relationship with Mom. I was responsible for making honest moves toward that, even if she hurt me again. I said, "Mom, I believe when you married Cal that you ignored the love I'd lost when you sent Daddy away. You had always told me Daddy loved me so you had to love Jessi. That left me all alone when Daddy was gone. You should have thought that through and realized that you needed to do something about the deficit of love in my life. Instead, you spent your time at Phillips's. Then after you were married, you didn't treat Cal kindly. The result was two people, him and me, feeling lonely and unloved in the same house. I feel that you contributed to my abuse in that way."

For a long span she silently watched her hands. Finally she said, "I can see that you are right and I am desperately sorry." Tears dropped on the table.

"I already forgave you," I said and walked around to her chair and hugged her. My mother and I were both subject to sin. The fact that she had admitted hers made me more willing to deal with her dysfunctional patterns, which I was sure would still plague us. She might not learn to watch for and meet the needs of others right away, or stop sending mixed messages. But she had apologized, and that was another giant step.

When I told Jane all that had happened, she literally applauded. "Look what God can do!" she said.

"I asked her if Kery can come visit us sometimes while she's gone and she agreed," I added.

Jane gave me a shoulder hug. "Kery needs to talk, so that's good. Let's try to finish the second chapter before she shows up;

then I can begin sending proposals to publishers and you won't have to work on the book while she's here."

Self-Assessment Guide

1. Ella wishes several times during the chapter that she didn't have to make the decision or do the courageous thing she faced. What principles did she employ to determine what to do in each situation? Make a list of them. If you don't yet spend time reading Scripture daily, start with five minutes a day. Along with trying to get to know God better during your Scripture reading, look for principles to add to this list.

2. Ella works through with Jane the sexual dysfunction of fantasizing during sex, a habit Ella set in order to survive during her abuse. Her fantasizing turned into a bad habit she had to work herself out of. What habits that you established during abuse do you struggle with today? Pick either the one that bothers you most or the one you think would be easiest to overcome. What first step could you take to break this habit? Set a date to take that step (not more than a month from now).

3. As Ella walks down the hill on her way to talk with Cal about his responsibility for her abuse, she feels herself regressing emotionally to the abused girl she once was. She begins to talk to herself about her position as God sees her. Look up 1 Corinthians 13:11–13 and Galatians 3:29–4:6 and write the verses using your name in order to define for yourself what God considers a spiritually mature person. Write one lesson you learn from each passage and how you can apply it to your life.

4. Look at Ella's confrontation with Myrna and Cal. How has she prepared for it? What facts does she state? What response does she expect? What results does she experience?

5. Ella is beginning to use God's principles to deal with the situations she faces. This indicates that she has come to trust God because of what He has already done in her life. What has God done in your life? What specific opportunity have you given Him to prove that He loves you? If you have given Him that opportunity, thank Him for the results. If you haven't, why not do it now? The Bible says, "You have not because you ask not."

Helper's Focus

Stepping Stones, First Baptist Church's Bible study/support group for adults abused as children, began when three people realized that God had brought them through recovery and that they could teach His principles to others who needed to recover. Jane and Ella discussed the idea with Art, whose master's degree in divinity provided the necessary spiritual direction. A proposal was written and presented to the pastoral staff. Initially, the idea was to minister to a group of ten to twenty people, splitting into small groups of five for discussion of *When Love Is Not Perfect* by Marie Sontag.

As time went by, Art and Jane wrote homework for twelve sessions, and the members now work through, and the small groups discuss, this homework. The group was the size we had anticipated during its first session, and all the members were women. But in the middle of the second session First Baptist had a conference on relationships at which Stepping Stones was presented. At that point 123 people signed forms saying they were interested, resulting in a group of almost sixty people, with 14 percent of them men. At the next session, the group grew to eighty people. The group continues to grow and change. The most challenging aspect of this growth is the training of leadership.

There are now three leaders of Stepping Stones: Art, Jane and a woman who replaced Ella. There are two leaders in training, five encouragement coordinators and six table assistants. The leaders train these comforters who can be available to group members to maintain crucial one-on-one time.

The first level of comforters is table assistants, whose only responsibilities are to hand out homework and other forms and take roll in the small group at each session. Each assistant must have been a member of Stepping Stones for a trimester before becoming a table assistant. These people also attend monthly leaders' meetings.

Second-level comforters are called encouragement coordinators. These coordinators are men and women who are becoming stable through their recovery process, who want to comfort others, and who have already served one cycle as a table assistant. They are the backbone of a support group. Not everyone who is abused will have the capacity to become an encouragement coordinator, for various reasons, but many will. Their function is to facilitate discussion of the homework in the small group and to call each small group member once a week. Besides attending monthly leaders' meetings, they are encouraged to take training through the church on leading small groups.

The time and families of all encouragement coordinators are protected by the leaders, and each coordinator is given the guidance she needs to be an effective comforter. Since adults abused as children are easy prey to the "fixer" syndrome (that is, we tend to step in and solve problems for people), encouragement coordinators must be taught the difference between fixing a situation and serving a person. A servant frees someone to do something. She provides tools, responds to *requests* for advice and encourages. But she equips people to solve their own problems, rather than fixing them herself. On the other hand, a fixer, invited or not, steps in and carries the person instead of letting her stand up for herself. Encouragement coordinators are taught to be servants. An encouragement coordinator tries to contact every member of her small group on the phone once a week. This talk may start out with a surface conversation of less than a minute, but we have found that as the session progresses and people get to know each other better, it is necessary to set a maximum of one hour per week for each group member to spend talking on the phone with her encouragement coordinator. The member determines the amount of time, up to the one-hour limit. The point of these phone calls is to help deal with the denial that is heavy in people abused as children. Talking helps to bring the abuse back into her reality where she can work on the attitudes, personality quirks, and so on, that are part of having been abused. The time constraints during the two-hour group meeting do not allow enough time for in-depth talk. The weekly phone call provides this time. Once denial has lessened, the weekly phone call can be used to clear up questions about issues or talk about whatever topic the member feels is necessary. Each encouragement coordinator is given no more than ten women to care for, no matter what. Five or six is a much more manageable group.

Encouragement coordinators do not counsel. They listen, they share what has worked for them, and if they hear a member express a desire to do something clearly unbiblical, they advise against it. Plans for suicide, adultery, abortion, and so on, are immediately referred to a pastor.

Leaders in training will one day be able to lead an offshoot support group alone or with a partner, because they are being trained in this way: A current leader first models for them how to lead, then lets them help lead a lesson, then lets them lead a lesson with help, then they lead a lesson alone while being watched. They continue to be an encouragement coordinator for small groups during their training. The lessons led are shifted each session, so that leaders have led all sessions by the time they are ready to take a support group on their own, perhaps on a different night of the week.

Leaders are people of prayer. They have quiet time on a daily basis and they meet for prayer prior to the beginning of each group meeting. Support group leaders also follow the weekly phone-call rule with leaders in training and encouragement coordinators, to track both their progress at learning to lead and their recovery. Since Satan probably would not have much greater joy than to cause a leader to fall into sin in this type of support group, all levels of leadership are accountable to the next level above them and to the pastoral staff of the church.

Chapter Ten

All You Can Do Is Enough

There were a few moments of twilight when the eastern sky slowly darkened beyond the treetops, casting a pink and purple shade on the campground. Our family sat in chairs around a campfire with Jane, Art and their children. This rated as one of my favorite times of day, second only to sunrise. Ageless redwoods stood sentry around the camp we had chosen for our two-family camping trip, and the encroaching night chill had crowded everyone close to the fire. I propped my feet on a hearth rock to warm them and could feel the heat radiating through the bottom of my tennis shoes. We had just finished a cutthroat game of Trivial Pursuit, the men winning by the skin of their teeth. Pete had gloated disgustingly and Art, more of a gentleman, had smiled knowingly. It was maddening.

Jane and I had completed the book after two years of writing and rewriting and more years of proposing it to publishers to have them say we had done well, but... . During those years I had also had the blessing of leading Kery to commit her life to Jesus. She struggled in her relationship with Mom, and I was coming to believe that her acting out stemmed from that bad relationship and not from a problem with Cal. The sad thing was that Mom and Cal didn't take Kery to church, so she had no chance to grow spiritually except during the snatches I had with her when we visited every few months. Her self-image was beginning to improve though, at least a little.

Jane interrupted my thoughts, "Ella, I don't know why it's not selling. But with more responsibility in my job at church..."

Art interrupted. "This is Jane's dream. She's told me ever since she started doing public relations writing that she wanted to do it to help people know God better. This is an answer to prayer." He stopped abruptly and looked somewhat embarrassed.

"Art's not proud of me," Jane said sarcastically. "Anyway, I think we should stop writing proposals for a while."

I impaled marshmallows on the end of a stick that we'd shaved the twigs from. "Maybe even though we've finished it, it isn't finished from God's point of view. I don't know. To tell you the truth, I'm discouraged about it," I said. "Letting it sit for a while could be a great idea." I held the stick just above the coals where the marshmallows could turn a golden brown that would delight a gourmet.

Jane looked relieved. "Good. Then it's done," she concluded. "Put to bed, but not forgotten. I still believe it would help somebody." She spoke obscurely because Petey didn't know anything about my past. Her kids knew that she had been attacked by a neighbor man and they knew I had been abused, simply from being around as Jane and I wrote.

Suddenly Laura said, "Hey, what was that?"

Everyone turned to look at the tree she pointed to. About halfway up the trunk two eyes burned in the darkness, an absolutely still shape surrounding them.

"What is it?" Maryann murmured, clutching Jane's hand.

"An animal," John said.

"No duh," Laura said derisively.

"A squirrel?" Petey asked.

"I think it's too big for a squirrel," Art said.

"Maybe a possum?" Pete offered.

"Where's the flashlight?" Jane asked.

"I'll get it," Laura said, running into their tent.

The animal suddenly ran down the tree and disappeared into the dark.

"Darn!" John exclaimed.

Laura returned with the flashlight.

"It's gone," John told her.

"Which way did it go?" she asked quickly, obviously ready for the hunt.

"You can't go off in the dark looking for an animal you don't even recognize!" Jane ordered. With Laura, you had to make your point fast and loud. She acted even more impulsively than Jane.

Laura couldn't stand it. "You mean we're going to sit here and let him get away?"

"Exactly," Jane retorted with finality.

"Petey, it's time to get ready for bed," I said.

"Do we get to read the story?" he asked.

"Art's reading tonight. But he can't start until you are ready for bed. So get hopping."

Petey loved the book we were reading, *Perelandra* by C.S. Lewis. It mystified his ten-year-old mind. As he turned to head for our tent, Laura smirked at him. I had guessed wrong about how old she was when I first met her. She was two years older than Petey, and Jane allowed more latitude than I about bedtimes on camping trips. So Laura was taking her advantage, the twerp.

When we had settled around the fire again, Pete said, "Remember what you were saying about the book helping somebody?"

"Yeah," Jane and I replied in unison, and then surprised at our stereo response, both laughed.

"There must be a lot of ways to help abused people," he mused.

Jane commented, "Some people say that all abused people need professional counseling to heal. But I don't see how, if one in four women were abused as children, they could *all* afford to pay professional counselors."

I pulled the burned marshmallows off my stick, which had been dropped in the fire when we saw the animal on the tree. "What do you think about groups like Parents United, where people who have been abused get together to work on their problems?" I asked. "I could never get up enough courage to face a whole group of people like that."

Unconsciously braiding a pine needle, Art said, "Something bothers me about those groups. People have told me that the group in Modesto puts the victims and perpetrators together, and they cuss and scream at each other. Sounds counterproductive to me. I wouldn't want to make judgments before I saw for myself, but I wouldn't think healing would be encouraged in that kind of environment."

My mind buzzed along ahead of Art. "But you know what might work?" I said. "A small Christian group, where people study the Word as it relates to abuse." I knew God had fostered this idea. I could feel the rightness of it, and I was excited.

Jane exploded from her chair. "Ella! You've had a revelation! Think of it! People who have been hiding their abuse, and found it so difficult to follow God because of all these problems hanging from their belts, could come and work together through the stuff that holds them back. There's a woman, Marie Sontag, in my critique group who is working on a book that could be used by a group like that. Man, we could do this, and I want to do it right now!"

Art verbally pulled her back into her chair. "Jane, Pastor Yaeger has been burned by a number of Christian counselors. It could easily be that he won't allow that sort of thing."

"He hasn't even heard it yet," Jane said, but she sat down. "Art, we could do it. I know we could. Look at all God has taught Ella and me. Look how you and Pete have pulled us through. All we did was use God's truth, His principles, maybe clumsily. But we've come a long way, baby." She looked pleadingly at Art. Impulse led her when she felt excited about something, and she combatted it by waiting on Art to think the issue through and say go ahead or stop. It was clear she desperately wanted the go-ahead. Art is a wise man, so I wanted to hear what he had to say too.

He began, "Neither of you has credentials. That kind of group could come under strong attack because of the dysfunctional people you may encounter. I think Pastor would feel you were unprotected in that situation, and he wouldn't allow it."

"I felt pretty scared to try to help anybody before. But you have a Master's in Divinity," Jane suggested. "And so does Pete. If you helped us, I wouldn't feel afraid."

Art smiled. "Ah, rock soup," he intoned. Rock soup was a story Pastor told about a man who manipulated a whole town into making a giant pot of soup by starting with a rock he had and suggesting that they could make the soup better by adding the vegetables and meat they had. He used the term good naturedly to indicate that he was being conned.

Petey came slapping back to the campfire in his slippers, pajamas and robe. "Okay. I'm ready for the story," he said, climbing up into Pete's lap. His Teenage Mutant Ninja Turtle night clothes were wearing out and he had informed me that he was getting too old for that sort of thing when I bought new ones.

"So you would like us to help you two lead this group?" Art asked.

"Only if you think God wants you to," Jane said looking back and forth at Pete and Art, hope peeking out from under her voice.

"We'll think about it," Art said as he picked up *Perelandra* from beside his chair and winked at Pete.

Just then a sound of metal crashing on concrete came from where the trash cans were. John grabbed the flashlight and said, "Come on, he's back."

We tipped over our chairs as we jumped up. Art cautioned, "Don't run, you'll scare him away."

"Look, it's a raccoon," Maryann said with awe as John spotted the little critter who had run up a pine tree.

"Nope, it's two raccoons," Laura said, as the second peeked its bandit face around the other side of the tree.

"Wow, I never saw a raccoon before," Petey whispered.

The trash can lid lay on the pavement, wadded up papers scattered around it. Times like this when I caught a glimpse of nature made me feel that God had given me a little gift, just for fun. "Let's leave them to their dinner," I suggested after a few minutes of watching them—and them watching us. We quietly slipped away. I never did get a toasted marshmallow that night.

A few months later Jane and I explained our idea to Don Ford, pastor of the age group I belonged to at church. Art had agreed to lead, but Pete said his intern responsibilities wouldn't allow adding another job to his list. He promised to help me think things through at home, though. That meant no small help.

Sitting in front of a whole wall full of theological books, Don said, "You have no idea how much time I spend counseling women struggling with childhood abuse. I think it's a great idea." He doodled on a note pad. "Here's what you need to do," he continued. "Put together a proposal: who, what, why, when, where and how. Bring it to me and I'll propose the support group to the staff. You may not wind up working under me, but I'll sure give it my full support."

My heart sang. Step One was passed. We had prayed the whole month and so far God had said yes!

When Jane, Art and I met to work on the proposal, Jane said, "See, it does a lot of good to pray your face off."

Art felt his face gingerly and said, "Mine's okay." Then he looked at me and said, "I don't know, Ella, I think you may have lost a cheek."

"Real funny," Jane said, smirking.

We sat at our huge dining room table, having anticipated the need to spread out papers. I had fixed Russian Tea and its spicy aroma drifted to my nose. Art suggested we start with our purpose statement. "Begin with a strong foundation and everything else will fall into place," he said. I wondered whether he ever had a frivolous thought. We threw around possibilities, finally settling on "Stepping Stones is a Bible study that equips and challenges adults abused as children to live whole and discipling lives."

Next we described ourselves, since we would be the leaders. We included that each of us had been abused as a child. Then we worked on who would be eligible to belong to the group. We decided that only adults, either male or female, who had been abused as children could participate, along with their spouses or friends helping them to recover. We wanted to avoid "onlookers" and keep the group focused. We also thought the recovery dynamics would be different for adults than they would be for children, so we began with adults. Members, we decided, could be referred by pastors, other members, or word of mouth. We agreed it was crucial that all members sign an agreement to keep confidential what they heard in the study. Members could continue participating unless they missed three weeks without a reasonable excuse. If they missed three weeks, the leader would encourage them to join the group later when they could be more available. By the time we got this far, we had scattered scribbled papers all over the table, just as we had suspected. We took a break and organized the sheets so we could tell how far we had gotten and what we needed to do next.

"Coffee?" I asked.

"No. The tea tasted great, but if you've got a Diet Coke, I'll take that," Art said.

"He can't drink coffee, makes his heart beat too fast," Jane added. "I don't know why he likes Diet Coke. Tastes like gasoline to me."

I got a Diet Coke for Art and Diet Pepsis for Jane and me, and we started in again.

We decided not to advertise the group so that we would have time to develop leadership. We would develop a study that consisted of two fifteen-week sessions, with actual material covered in only twelve of them. Two meetings would be socials with time for questions, and one would be a vacation week in case of church activities. During the first fifteen weeks, and perhaps the second, a member simply studied the material. Before the second fifteen weeks, some members would be approached to be table assistants who helped with attendance and materials in the next session. This might lead into serving as an encouragement coordinator and on into full group leadership. We decided that some people who hadn't been through the classes at our church for evangelism or for Home Bible study leaders would be filtered out there. For the meeting itself, we planned a fifteen-minute opening to serve as a time for everyone to arrive, get coffee and catch up with each other. A thirty-minute small group session would follow the opening. Next would be a one-hour general discussion session led by Art, in which application of what the members had been studying would be the major activity. Fifteen minutes for prayer and closing concluded the meeting and our plan.

Standing to stretch, Art said, "I think it's a good proposal."

"I'll type it first thing in the morning and send it over to Don Ford," Jane offered.

As I got their coats, I assured them, "I'll pray."

"Amen," they agreed as they scurried through the cold to their car.

It seemed like forever before we heard that the pastors had liked the proposal and given Marie Sontag's book to Pastor Ron Blanc to read. He was Pastor Yaeger's preaching partner, who did much of the short-term counseling at the church. In reality, it took only two months before Don told us that the pastors approved the abuse support group, and Pastor Jim Talley had been chosen to be what Pastor Yaeger calls our "umbrella man." Pastor got the concept of the umbrella man from a story about a teacher who saves his whole class in a lightning storm by holding his umbrella over them, acting as a lightning rod, and losing his life in the process. Pastor Yaeger considers a pastor a *spiritual* umbrella man, who should spend his life on his sheep.

My dad called one day before we had our first appointment with Jim. Although I had never told Papa about Cal, I was really excited that we were about to start the group and told him all about it.

"Why do you want to work with people who have been abused?" he asked.

This was my dad, who told me never to lie; my dad, who had been closer to me than anyone except Pete. A lot of water had gone under our bridge, and there was no need for him to protect me from Cal now. "Papa, when I told you Kery was the result of rape, I lied," I answered. "She is Cal's child."

"I knew that when I saw her at your wedding," he told me, sounding misunderstood. "I wondered why you didn't tell me before."

"Because you love me and I thought you might do something foolish, like try to kill Cal and get yourself thrown in jail." Merely saying it brought back the fear and confusion of those days.

"Well, you never can tell," he said, the good humor with which he generally faced life returning to his voice.

"I missed you bad after the divorce, Papa," I whispered, trying to cover the lump growing in my throat. I remembered running to get his picture when I forgot what his face looked like. I swallowed hard to release the pressure on my throat and continued, "I felt alone and unprotected. But you know what? I think when God saw what Satan had planned for me, He stood in for you. He made up His mind that no matter how bad the abuse, He could make it come out for good. He gave me you when I was little so I would know who I am, and then He turned Satan's plan to destroy me into His plan to save lots of women—and maybe men—from being destroyed by abuse. I know a lot about how to recover from abuse. How about that?"

"It's a good way to look at it, Ella. And if you aren't living in the past, but going on with your life, then more power to you."

"Papa, you told me once, when you were drunk, that you asked Jesus to be your Savior when you were sixteen. I see that you go out of your way to be kind to people around you, and to your family, us. But you don't go to church. Did you tell me the truth about your relationship with Jesus, or are you doing the good things you do under your own steam?"

"Yes, Ella. I told you the truth. But other things happened. I don't trust church people very much. And there was the war. And other things."

"You know that God forgives us for what we do wrong?"

"I imagine. Listen, you just take care of that little family of yours. You'll be all right."

"I will, Papa."

"Okay then. I love you, goodbye."

"I love you too, Papa." The line buzzed.

"What is it that I sense under his words, Lord?" I asked. "If there's something I don't see, please show me. I love him and I can't imagine heaven without Papa. I hope he's telling the truth about being a Christian."

I guess I had never stood close enough to Jim Talley before to realize how big a man he is. When he stood as we walked into his office, he kept going up. He seemed a hundred feet tall. I felt better after he sat down. I noticed a sign on the wall that read, "All you can do is all you can do, but all you can do is enough." Jim was singles pastor at the church and Jane had said he had an incredible counseling load. He probably meant his sign as much for himself as for anyone else. I liked it. It made me think of what the Bible says about Jesus' burden being light.

Art and Jane had known Jim a long time and they started talking about interning together and the funny things their children had conned each other into. In the old days I might have felt left out or envious, but Pastor Yaeger had told us never to envy someone else's ministry. He said God purposely made us all different and there are lots of needy people to minister to. That freed me to enjoy and feel honored in the presence of these people who followed God closely and had such a good time at it. And I wondered where God was taking us.

Finally Jim said, "Listen, Art, you know what to do here. So I'll give you a few guidelines and you run with it. We want to start small. You already know that. Be careful to be supportive, but don't allow anyone to consider you professional counselors. What you have to offer are biblical principles and what worked in your own recovery. That's all. When you come to meet with me once a month, you make out the agenda since you are the ones in the trenches."

As Jane would say, "a piece of cake." After months of waiting, it seemed almost too easy.

"I'll also want all three of you to take the Taylor Johnson Temperament Analysis sometime soon. Have you ever taken that, Ella?" Jim turned to me.

"No."

"It's designed to show your relational strengths and weaknesses. How do you feel about helping to lead this group?"

"Kind of amazed that God has opened all the doors," I answered.

Jim pulled his electronic pocket calculator out and made a note. "Good attitude to have. It will keep you humble," Jim said. "Okay. We'll start filtering names to you right away. You should meet Wednesday nights so your members can take advantage of the child care at the church. We'll give you a cozy room off the beaten path. Call people before the first meeting and let them know where and when. Stop and pick up the Taylor Johnson from Jo Ann on your way out. Ella, get one for Pete too, and schedule an appointment when he can come with you so I can interpret them for you. That ought to do it. Let me pray for us before you leave."

I turned in our Taylor Johnson Temperament Analyses, TJTAs for short, the Monday after Kery's graduation from high school. It had been a bittersweet time. Again I juggled being a public sister and a hidden mother. Mom had dropped a few bombs, and that probably colored how I felt when I filled out the analysis.

When Jim called us in to go over it, he handed each of us a white paper with a blue grid on it. At either end of the grid were temperament traits. Jim said, "First I want you to put a little circle where you think you fall between each of the traits." When we finished that he gave us a clean sheet and had us plot our spouse. Then he gave us our original sheet back and I put a "P" where he told me Pete had plotted me. When we had finished, he told us to mark little X's at various places on our sheets and then connect them with a line. Finally he said, "Ella, we'll do you first. Did you realize that you are a somewhat nervous person?"

Pete smiled and looked meaningfully at my finger rotating on my thumbnail. I had never considered myself a nervous person at all, but there was that finger. "No, I didn't," I said.

"Here is where you put yourself and here is where your test

and Pete put you." The marks of the test and Pete were nearly on top of each other and far closer to *nervous* than I had marked myself. Jim smiled gently and said, "I think you may have learned to hide some of your feelings so well that you even made yourself believe you weren't being affected by what happened around you."

I remembered my aunt asking, back when I was eleven, if I was surviving my parents' divorce; I responded "I'm okay," wishing she wouldn't ask. Could that refusal to feel have carried down all these years?

"On the next trait, you see yourself as lighthearted," Jim continued. "But Pete, who appears to know you pretty well, and the test both mark you as mildly depressed."

I began to wish we hadn't done this. Pete had always said intelligence tests were unreliable. Could this be compared to an intelligence test?

Jim continued, "On whether you are more socially active or more quiet, you fooled Pete. That means you do a good job of covering up in some areas. You actually like to be alone and read a book about as much as you like to be with people. But you project a different image. Probably another cover up."

I don't know how I looked about then, but I wanted to leave. Pete said, "Maybe she was comparing herself with me. She is more social than I am."

"Yeah," I said. "Pete's a home boy."

"We'll get to Pete," Jim said. "For now, if you don't want to invite people over or go out, don't. There's nothing to prove to anybody. On *expressive-responsive*, you are closer to reality. You aren't too inhibited."

I smiled involuntarily, feeling satisfied that at least I came out right there.

When Jim came to *hostile* versus *tolerant* I needed work there too, and I began to feel like a bad person. Jim must have noticed and he stopped. "When the staff did the TJTA on me the first time, I went off the scale on *hostile*. I am pretty imposing, and none of them wanted to read my results to me. Finally Bill Stewart got saddled with the task." Bill used to be the youth pastor at First Baptist. After nearly twenty years of ministry, he went to Arizona to teach at a Bible college. Jim smiled. "Bill took me to a very public restaurant so he'd have help if I attacked him." We could see Jim's laughter inside before it exploded at the end of the story, and somehow his laughing at himself made me feel less like I had been tested and found wanting.

When he did Pete's TJTA it turned out that I had interpreted Pete wrongly in several areas. Jim gave me a whole pile of homework so that I could get God's perspective on the areas where I needed work. "Now, Ella, I can tell this threw you a curve. Don't start doubting yourself or your ability to lead. Just do the homework."

As soon as we were out the door, Pete asked, "How do you feel?"

I burst into tears. "I feel like I have no idea who I am. Do I know the truth about anything?"

"It's not that bad," Pete soothed. "The test is designed to show you your weak areas. That's all. Honey, I don't think it's so bad that you would rather curl up in front of the fire with me than be with crowds."

I smiled a little. As we walked down the street, Pete put his arm around me and said consolingly, "You are too hard on yourself. We both know your secret dream is to be perfect. I think this will help you cut yourself some slack. Pastor says a strong man knows who he is, but more important, who he isn't. I think strong women do too."

"Okay then," I said, and rubbed tears out of my eyes.

While I studied Jim's homework, Jane and I divided the names he'd given us and called the women with the details about the first meeting. I prayed about every aspect of the group, from who would come, to all of us being open and kind.

Art worked on the meeting format and which of us would do what. We had barely completed our preparation when we came to the first Wednesday night in May 1990.

Art arranged the room so that no one could see who was inside through the windows in the doors. He situated the overstuffed furniture and oak tables in a big circle while Jane and I prepared the coffee; only coffee, nothing fattening to work as accomplice to our bad habits. Art appeared calm, but Jane and I wandered about studying the room from different angles, and pausing to check our hair in the mirror. First impressions are lasting, after all.

Finally, a woman with a blond spiral perm opened the door and stuck in her head. "Is this Stepping Stones?" she asked quietly.

"Yes," Art answered, "come in." His outstretched hand beckoned her in. *How careful he is,* I thought. *He didn't offer to shake her hand or touch her at all.*

"Hi, I'm Ella," I said. I shook her hand. "And this is Jane."

"I'm Donna," she replied.

"Pick a seat anywhere," Jane said. "You're first, so you can pick wherever you like."

She perched at the end of one of the sofas and laid her purse and Bible next to her on the middle cushion.

"Did you have any trouble finding the room?" Art asked.

"No, I go here. I knew where it was. I'm in Singles. Jim Talley told me about the group."

"I think I talked to you on the phone, didn't I?" I asked.

"Yes, I think so," she answered.

I remembered that when I asked her if she had been abused as a child, she told me her father had abused her and that when she confronted him about it, he said it wasn't true. *What would I have done if that had happened to me?* I wondered.

The door opened again and one woman came in followed closely by another. The first was a petite woman with dark hair cut in a shingle. The second dressed in jeans and a halter top. *Whoa, what's this?* I thought. Her black hair cut very close to a butch, she wore bangle earrings at the sides of a face that screamed, "I am angry!"

Jane extended her hand to the first woman and introduced herself. I waited so I wouldn't miss anyone's name—or perhaps because the second woman looked kind of scary?

"My name is Heather," the petite woman told Jane. I smelled Chantilly perfume as she turned to find her seat. I hoped I wouldn't have trouble liking her. One of my *philosophical* thoughts on life was that petite women were often stuck on themselves.

"Hi, I'm Melanie," the second one said, sticking out her hand without waiting for Jane to turn to her. She smiled and her whole face changed. She looked like a little kid. "I talked to you on the phone."

"I remember," Jane said. I hated it when she said things in a way where you couldn't tell what she thought. It reminded me of Mom, I guess. But it was one of the only things that bugged me about Jane, so I could live with it. I wondered how it made Melanie feel.

Jane sat with these women, and the next one was up to me to greet. She came in, a heavy woman, but coiffed and nicely made up. She wore a pressed shirt over new jeans.

"Hi, I'm Ella," I said.

"I'm Pat. Is this Stepping Stones?" she responded.

"Sure is and you're right on time. Here, sit next to me," I suggested as I took the seat where I had left my things.

As Art finished talking with Donna, he looked around the group and said, "If you came to Stepping Stones, you're in the right place. Let's start with prayer."

The door opened. This last woman looked disheveled and came in apologizing. "Oh, you're praying. I'm sorry. I had to take my kids to child care. This is Stepping Stones?"

"Yes," Art said. "Don't worry, we just started. What's your name?"

"Valerie," answered the woman, whose hair was the color of a new penny.

Art finished the prayer and then we each told our name and one good thing God had done for us that week. We'd purposely picked that icebreaker because abuse survivors tend to look at the down side of life. Some of the women had a hard time thinking of a good thing that happened to them that week. When one couldn't, Jane said, "Well, you've managed to get here, that's a good thing."

Art, Jane and I took a short time to say we were each abused as children, so they would realize that we weren't going to ask them to share things we weren't willing to share ourselves. Then I explained that we would pray for, listen, accept, protect and share honestly with one another, and that we were in for a lot of hard work with God on our way to recovery.

Jane helped them fill out a confidentiality agreement and enrollment forms and explained that we were available to talk with them up to an hour a week on the phone. She said if they chose to call one of us, that person would be their helper during the session. If they didn't call, we would assign a helper. They chuckled a little at that. Jane told them that she and Art would take calls whenever they needed to talk, but that if they called her during working hours she could only talk for a few minutes.

Art took it from there and related the importance of doing their homework. He told them that if they only showed up at class, the group would be nearly useless to them. "The interaction between each of you and God during the week will help you recover," he explained. He encouraged them to start a personal journal to record what they learned about themselves as well as biblical insights on how to recover.

He warned them that to get thrown out of the group they only had to talk outside this room about something someone else said in confidence to the group. Finally, he explained that support sounds like: "You've been through a lot, but you know it hasn't gotten you down. You're still here plugging away." He said hugs and pats on the back are support, and so are listening to and crying with someone. Then he said, "What we won't do is give advice and counsel; that sounds like this: 'Here's what you need to do to get your life straightened out.' Nobody will do that here." Then he went over the outline of the sessions.

We didn't seem to be clicking yet. I wanted to hear who they were and what they wanted to see happen here. I had hoped to see that begin tonight.

Art finished and said, "Now we'll take time for prayer. Make your request something for yourself. We know how much effort you put into appearing to have no problems." They all chuckled again. He continued, "But this time it is an assignment. We don't want you to pray for Aunt Minnie's lumbago, but for yourself."

Deep silence and staring followed. Jane said, "I yelled at my son, John, last night because he hasn't been studying for finals. He's in high school, for Pete's sake—I need to back off and let him sink or swim."

Melanie scratched the top of her head as she prepared to speak. "I, uh, I need some help with my old man. He keeps bringing drugs into our house." She rubbed her hands against each other. "Actually, he's not my husband and my mom says I ought to get out of there and take the kids. But they are his kids too."

Valerie said, "Man, that's tough. You can make it, though. My husband kicked drugs. I had to walk out first, but he finally did it." She stopped suddenly, realizing, I think, that she had said much more about herself than she had intended to. She cleared her throat. "Our finances aren't very good. In fact, I, um, I don't know where we're going to get the rent."

There was a long pause. I said, "I took this test the other day that showed me all this stuff I didn't know about myself. Now I have all this homework to do. I think the homework is helping, but I'd like somebody to pray that God can get through to me."

Art followed with, "Mine isn't as spiritual as most of yours. I just want a raise at work."

Donna and Pat both started to talk at once. Donna quit and encouraged Pat to go ahead. Pat said, "I have a job right now, but it ends in a month and I have no idea where I can find another."

Donna looked at her lap as she said, "I wish my dad would admit he molested me. I'd like to pray for that, or else that God would help me be content the way things are."

"Amen," Jane said.

There was another long pause as the group waited to see if Heather wanted to talk. She didn't take advantage of it, so Art said, "Pray for whoever's request you want. Don't pray too long. It's intimidating. And you don't have to pray at all if you don't want to."

I thought, *There is something important happening here. Now we're clicking. I think it must be impossible to pray for someone and not take an interest in them. Prayer is how we communicate with God and how we care about each other.*

Then it was over and no one wanted to leave. We stood talking for an hour.

Jane caught me in the street after church on Sunday. "Jim wants us to do a presentation in Sunday school on the group," she said. "We would tell how we put it together, some stuff about abuse, but what has me freaked is that he says to finish the cycle of recovery you and I and Art should say we've been abused." While she waited for me to reply she ran her thumb around her lips.

Finally, I responded with great intelligence. "Wow." Then I exhaled.

Jane smiled ruefully, "The good part is that he says we don't need to say who abused us or give any details. In fact he says that's telling someone else's story and wouldn't be biblical. I think I could do it if I don't name names." She hesitated. "At least I *think* I could. It feels different to tell a big group of people, some of whom might not have been abused and so could misunderstand."

I felt my finger make contact with my thumbnail. "If you're going to do it, I'll be with you," I assured her.

"Jim said he wouldn't let anyone pick on us," Jane offered. "And Art will take the lead."

The morning we spoke, people had already filed into the meeting area as we walked to a side room to pray with the leaders. I had hoped a lot of people would stay home because of the subject, but they were coming. To make the situation a little more interesting, Jim would record our presentation to play for the pastoral staff.

We had asked the women in the group to come for moral support, and I could see some of them sitting among the crowd. I had also asked everyone I had told about my abuse to pray for me, but I still shivered as we climbed the steps to the stage.

Jane and I sat down while Art began speaking. We each explained our background, and although when I finished I had no idea what I'd said, there was something about not being real glad that I had this story to tell, but very glad that God had orchestrated the outcome.

One event struck me during this meeting; it happened when a woman raised her hand during the question and answer session and asked Art, "If God loves me so much, where was He when I was being abused?"

I exhaled like I had been punched in the stomach. Jane leaned over and said, "Pardon me while I swallow my tongue."

But Art looked down at the woman in his gentle way and said, "He was right there, and He was crying."

I felt myself starting to cry. I knew Art was right. God loves us enough to give us *choice* that is part of honest love. And He has the capacity to love us more than we love, because He has the power to rescue us from the wrong choices we or others make. When Art said God cried when we were abused, I remembered how Jesus cried when He learned his friend Lazarus was dead. I wondered whether He had cried because, to work God's plan, He had to bring Lazarus back from heaven? And did He cry when I was abused, because God's plan includes letting Satan run loose long enough for us to have the opportunity to decide about Jesus?

Before I knew it we were finished and people were coming up to each of us. I explained to several women when and where the group met, and they each thanked me several times for having the courage to share with this group. Not one soul came up to me and said, "Why don't you keep your dirty laundry to yourself?" or "You must have done *something* to bring that on yourself." No one. The scared girl I so easily regressed to looked up and said, "They like me. They understand me. They want me to help them." Her face changed from that of the frightened girl I used to be, to the woman's face I now see in the mirror.

After everyone had drifted away, Jim came up to us and said, "Well, did you survive?"

"Survive!" Jane exclaimed. "I feel freer than I ever felt in my life."

"What did I tell you?" Jim asked rhetorically.

He ruffled the hair on top of my head and said, "How about you, Ella?"

"What is God doing?" I asked.

"We'll see," he answered. "Keep praying, and we'll see."

Self-Assessment Guide

1. Ella says that God provided her father in her early childhood so she would know who she was. In your opinion, what affect does a father have on a daughter's image of herself? What influence did your father, or mother, have on your self-image? Is there an abused little child in you? What is this child wishing for?

2. Why do you think Ella felt so upset after Jim interpreted the Taylor Johnson Temperament Analysis for her? Do you think there could be leftover defense mechanisms or survival tactics inside you that keep you from truly knowing yourself or relating well to others? What are they?

3. Pete, Ella, Art and Jane discuss the advantages and disadvantages of support groups. How does the little child inside you respond to the idea of attending a support group?

4. What is your inner child wanting when she asks where God was when you were abused? How do you feel about Art's answer to the woman who asked where God was when she was abused? Draw a picture or write about where God was when you were abused.

5. There is a balance to questioning God. After all, He is the Creator. Apart from Him we wouldn't exist, abused or otherwise. Read Job to help you gain a perspective of Who God is and what our relationship should be with Him.

6. What negative things will Ella stop doing now that her abuse is public? What restrictions did Jim place on how much Ella, Jane and Art should say about their abuse? What would be the effect on the scared child you carry inside yourself if you were to make your abuse common knowledge?

Helper's Focus

> Therefore confess your sins to each other and pray for
> each other so that you may be healed. The prayer of a
> righteous man is powerful and effective. (James 5:16)

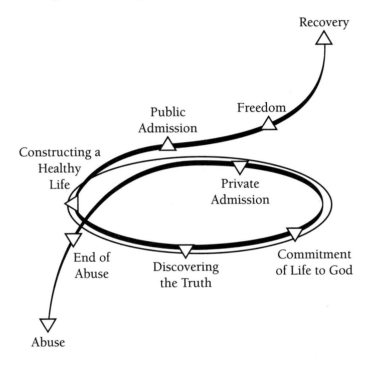

This diagram illustrates the cycle of recovery. We have said
before that ending the abuse by making authorities aware of it
is the only sure finish. It is step one of the recovery process and
no other step can legitimately be taken until the abuse is over.
It is best when the adults in the family disclose the abuse to
authorities, because their self-image is affected by the fact that
they have done the right thing. If they will not, the other people
aware of the situation must report the abuse themselves.

Rationalizing the abuse of a child by an adult into a minor offense or a learning experience ignores reality and God's promise to give us good lives. When a person in a helping role does this, she is probably avoiding having to confront the situation. Abuse is ugly, but becoming involved with abusers and the abused won't taint the helper or destroy the family. Allowing the circumstances that promote abuse to continue is hideous, and a would-be helper who stands idly by becomes "soiled." You may wish it weren't you who knows about the situation you are dealing with. But God apparently thought you could help or He would have alerted someone else. Gather His strength in prayer and the Word, and then do what is right.

Every local church needs to teach its members to avoid blaming a victim or suggesting that she leave it in the past, thus taking away her opportunity to cleanse her wound. It would be better for the church to actively participate in her recovery. Spiritually mature people who desire to help in these circumstances could be educated about recovery from abuse. These people could walk with the victim—and perhaps the family—through the recovery process, providing the opportunity for private confession for all members of the family.

Admission of abuse in the family will differ for each person, but whatever way each wishes to reveal the truth of the situation should be accepted and reflected back to them, to help clarify their thought processes. In Chapter Two we covered how to help the person who privately admits being abused for the first time.

Keep in mind that until we ask Jesus to take control of our lives, we may apply all the biblical principles and find some measure of recovery, but something will be missing. That something is Jesus Himself, who comes to live inside us when we ask, bringing with Him power and truth that are not available to those who will not ask. Without Jesus, recovery is never complete.

We believe that discovering the truth happens best in a support group. The benefits are:

- You have people leading you who constantly study abuse issues.

- You attend with others who have been abused and understand what you face.

- You receive instant feedback on the thoughts you voice.

That doesn't mean that one-on-one time with a sympathetic individual isn't worthwhile. Perhaps it should even come first in the process. But the recovery process is accelerated and enhanced through attendance at a support group.

The fifth step in recovery, *constructing a healthy life,* is completely up to the individual who has been abused. The helper can explain Christianity, provide truthful and healing principles, listen, explain, give feedback and befriend. But the abused person must do the work of restructuring her belief system. This will happen as she works at hearing her helper as well as her own feelings. She has to apply the medication of truth to her wounds and make a concerted effort to heal. Some people refuse to do this. We will address dealing with them in Chapters Eleven and Twelve.

Public admission, the last step to freedom, is the most frightening and yet the most freeing step for the abused. It frightens her because she is still certain that "they" will brand her dirty and disgusting. But it actually frees her because when she speaks the truth of the responsibility for her abuse aloud, her own shame must leave. At this point her comforter will help more than ever. Hiding has become comfortable to the victim through the years. The openness and vulnerability that will bring healing to the survivor, as well as others, leads toward freedom, not more pain. But the helper can see the light of freedom, when the abuse survivor still can't see it and fears the further pain she suspects lies in wait for her. The helper can describe the light of freedom to her and encourage her to walk toward that light when, for her, the path is dark. The comforter can arrange a public admission at a time and place least threatening to the survivor, most likely in a church class or support group. If the victim will not take the step of public admission, she must go around the recovery cycle again, until she allows God to work through her in public admission.

Finally, freedom. She has revealed her secret and is on the road to recovery. What happens when she's free? If she confesses her sin consistently, communicates with God in prayer, takes instruction through His Word and enjoys the company of other Christians in worship, she lives a new life.

The survivor is free from spending great quantities of energy on protecting herself. No longer is she frustrated by her lack of comfort and affirmation from dysfunctional relationships. Isolation doesn't plague her. Hiding, lying and shame cease to be her constant companions. She leaves behind her image that she is trash.

But most important—because when the survivor asked God to take over her life, His truth set her free—now she can choose not to sin but to follow God instead. Now she has the power to say no to self-demeaning behaviors. She is free to protect, be close to and comfort someone else. Her vulnerability allows her to relax, to rest. The courage to try new things may be hers for the first time in a very long time. She may follow the Great Commission to go into all the world and tell how He changed her life. She is free to live as a servant of God, doing what Galatians 5:6b says is "the only thing that counts...faith expressing itself through love."

Chapter Eleven

Out of the Closet—
Now What?

The ceiling fan only served to swirl the steam from the canner around the kitchen. The room had taken on the feel of a dry-cleaning establishment, humid on top of hot. It was only 9 A.M., but September in the Central Valley is about as close as I want to get to hell, and corn has to be canned when it's ready, first thing in the morning. Amanda rubbed the sweat off her forehead into her streaked hair. Although our current boarder generally proved helpful, she was a city woman who had to be told everything about canning. She moved as slow as the seven-year-itch slicing corn kernels off the cobs. But she was company.

"Ella, how much longer do you think it'll take?" Amanda complained.

"I planned for us to be done before lunch, but you've got to move that knife a little faster. Otherwise, we could get old here," I answered, grinning.

"Seems to me it would be a lot easier to buy your vegetables in a can."

I dropped more ears into the freshly boiling water. "When you taste this, you'll change your tune," I assured her. "I'll tell you what. Grab one of those ears and bite into it."

In horror, she said, "They're not cooked enough! Won't I *get* something?"

"Cryin' out loud, Amanda, they're vegetables, not pig fat. Taste one." I sounded like Pete's mother to myself; she spoke with a country charm I admired.

Amanda bit into an ear and juice squirted on her chin. "Man, this is tasty," she declared around the ear, which she went at like a typewriter. I pulled more ears out of the ice water in the sink and sat them next to her. Taking a particularly succulent one, I joined her in munching. "Food of the gods," I remarked.

She had devoured her cob. "Nevertheless, it takes forever and it's a slave's job for slave's wages," she grumbled without picking up the knife again.

"Don't be a quitter," I warned. "Us country folks will think you city folks are feeble if you don't hang in there. Could you get me another box of those quart bags on the top shelf?"

Amanda walked over to the cabinets and reached onto the top shelf. She was as tall as Pete and saved me having to get the step stool off the back porch when she worked with me.

I loaded my arms with plastic bags full of corn and headed out to the freezer. At the front of the top shelf stood a half gallon of chocolate ice cream, calling my name.

"Hey, look what I found," I said as I came back into the kitchen. "Want some ice cream to wash down your corn?"

"I don't think so, but you go ahead," Amanda said, returning to cutting corn off the cobs. She glanced down at my over-stuffed thighs and quickly away. "Tonight you'll be gone, huh?"

I dragged the ice cream scoop through the solidly frozen chocolate. "Yeah, Stepping Stones, fourth meeting of our second trimester."

"You care if I invite a couple of people over to watch movies?"

"As long as you're finished with the corn first," I teased.

It was a good thing we were coming to the end of the corn; we were running out of ice. When the buzzer went off, I took the hot ears out of the canner and dropped them in the ice water. While I waited for the water to boil again, I smoothed ice cream off my spoon and into my mouth with my top lip. I really shouldn't have eaten ice cream in the morning, but the tedious work made me hot and ice cream made me feel better. I dropped the last ears in the water and grabbed another knife to help Amanda.

At last we cleaned the corn off the table and floor and stacked the last bags in the freezer.

I showered and changed clothes in the afternoon and even had an hour for a nap before Petey got home. We fed the animals, ate dinner and arrived at church a half hour early. Petey hustled off to Campaigners, a children's organization the church had imported from England that helped Petey learn the Bible and have great fun at the same time. Pete kissed me goodbye and headed for a Bible study he led. As I unlocked the Fireside Room and turned on the lights, in came Melanie, wearing short shorts and another halter top.

"I'm glad you're here," she said. "I gotta talk to somebody."

Heading for the kitchen, I said, "Okay, you can help me make coffee while we talk." Melanie hadn't shared much during the group. Maybe this meant a breakthrough.

She followed me, talking. "Remember how, way back when Stepping Stones started, I said my old man did drugs?" she asked.

I turned on the coffee maker. "Yes, I remember," I answered.

"Well, I didn't tell the whole truth. I do them too, and I drink, too much."

Man, where are Jane and Art? I thought. "Not a good plan," I said.

"Well, it's not like I want to. I mean, I want to—but I know I shouldn't." She stopped.

I hadn't looked at her since she'd started talking and I imagined by now that she could feel my discomfort. What did I know about drugs? Alcohol was a little closer to home because of Papa, but not personally. I looked up at her, trying to hold acceptance in my eyes. Stalling, I said, "Here, pour this coffee into the filter."

"I want to follow God. I want to do what is right. What do I do?" she asked.

I was afraid you were going to ask that, I thought.

The door opened and Jane lugged her "group box" in and sat it on a table. Art came in right behind her, a load of notebooks and manila folders in his arms. I smiled at Melanie and said, "Here are the people with the answers."

Art heard me and said, "What's up?"

"Tell him," I urged Melanie. She walked back into the Fireside Room where I couldn't hear what they were saying.

Thank You, Lord, I thought. *Perfect timing.*

This trimester, the group was studying homework that Art and Jane were writing. Tonight we would work on "trust." As I had done my homework during the week, I realized that I trusted some people extremely slowly, who actually deserved my trust, and far too quickly trusted others who should be encountered with care. I never seemed middle-of-the-road about trusting someone. I either trusted them instantly and without any concrete reason or felt extremely suspicious of them, usually because they had a position of authority over me or reminded me of Mom or Cal.

As we worked through the questions, we came to a section that talked about Gideon. The question we were on said Gideon acted in many ways the same as an abuse victim does. Art told us Gideon's folks could easily have been idol worshipers, so it seemed likely that he had been subjected to some kind of abuse. Donna said, "My irrational actions were what first made me think I might have been abused as a kid, kind of like Gideon. I felt mad all the time and I couldn't figure out at what. I expected my husband and kids to treat me exactly as I wanted to be treated, and if they didn't I went crazy. I was afraid of men big time, except when I threw myself at one. Everything I did was irrational. Then I started to have flashbacks. I would see my dad with me in places he shouldn't have been. Finally, I saw what happened. I don't know if he abused me only once or not. And a little later, I began to doubt what I remembered. It was really tough."

"How did it all come out?" Pat asked.

"I went to counseling and to the Parents United group. They encouraged me to confront my dad. I did. But he said he had no idea why I accused him of such a preposterous act." She stopped. "Man," she said with exasperation. "But at least I put the responsibility in the right place."

Art said, "Sounds like you stood up for yourself, told the truth as you knew it and left his response to him. That's what you're supposed to do."

Donna looked at him. "I know, but it feels so weird. Are my memories real? Am I crazy or not?"

Pat waved her hand in the air as if she needed permission to talk and answered Donna's question. "No, you are not crazy. I don't have the exact same problem you do, but mine makes me feel just as unfinished," she said. "My uncle got killed in a car wreck before I could confront him."

"You're right, Pat. Donna isn't crazy," Art answered. "And I have an idea for you. But first, let's answer Donna. Trust the facts, Donna. It's hard for most people to remember what happened five years ago, much less in childhood. And when something horrid happens to a child, the natural thing for the child to do is bury it, forget it. The child doesn't realize that abuse can't be buried, that it will come out in physical, emotional or relational problems. That's what happened to you.

"Something you might do to help yourself heal is to write your dad a letter. Tell him everything you know about his abuse of you, about the parts of your personality he took advantage of, and about the issues you deal with now. Then mentally hand your letter to Jesus. If God thinks it best for you, He will motivate your dad to make the next move. If not, you can be certain that God will take the contents of your letter, one at a time, and work through them with you."

Art reached for the insulated mug full of Diet Coke that he kept at the ready, then continued. "If you need to hand the letter to someone you can see, you can hand it to me." He smiled gently at Donna and tears began to drop on her cheeks. Jane grabbed a tissue and put her arm around Donna's shoulders while she dried her tears. I noticed Melanie scowling at her clenched hands.

"Okay, I can do that," Donna said. "But I can't trust my dad, and the Bible says I should forgive him. It's a Catch 22."

"You are misunderstanding forgiveness, Donna," Art said. "Forgiveness is simply giving up your right to exact the penalty for the wrong done you, refusing to take revenge. In the Christian's view, it is allowing Jesus' crucifixion to pay not only for your sin, but for the sin of another against you.

"It doesn't mean trusting someone who is unrepentant and therefore untrustworthy. You should exercise extreme caution around your dad, not just to protect yourself, but you also have a daughter, am I right?"

"Yes."

"Until your dad has a change of heart, and actually until he receives therapy, he is not to be trusted," Art concluded.

"I see," Donna said. Jane handed her the tissue and went back to sit next to Melanie.

Art looked at Pat. "Another thing victims can do is role-play, confronting their abuser using someone else as a stand-in. Some victims do this as practice before actual confrontation. You could do it this way since your abuser has died. The reason this is important is that when you place responsibility on the perpetrator, you remind yourself that if he is responsible, you can't have caused the abuse and therefore are not guilty."

Pat said shyly, "Would you role-play that with me, Art?"

Art flipped a page of his homework and said, "Jane and I will be glad to help you, Pat. You write what you want to do and show it to Jane. Then we'll take it from there."

Pat looked at Jane and smiled. Jane smiled back.

Art turned to me. "Ella, how did you answer question nineteen?" he asked. "Did God condemn Gideon for having trouble trusting Him? What did God do that showed He understood how hard it was for Gideon to give Him true trust?"

I read from my homework. "No, God didn't condemn him. He even did what Gideon asked about those dumb fleece tests and kept telling Gideon that he was strong enough to do what God wanted."

When Art focused a question on someone else, Jane leaned over and handed her office keys to me. "Good answer, good answer," she said. "I forgot next week's homework. Could you go get it? It's green papers on the top shelf."

"Sure," I said and left, quietly shutting the door, as Pat said, "I thought we weren't supposed to test God."

It was a starry night. The crispness of fall woke me up after the warmth of the Fireside Room.

Crossing the street, I thought, *God, what is my problem with trust?*

The answer flowed into my mind, *You don't trust Me.*

I kicked a crumpled pop can up onto the sidewalk. *But I love You*, I thought. *You saved me from abuse, and You answer my prayers.*

The thoughts murmured, *Your love for Me isn't complete because you don't trust Me. You protect yourself from being abused again, because you don't think I protected you before and you don't believe I have your best interest in My heart now.*

I stopped walking and looked inside myself for what I truly believed. Seeing, I cried, *Oh God, I blamed You.* I felt so sad. I said to Him, *You're right. It's true. I haven't trusted You for years. Maybe I did in little things, but not fully, not to protect me.*

I started walking again, distractedly kicking the can in front of me. *Father, can You understand I never want to hurt that much again? I have taken upon myself Your role of determining my life and thrust You out because of the pain. But I didn't do it on purpose, or because I didn't love You.*

Words came into my head again. *I know you, Ella. I understand how much you hurt. But I want the best for you, and you can't have it if you don't trust Me with every tiny aspect of your existence—if you don't leave it to Me whether pain will slice your life. Didn't you see how I treated Gideon? He was like you. I had great plans for him but he had to trust Me first. What will you do now?*

I stopped kicking the can and shoved my hands in my pockets. *I do not feel strong. Are You my strength as the Bible says? You know that the most obvious way I protect myself instead of trusting You is using my enjoyment of food as an easy way to distance myself from men. I began by thinking that evil men aren't interested in heavy women. But I've read many newspaper stories that say my theory is full of holes. Thinking I could protect myself is a big lie, isn't it? Will You help me give my life back to You?*

I stood quite still, looking up at the sky. Although I knew Jesus lived in my heart, I still looked at the sky when I wanted to feel close to Him. Peace filled the night, the world and me.

Yes. As I have ever been with all people of faith, I Am your strength and your salvation, came the quiet answer.

I had arrived at Jane's office. Quickly I grabbed the homework and ran back to the Fireside Room.

Bursting through the door, I said to the group, "I have to tell you something. I found out that I don't trust God. Nothing else works if you don't trust God." I tried to repeat word for word to them my silent conversation with God.

"I don't trust God, either," Valerie said quietly. "I know Art said God cried when I was abused. But I didn't want Him to cry—I wanted Him to save me."

Worrying whether my joy would overwhelm her, but hoping that she could catch up, I began, "Valerie, He reminded me that His heart is set on my good. I'm not more special than you. His heart is set on your good, too. I don't understand justice very well, but I know that our abuse is going to come out to a marvelous good, because that's what God wants."

In my excitement, I realized I was still standing. I sat where I had been before and continued, "I tried to protect myself from losing love or being manipulated into twisted love ever again, but becoming overweight didn't protect me. Only God can truly protect me. Hiding behind my weight only kept me from the relationship with God that I could have had if I weren't concentrating on protecting myself. The pain He allows in our lives is going to produce wonders, miracles. We just have to believe Him when He says He loves us and will make it all work out. I think the end will be so incredible that the pain will seem like a minor irritation."

Jane said, "I think I have a part of the help He promised you, Ella. I'll tell you after class."

Valerie's turquoise eyes transformed from despair to hope as I talked; they were fairly twinkling. I could see that she had caught a glimpse of what God had shown me outside. "This is good," she said, thoughtfully twisting a curl of her copper-colored hair around her finger.

Art smiled his huge Mickey Mouse grin. That grin popped onto his face whenever he saw God obviously working in someone's life. We all teased him about grinning so big because he became so transparent, and he looked like a little boy when it happened, despite his grizzly beard.

He had been explaining how to tell whom we could trust when I burst into the room. Returning to the subject, he said, "I think God had the lesson tonight. But we'll finish anyway. Matthew 7:20 says you will know them by what they do. In other words, it's okay to hang back and watch someone for a while before you trust them. It's also a good idea to check with others who know the person to get their opinion, especially others who know the Lord."

Heather said, "That would help us not to trust too quickly or too slowly, but find the middle road, wouldn't it?"

I thought, *Hey, she may be all right after all. She obviously deals with the same issues I do.*

"Absolutely," Art answered. He picked up his purple prayer card. "Have you all got your prayer request cards filled out?"

"I just have to tell you..." Valerie said, more as a request than a demand. "A company that Dan had written off paid him for work he did three years ago. Our rent is paid! We prayed about it last week, remember?" We often prayed for Valerie's rent because Dan was a contractor who could pay his bills only when he was paid. Lately business hadn't been too good. Every time we prayed, Valerie got the rent somehow. I wondered what would happen if we didn't pray.

Jane said, "Let's hear it for God!" She said that all the time. But Pat took her literally, started applauding, and everybody else took it up. Joy filled the room. I looked around at all the smiling faces—on everyone except Heather.

We finished writing our prayer cards and traded with each other. Jane prayed for Melanie's addictions, Pat prayed for Donna's letter, and Valerie prayed for me to stop using food instead of God to protect myself. The rest prayed for each others' versions of lack of trust. Heather still didn't pray.

When the group ended and we were cleaning up, I said, "You know, Jane, I show a very stable front to most of the people who know me. Just this morning, I busily exhibited my expertise at canning to Amanda. I probably have shared more of my weaknesses with you than anyone. Generally, I act the strong one. But under all that, God knew I also cringed, because I didn't trust Him."

As she wiped the table, Jane said, "You probably already know that when you were abused you felt weak and manipulated. You responded by trying to control everything you could in your life and being as strong as possible. I think you are going to find less of a need for your strong, competent image. From here, you'll deal more honestly with yourself. I've been reading a book called *Love Hunger*. The thing it says that struck me hardest is that people from dysfunctional families often use food as a substitute for love. I think you are close to realizing that. As I've been practicing eating better, I remind myself that when I'm bored, lonely, tired, mad, happy, etc., the answer isn't food, it's talking to God. I think your U-turn to trusting God will be easier if you practice talking to Him when you feel like eating. It will give you prayer to fill the void left when you refuse to see food as love."

She put the leftover cups in the group box. "Did you notice the change in Valerie while you were talking about trusting God?" she asked.

I nodded.

"You have much to give. I think you might make a good leader. You ought to talk it over with God."

"I don't know," I said. "Trust is only one of the issues I have to deal with. There seem so many things to heal."

"Abuse leaves a deep wound," Jane responded.

I pushed back against the wall the oak hall tree that we used to screen off the people sitting in the room. "Dealing with Mom and Cal seems to keep breaking open the wound."

Jane handed me the box while she flicked off the lights. "You're learning to deal with them, though. You don't have to heal completely before you share what you have already learned with others. I mean, people can walk on a broken leg. At first there are crutches and then a cast, and all that is clumsy. But walking helps them heal. When they keep walking, sooner or later the cast comes off and they can run again."

"Yeah, I guess you're right," I said. I longed to run and feel the wind in my hair again. And I wondered if I could teach someone else to run again.

Self-Assessment Guide

1. How do you think Stepping Stones affected Donna's inability to close the book on her abuse when her dad refused to admit he victimized her?

2. Art encouraged Donna to write a letter to her dad and mentally give it to Jesus. If your abuser has not admitted what he did, you should follow this advice.

3. Read about Gideon in Judges 6:11–40. What characteristics in Gideon can you identify in yourself? Enjoy imagining God responding to you the same way He did to Gideon.

4. What are you holding back from God? Ask Him to show you and guide you to give it back to Him.

5. Addictions of several kinds, used to numb the pain of abuse, have appeared in the lives of the women in Stepping Stones.

Have you struggled with an addiction? What is it? Where will you go for help? Set a date within the next week to do this.

Helper's Focus

The cycle of recovery is complete when the survivor has disclosed the secret, dealt with the feeling of culpability and resultant guilt, placed responsibility on the perpetrator, found a healthy way to express her anger, confronted the trauma she's gone through in a way that allows her to reclaim her personal power, and finally considered herself a survivor who can integrate her abuse into her life so that it becomes a source of strength to her. Some of these issues may be inseparable, so that the survivor is dealing with more than one at a time. Sometime soon on the path we've taken toward recovery, the helper and survivor should be attempting to integrate abuse into the survivor's life so that it can become a source of strength to her.

Until the decade of the '70s, the stigma attached to child sexual abuse impeded the development of therapeutic methods for recovery from abuse. You can't study something you are hiding. Therefore, research being done now on recovery from abuse has not had time to measure the results of therapeutic methods. Due to the short time frame of the research, these methods must be considered experimental. Currently, the importance of clearing the air between the perpetrator and the survivor is being studied. Results of this research are inconclusive because of the lack of results over time. However, many survivors have had success at healthy integration of their abuse into their lives when they used one of a number of methods to get the "why me?" answers from their abusers. A helper may borrow from this research with extreme caution. We believe that any communication past unsent letters or role-playing with a non-offender should be accomplished with the guidance of a trained, professional therapist.

In the article "The Use of Victim-Offender Communication in the Treatment of Sexual Abuse," Yokley and McGuire use a set of guidelines to determine the advisability of attempting this type of therapy in an individual case. Parts of their list can assist support group leaders to borrow from their research.

1. The victim chooses whether to communicate with the abuser without pressure from anyone regarding the hope of complete recovery.

2. The victim's safety must be assured. The victim defines what is safe, whether that be indirect communication, talking with and listening to abusers who didn't abuse her, physical distance between the two people, a wall separating them, or communication only by letter or through a go-between.

3. Only offenders who have undergone professional treatment are allowed direct contact with the abused.

4. The offender is prepared beforehand to communicate with the victim in responsible, victim-sensitive language.

Given these guidelines, it is clear why the distance of unsent letters or role-play with uninvolved parties is essential when the helper lacks credentials.

The following are possible questions to help the victim begin this type of communication:

1. What would you think if _____ wrote you a letter to apologize?

2. If you could talk to _____, what would you say?

3. If you were talking face to face with _____, what would you want to understand about your abuse?

In role-playing, the non-offender should take a position consistent with an understanding of the high position in which God has placed man, and the mandate He has given us to right the wrongs we do. The survivor defining what she needs from this role-play will give the non-offending helper insights into how this conversation should go. Again, if there is any hesitation on the part of the helper or victim, the lay role-play or letter writing should be stopped, and if the victim wishes, a professional therapist should be enlisted to help.

Obviously, there are many issues involved with abuse where creative strategies could be employed to assist in healing. The concern of all involved must always be to avoid further traumatizing the victim. If there is the slightest possibility that the victim will be hurt rather than helped by a course of action, it should be avoided. Comparing therapy methods with scriptural directives can ferret out much that might be counterproductive to healing. If a professional therapist is needed, choosing a Christian counselor with a reputation for integrity is essential.

One area where intensive counseling may need to come into play is that of addiction. Substituting an addiction for lost or mutilated love is common among the abused. The addiction can range from alcohol or drugs, through illicit sex or pornography, to food or fitness. The key that identifies the behavior as an addiction is that the addictive agent is used to supply love, comfort, diversion or release of tension. A helper or a support group can often assist the abused person to kick a habit, simply by helping to identify the addiction and apply basic principles for breaking habits. In some cases, all it takes is supplying a constructive action for a destructive one, a phrase of truth to repeat when tempted, and personal support during the first several months. In others, where the desire for the addictive agent is genetic as well as emotional, professionally managed withdrawal is crucial.

Chapter Twelve

Into the Second Generation

Pete and I sat in church next to Art and Jane in the second row back, center aisle, right under the pulpit, where God had our direct attention. Pete had completed his internship and we were anticipating his first pastorate. Whenever I arrived early enough to have an opportunity to look around our concrete auditorium, I marveled at how many people wanted to know what God thinks. There were two churches in Modesto almost as large as First Baptist and many smaller ones. Think of the faithful people in the whole world!

Probably 2,000 people had come for the opening session of this conference on relationships. They covered the main floor and the balcony, from gray-headed folks who sat talking quietly with friends waiting for the service to start, to junior high students milling around in their section. The boys were occasionally punching each other, the girls smoothing their hair or adjusting their clothes.

Tom Payne, the orchestra conductor, lifted his baton and the orchestra began the service. Wade Estes, who would soon be senior pastor, and Bob Horner, the speaker for the week, strode up the ramp onto the platform. Wade came to the pulpit and said, "Welcome to Interchange 1991! We are glad you're here. You are in for a week that we expect to change your lives. When you came in tonight, you were given a flier about support groups that we will start after the conference. There should be something for everyone here, from *Stressed Out* to *Marriage Building* to *Stepping Stones*." I glanced at Pete and smiled. It was the first time we had publicly advertised Stepping Stones.

Wade continued, "Stepping Stones is a support group for adults who were abused emotionally, physically or sexually as children. The leaders are biblically-trained people who were abused as children. If you've been hiding the fact that you were abused as a child, or you feel your abuse has kept you from maturing, you will find in this support group the acceptance and scriptural principles you need to free yourself of the bonds of abuse. I highly recommend this group."

I didn't hear what Wade said next. Tears were running down my face. I hadn't realized he thought so highly of Stepping Stones. Through my tears I could see that Jane was crying too. Art wasn't, but I heard him sniffle.

That's how everything changed for Stepping Stones. One hundred twenty-three people expressed interest on a tear-off section of the flier Wade had pointed out. Some went to other support groups first, but fifty-eight of them came to Stepping Stones. They were members of First Baptist, members of other churches and members of no church. Fifty were women and eight were men.

The group had been in the middle of a session when this happened and we asked the current members to allow us to start the session over with this new set of people, who numbered almost four times as many as presently attended the group.

I was polishing furniture when Jane called me a few days before the new group came in.

"Art and I were talking last night and we think we should meet as a large group, but then break into small groups led by you and me, and one led by him for the men. I know you are hesitant about leading, but I think God has made your decision for you. We could give them the orientation this week and begin the small groups next week if you will lead," she suggested.

I could see that trying to minister to fifty-eight people all in one group would be impossible. But was I well enough prepared to lead? I shot up a quick prayer. *If You want me to do this, I need Your wisdom and guidance. If You don't, throw up a road-block, quick.* That peaceful feeling came that God used to let me know that He approved things I wanted to do. "Okay, I'll do it," I answered Jane, absently rubbing the oily rag over the burnished finish on the hall table.

"Praise the Lord, there is a God in heaven," she exulted. "You can do it, Ella. I have great faith in you," she ranted on.

"Give me a break. You're just in a bind," I replied.

"You know I talked to you about leading before any of this happened," she corrected me good naturedly. "Don't give me any of your garbage."

"No telling what will happen now," I said. "I may lead them down the garden path."

Jane laughed, which nearly broke my eardrum. "Nope. Because you are going to pray a lot," she said. "Just think, you have a whole week and a half to get petrified about it." She became serious. "You know, Ella, God has been wiping out some things I've been petrified about lately."

"Like what?" I asked.

"A couple of things. I have been nearly as leery of men as you are. Lately, besides all the pastors, God has sent a man to work as a graphic artist with me. I had asked to have a female graphic artist because we work alone nearly all day. God had a lesson for me, so I didn't get a woman. This man has behaved as a complete gentleman—no sexual innuendos, coarse language or dirty jokes. I was used to a having a macho sexist around in most of the secular jobs I've had, and I kind of yelled at God when He sent this man. But I prayed the other day, and asked if He is trying to point out to me that Art and these men I work with are all trustworthy. I could almost hear Him chuckling. I wrongly indicted the whole male gender. They are not all untrustworthy, as I once believed."

"Add Pete to that," I said. "He's incredible."

"I'll bet he doesn't sing *Amazing Grace* in his head when he sees a pretty woman," Jane responded.

"Who does that?" I asked.

"Art does," she answered, as I got another earful of laughter.

"And it isn't just trusting men that God is working on with me," she continued. "When we first got a new boss, I wouldn't mention problems that I should have, like our work needing flexible hours. I guess I expected every authority to rage and scream like Mom did when crossed. So I avoided situations where conflict might occur. But I can't do that; it only leads to more complicated situations. I have to lead the department, and if I don't explain what needs to happen, we can't do our work right. So God forced me to talk. Every time I've talked, I've been understood—no screaming, no inflamed eyes. We work it out and do what is needed. Why did I wait so long to learn to stand up for myself?"

"It's a long haul out," I observed.

"Amen to that," she said. "You know, I am also experimenting with telling people what I really think about something, even when it is possible that they'll get mad. You're going to have to do that too, when you lead a group. There seems to be someone who wants to talk constantly in each session of Stepping Stones. You'll be responsible to keep her under control."

"Oh, good," I said sarcastically. I guessed I wasn't any more excited about confrontation than Jane was. I sat on the floor to polish the legs of the table, balancing the receiver against my shoulder.

"Well, nice talking to you," Jane said.

"Yeah, right," I answered, hoping my sarcasm dripped out her end of the phone. "How did you get like this?"

"Don't know," she answered. "Just lucky I guess."

The two and a half weeks before I led a small group passed in a flash. We moved Stepping Stones to a larger room that could be divided, with lots of round tables and no windows in the doors. Art had struggled through this first meeting of the large group because Tina, a woman with long, gray hair, interrupted him every two minutes with a comment like, "Well, that may apply to everyone else, but it doesn't apply to me."

Jane and I had divided the group between us and I already knew that Tina belonged in my small group. I also had Heather, who consistently had done the homework last trimester but still would not pray with the group. She only spoke when required to answer a question. Then she would spill out bitter, angry answers that showed the homework and class sessions were definitely not getting through to her. I was despairing about this trimester when we broke to move to the small groups. Jane passed me and said, "I'm praying for you. Let us know if you can't handle her."

When my group was settled around the tables we had pushed together, I tried to see how many homework sheets were written on but the tables were spread too far. The women close to me had all done their homework. We spent a few minutes on an icebreaker and then I explained the group rules. If a member hadn't done her homework, she had to wait until we got through the questions to talk. I reminded the women that we didn't give advice and added that one who had already

talked should not speak again until all others who appeared to
want to talk had the chance.

Tina raised her hand. "I think you would create much more
spontaneity without all these rules about talking," she said.

I smiled at her. "For people like you who have no difficulty
talking, you are right," I answered. There was a small twitter.
Apparently Tina had made others feel uncomfortable. I continued, "But there are women here who are shy. They want to
recover, but it takes them a little longer to get their feelings out.
We need to be sensitive to everyone."

We started around the room answering questions. It went a
little stiffly at first, until one woman, an athletic-looking, dark-
haired woman named Nell, said, "I don't know if I belong here.
I've about given up on God. My husband abuses me as much as
my relatives did when I was a child. Is there any hope? Does
God really exist?"

Tina jumped right in. "Of course there's a God. How do you
think *you* got here? I read the Bible. You should do that. What
does your husband do to you?"

I prayed quickly, *Father, give me gentleness.* "Tina," I said.

"I was just telling her what works for me," Tina shot at me.

"That's called advice," I said. "We don't do that."

"Oh, I see," she said cryptically.

"Nell, I'd like to talk with you after the group is over if you
have time," I said.

Her embarrassment showed on her face. "Okay," she replied.

We finished the group and Tina fairly stalked out of the
room. I wondered whether she would return the next week. A
couple of women hung around to get a question answered.
When I finished with them I went over to Nell, who waited
where she had sat during the meeting. She twisted a flowered
handkerchief around her fingers.

I sat next to her and began, "Tell me about you."

She looked at me defiantly. "Seven different men abused me when I was growing up, all family, or friends of the family. Then I met Hal and thought I was rescued. Nope. He berates me in front of his friends. He uses pornography. What kind of example are his magazines for our children?"

"A bad one," I answered.

"If there is really a God, and He has the power to keep little children from being abused, why doesn't he?"

Funny you should ask, I thought. "I've begun to find the answer to that," I said, and we talked until about 10:30. I noticed that a man named Lenny who attended Art's group had waited for Nell and walked out with her.

Walking to the car, I told Pete about Tina. "What would you do if you were me?" I asked as he unlocked the car door.

"Give her the opportunity to change her behavior next week. If she doesn't, you need to have a serious talk with her right away. A person like that can kill a group."

Getting into the passenger seat, I said, "Oh good. Just what I wanted to hear."

A couple of days later I walked across the pasture exulting in having mentally stayed in the room with Pete the night before, not fantasizing at all during sex, and feeling no guilt. My progress made him happy and me ecstatic. A gentle breeze had blown the pollution from the sky and wisping clouds floated lazily. The pansies and shrubs close to the gate looked perky and the smell of gardenias floated in the air. I enjoyed the rough feel of the old wood as I unfastened and refastened the gate letting myself out of the pasture. Suddenly wild abandon that I recognized from long ago flooded me. *What is this?* I asked myself. I felt like dashing around. *Lord, You answered my prayer!* I exclaimed soundlessly. *I'm running!* I ran into the driveway, faster and faster until my hair flew out behind me. I threw my arms in the air like Snoopy does in the Peanuts comic strip. When I stopped I said to God, *I am regaining myself, aren't I?* and there was that peace again.

As I walked toward the house, bending now and then to pick up trash that had blown into the yard, Pete's comment last night came back to me. He mentioned a church in Canada that had called Pastor asking for a recommendation of someone who could preach and start a Bible study ministry. Pastor had recommended Pete, and I felt torn. Of course I would go with Pete, and support him in every way, but there were so many reasons to stay in Modesto. I did another of my on-the-spot supplications. *Father, I'm giving this to you. The group is off to a great start. I feel like family here. I am secure. I know You love me, and I will do what You want and go where You lead. Please show us.*

The phone began to ring. Jumping the steps two at a time, I answered it on the third ring. "Hello."

"Ella, this is Melanie. I know I'm not in your group, but Jane's not home and I need to talk. Do you have time?"

I thought her voice sounded agitated. "Sure," I answered, dumping the trash I'd collected in the garbage can. "What's up?"

"I'm not doing very well." She paused.

"What's the matter?"

"My life is nothing, nowhere. It's the pits. I don't know why I'm even living."

I sat down at the kitchen table. "Um," I said brilliantly.

"I fight a half-hearted battle with drugs and alcohol constantly. Is life going to be like this forever? If it is, I can live without it. Or *not* live without it."

"What are you saying, Melanie?" I probed, while I drummed my first two fingers on the table.

"I'm saying that I don't know if I want to live anymore. Nothing gets any better. I mean, coming to Stepping Stones has helped me, but everything here stays the same. My old man is in jail again and the welfare people are telling me if I don't stop leaving the kids alone, they're going to take them away."

"Why are you leaving them alone?" I asked, trying to sound gentle.

"I have to get groceries and, oh who cares." She stopped.

"Melanie, are you considering suicide?" I questioned her straight out because she sounded desperate. It didn't appear to be a time for pussyfooting around.

"Well I, ...why?" she hedged. I heard a child cry in the background.

"We care about you, girl," I asserted strongly. "If you're in trouble, I want to help." Where was this boldness coming from? I sure didn't feel very tough.

After a long pause, she whimpered, "Ella, you don't understand. It's hell where I live."

"I want to understand," I said. "Tell me."

"I never started out to live in a hole like this with pushers and scuz bums all around. I dreamed the same dreams everyone else does, of white picket fences and roses under the window. I don't want to be me anymore." She wept.

"Melanie, I think you need to talk with a pastor," I said.

"I tried to talk to a pastor in another church once," she said. "He told me I was sinning and should expect to feel like this until I stopped. It made me feel like getting in my car and driving as fast as I could go down the freeway into the biggest tree I could find. I don't need people like him. I needed him to tell me *how* to stop. What do I do?"

I heard the plan she'd made about the tree. Jane had told me that suicidal people who have developed a plan are serious. It crossed my mind that I didn't hear any help from the Holy Spirit coming through her conversation. "Melanie, do you have a relationship with Jesus?" I asked.

"Sure. I'm a Christian, I believe there's a God."

"Being a Christian doesn't mean believing there's a God. It means committing your life to Jesus, letting Him run the show. It's like the difference between watching a guy walk a tightrope across Niagara Falls, and getting in a wheelbarrow and letting him push *you* across the tightrope. Watching is uninvolved; riding is total commitment, life and death." Out the window I saw Petey swinging on a rope in the barn.

"How do you get that?" Melanie asked.

"Simple beyond belief. You pray."

"That's all—pray?" she repeated incredulously.

"God made it easy so that conceited people who are sure they can handle themselves without Him won't lower themselves to do a silly thing like pray. God wants people of faith, people who recognize that He's the Creator and submit themselves to Him." Where was all this coming from? Did *I* form these words coming from my mouth? I sounded so sure, so bold, and on the *phone*. "Would you like me to pray with you?" I asked.

"Yes, I would."

She said yes, I thought ecstatically. *Lord, You are letting me help someone find You!* My mental Snoopy ears were flapping in the breeze again.

"You pray, and I'll pray after you," I urged. "Tell God what you've been telling me. Prayer is talking, but to God. Tell Him you don't want to do drugs and alcohol and that you know He can save you. Ask Him to be your Savior."

Melanie didn't say anything.

"Melanie?" I said.

In a tiny whisper, she said, "I'm not worthy."

"We aren't worthy beforehand, Melanie. Jesus said that people who aren't sick don't need a doctor. God's the doctor. God cleans us up, we don't."

"Okay then." She paused and then softly, reverently, said, "God, You know me. I do drugs and I drink, and I can't stop. I don't know why You would want me, but Ella says You do. I don't want to be who I have been anymore. I want You to save me. Please." She was done, and yet just begun.

I felt honored to share her prayer. "Father, thank You for Melanie. Help us who love her to help her follow You out of the pit she's been in. In Jesus' name, amen."

I paused, feeling the beautiful wonder. *Now what?* I thought. "Melanie, where is Jesus now?"

"He's inside me," she said without hesitating.

"Welcome to the family. Now, our pastors are different from the other one you talked to. I think you need to go see Rick Thompson. He's the pastor who looks after people your age. I'm going to call you everyday for a while. Will you call the church and make an appointment with Rick?"

"Yes."

"Next Sunday you need to say publicly that you are a Christian. Jesus said if we confess Him before men, He will confess us before the Father, God. You know how the pastor invites people to go forward at the end of the service. Do you want me to walk with you?"

"I think I can do it myself."

"Great. I'll be there, absolutely dancing and singing, and praying. Do you feel better?"

"Lots."

The next day when I called, Melanie had made an appointment with Rick Thompson that afternoon. When she went forward on Sunday, gone were her halter tops. Instead she wore a conservative blouse and her only skirt, a mini. When she came to Wade, she shook hands with both her hands. I was delighted to see her make these steps, and to know that God welcomes us as we are and understands us, lovingly allowing our growth to be a process.

We had a monthly meeting with Jim Talley to look over how the group was developing and work out trouble spots. Art came straight from work and looked like a lumberjack sitting there with his thumbs under his suspenders. Jane walked over from her office. The two of them were quite a contrast, her in a dress and heels smelling of White Shoulders and him in blue jeans and his Greek fisherman's cap, smelling of wood chips. Jim had his laptop computer on the desk between us taking notes on what we were telling him. He was known as the church computer whiz. I had grown to love these people in a more mature way than I loved my mother and stepfather, and I dreaded telling them that Pete had accepted the call to the church in Canada. We would leave in a few weeks, when school ended for the summer. Pete and I had traveled to Canada twice, and Art, Jane and Jim knew we were considering going. But Pete had only determined for sure what God wanted him to do the night before.

Jim pointed at me. "I don't know whether you did it on purpose, Ella. But you did exactly right to connect Melanie with a pastor immediately. We have a form for you to fill out when someone talks of suicide, and the next step is to give the pastor the form to alert him that the person is in trouble. Get a supply from Jo Ann when you leave," he said to Art.

"Let's hear it for you," Jane said, patting me on the back.

"Can I trust her to be all right now?" I asked, leaning forward. I was sitting in a chair that squeaked every time I moved. I grimaced when it squeaked now.

"Little trouble with your chair there, ma'am," Art teased, looking toward the bottom of it to see if he might know how to make it stop squeaking.

"Just needs a little oil," Jim said and then continued, "Trust isn't earned, it's given. Give Melanie little opportunities to be trusted. If she manages those, give her bigger ones."

"Okay," I agreed, then continued. "You know the other woman, named Heather, who I talked to you about before?" I asked.

"Yes," Jim answered, clicking away at the computer.

"I talked to her the other day on the phone. She's still spewing bitterness and anger over the group. When I talked to her this time, she said, 'Why did God give me a body, anyway?' I had wondered about that myself, and one day I found the answer. It's in 2 Corinthians 4:7. It says we are flesh and blood because that shows we're a creation of God's power, and not something of our own making. When I told her that, she said, 'Forget it, I don't need or want a body, for any reason.'"

I leaned my elbow on Jim's desk. Jane laughed when the chair squeaked again. Ignoring my problem, I said, "I can sort of understand it. Abused people feel that our bodies only brought us pain. But after all the other discussions I've had with her about God loving us and wanting good for us, and her refusal to even consider the possibility that those things could be true, I am frustrated. She refuses to move out of the mire she's in. I don't know what to do."

"Call her this week and tell her that it is time for her to move on to another Bible study for a while," Jim said without preface. "You have given her plenty of input and time to grow. Her attitude will begin to influence others and she needs to be faced with it."

"Okay," I said uncertainly.

Jim looked at me sternly. "No, Ella. You are the leader of over twenty people. You are responsible for the truth getting through to all of them. If one person clouds that happening, you sideline her. Not forever, just for the time being. You will do her a favor by making her consider her effect on herself and on the others."

"I will," I asserted more firmly.

Art and I were both dealing with Tina's will to dominate the group. He probably thought of it when Jim talked about our responsibility for getting the truth through to all the people in the group. Now he said, "Jim, there's another woman in the group who talks so much that we can't get the whole lesson taught. I think Ella has trouble giving the shy people in her group an opportunity to talk because of this woman taking up so much time. We've tried to confront her gently."

"Now tell her she's in danger of leaving the group," Jim answered matter-of-factly, without further comment.

When there was a long pause I thought, *Uh oh, are we coming to the end? Do I have to tell them now?*

But Jane said, "We did a really smart thing that helped that situation a little. We used to have the large group time first and then break into small groups. Now we do the small groups first and have questions that weren't answered written down for Art and me to answer at the end. That gives all the talkers the opportunity to ask the 10,000 questions they thought of while doing their homework."

"Good," Jim said. "Anything else?"

I swallowed and said, "Yes. Pete has accepted the call of the church in Canada."

For a moment everyone stared at me without saying anything.

"There it is," Jane said, a catch in her voice.

"Now come on, Jane," Art coaxed. "We knew they would be going someday. God has plans for them, and we should be happy, not sad." Looking at me, he added, "You're going to make Ella cry."

"I don't need any help," I said, wiping my cheek with my sleeve.

"What about the book?" Jane asked.

"What book?" Jim asked.

"It's done. When you're ready to send it out again, do it," I answered.

"What book?" Jim asked again.

Jane turned to him and said, "Ella and I wrote a book about her abuse, but although several publishers have said they liked it, they won't publish it. It's a good book, though."

Jim had published several books, on subjects like how dating relationships develop, marriage reclamation and dealing with singleness. "If you want me to co-author it to get you published, I probably could help you," he offered. He had just finished co-authoring a book with a man who worked in the singles ministry with him. "I told a publisher once that I'm sure there are at least ten books in this church," Jim added.

I looked at Jane and she shrugged.

"Talk to Terry Benner about how it is to work with me," Jim suggested. "It's just a thought."

The day after our meeting with Jim, Nell called. "I've left my husband," she reported. "I couldn't stand being degraded anymore. You know Lenny?" she asked.

Lenny was the guy from Art's group who had walked with her from the meeting after I talked with her.

"Yeah," I said.

"He said there was no reason for me to take that kind of treatment anymore."

Lenny had been hitting on women in the church for several months. Jim threw this kind of man out of the singles group because he was a wolf in sheep's clothing looking to pick off a tender lamb. The timing of his consolation of Nell appeared too convenient.

"Nell, you are too strung out to start rearranging your life like this. What's Lenny got to do with your marriage?"

"He's just a friend."

"Where did you meet him?"

"At Stepping Stones."

"I think you should stay away from him."

"He treats me so sweetly, like I've always wanted to be treated."

"Nell, you have a husband and children. You have a commitment to them that you shouldn't walk away from."

"You mean God wants me to live with the pain my husband causes instead of to be happy?"

"What guarantees that Lenny will make you happy?"

"Oh, Ella, you don't know him. He's gentle and kind."

The next Wednesday they were both absent from the group. Art alerted Jim about the phone call as soon as I had told him. But it was too late, they were already embroiled in an affair and left the church. My heart hurt. It seemed that as a leader I dealt either with great happiness or great pain. The women who grew steadily didn't come to my attention often, just the ones who were about to grow mightily or fail mightily.

When I called Heather and Tina, neither of them changed their attitudes. Heather said she had been thinking about dropping the group anyway. Our conversation was short and we didn't hear from Heather again. Tina listened and said in a staccato cadence, "You will not hear another word out of me." I had been very straightforward with Tina because she behaved that way with others, and I thought she would appreciate a straightforward message. When I hung up I had the feeling that she wasn't as tough as her exterior had led me to believe. She continued in the group, but in total silence. Later she told Jim that I had been unkind, and she criticized the group strongly. But she sent her cousin the next trimester, and we have used some of Tina's criticisms to improve the group.

Pete and I made the trip the next weekend to say goodbye to my family before we went to Canada. Jessi had long since left home, was married and had a little girl, Lisa. Her family would be there. Kery worked as a secretary in Maplewood Springs and had recently moved into an apartment with a woman who worked in her office. She told me that she wanted me to meet somebody when we got home.

Driving up that beautiful road Pete and I had traveled so many years before when life was twisted beyond recognition, I let the scenes of my recovery drift through my mind. I was not the girl I had been. In fact I had come so far that I thought of myself as another person as I played back my memories.

Kery walked up and threw out her arms as I shut the car door. We hugged hard. Jessi stood with her husband. Lisa rested in her arms, and grinning, Jessi gave me a kiss over Lisa's head. Mom waited for a kiss and then hugged me long enough that I felt embarrassed. It was a greeting that was a farewell. There was another man. He stood over six feet tall, with dark hair and kind brown eyes.

"Who's this guy?" I asked rudely.

Kery went to stand next to him. The top of her head met his shoulder. "This is Bill," she said proudly. "He and I are engaged." She stuck out her left hand on which sparkled a ring with my grandmother's gigantic diamond in it.

"Say what?" I exploded. "I just want to know if anyone has locked this guy in the chicken house yet!" I said, looking around me as if for a key to the chicken house.

Pete walked up to Bill and clapped him on the back. "You got a keeper," he said. "You be good to her, or we're coming back."

I said behind my hand to Kery, "Wow, what a rock!"

Bill smiled down at Kery and said, "If only she could cook."

Everybody laughed, except Kery, who was fussing at him under her breath.

We all went into the house. Cal was working at the sink. I walked over and kissed him on the cheek. "Hi, Cal," I said.

"Hi. So, you're going to Canada, huh?"

"Yep. The call of the wild, or something like that."

"It's pretty country up there."

"Pete's sure he'll freeze solid in the wintertime."

"Could be."

"You going to come visit us?"

"Take me fishing?"

"Without a doubt."

"We can probably find our way."

The weekend ended before I knew it. I had enjoyed the smell of the pines, riding up Digger's Ridge on strange horses and swimming in the lake at sunset with Jessi and Kery. Mom had wanted to know all about the church, its people and what Pete would do. Pete and Cal and the men had worked in Cal's shop on a cabinet Cal was building for Kery. The closer we had come to Sunday night, the more distant Kery seemed. When I started loading the car she followed me. The old squirrel must have had grandchildren, because a mighty disgruntled squirrel still lived up in the pine tree.

"This reminds me of the bad old days," she lamented. "I feel like that little girl you left when you went to seminary."

I finished putting the suitcase in the trunk and turned to her. "Sometimes God's will isn't easy to follow," I said, trying hard to hold my emotions in check. "I'm barely hanging on. But I think it's because we can't see the future." Looking back at the house where Bill talked with Pete, I added, "I think your future is in good shape."

"You like him, then?"

"He seems devoted to you, and that's what matters to me." I patted her on the arm. "Is he a Christian?"

She looked me in the eye and said, "No. But he's interested."

I winked at her. "That's good," I said. "You tell him the whole story. Don't fly in God's face by marrying him before he becomes a Christian."

She made a line in the dirt with her tennis shoe. "I'll work on it," she said.

Pete came out with the rest of our stuff and Petey in tow. I began to kiss and hug everyone quickly. I hated long goodbyes. "I guess we're going north with the geese," I said, moving quickly for the car. Mom grabbed me and cried, "Oh, we're going to miss you so much." I had to wiggle out of her grasp.

Pete started the engine and Jessi said, "Be sure to honk." It was a family tradition to honk goodbye. As I looked back in the mirror watching them on our way down the hill, I saw Kery turn and bury her head in Bill's chest, and I heard a curly-headed little girl's cry from long ago. "Honk," I said to Pete.

Back in Modesto we went to a farewell party in every group we had anything to do with. If it hadn't ended when it did, we would have had to ride in separate cars to get over the load limit bridges on our way to Canada.

Then the day came when Jane and Art helped us pick up the last umbrella left in a closet, an unmatched slipper and Petey's discarded teddy bear. We stuffed them in the last space in the truck and slammed the door shut.

"Write to me," Jane said, tears in her eyes.

"Only if you write back so I'll have these priceless letters from a famous author that I can sell for millions someday," I teased.

"Well, if you'll settle for letters from me, I'll still write," she countered.

"Shepherd the sheep," Pete said to Art and climbed behind the steering wheel.

I looked eye-level at my son and said, "Come on, Petey." He clambered into the cab and I followed him.

We headed north. This time I couldn't look back. Petey soon lay his head in my lap and fell asleep. My feelings found prayer.

Father, I said silently, *thank You for making me a survivor whose journey to recovery led through Modesto. Thank You for letting me help You heal others. I don't know what is at the end of this road. But I know You have used me before and will use me again, in happiness and pain. I don't know if there is more in me to heal, but I know that whatever is needed You will supply. Thank You for providing my earthly father and for being my heavenly Father. I see Your love for me in Your going ahead of me to meet my needs and in*

Your allowing situations in my life that make me grow more like You. Help me to know You completely as a Father, the way You intend daughters to know fathers, more intimately than I understand my earthly father.

The Bible says those who love You can be identified because we keep Your commandments. Please keep guiding me and protecting me so I can keep Your commandments. Help me not to lie, even a little deceit now and then, and help me not to commit the adultery that doesn't put my husband first. I want to be the best wife and mom there has ever been, the caliber of the woman in Proverbs 31. Give me what it takes to put my entire heart, soul and mind into loving You day-to-day and help me to look forward and not back. You are my Father. You love me, and I love You. Thank You for Jesus, amen.
I looked out at the familiar valley scenes slipping away, and I traveled in peace.

> The Lord turned to him and said, "Go in the strength
> you have and save Israel out of Midian's hand. Am I not
> sending you?" (Judges 6:14)

Beatitudes for the Abused

Blessed are the abused who know their weaknesses by
experience, for they may live in God's house.

Blessed are the abused who pray that all abuse will one day
be no more, for God will take its pain from them.

Blessed are the abused who keep their hands in God's,
healing hurts and stopping the cycle, for their influence
will change the world.

Blessed are the abused who pray that God will transpose
victimization to humility, for their prayers will become reality.

Blessed are the abused who forsake bitterness and revenge
to follow God, for He will show Himself to them and
through them.

Blessed are the recovering abused who help those still in
darkness, for their own healing will be multiplied.

Blessed are the abused who seek peace,
for they will draw others to God.

Blessed are the abused who tell their secrets and stand alone,
for God has a reward for them in heaven.

Blessed are rescuers who are attacked for their work,
for they walk in the power and protection of God.

Self-Assessment Guide

1. Where are you in your recovery process? Write a description of who you are, where you stand with God and what you have dealt with in your recovery so far.

2. Continuing to recover is a matter of taking the next step. If you need to take a step toward God, what is it? How and when will you take it? Look back through your answers to the Self-Assessment questions. What is your next step toward recovery and when will you take it?

3. Can you identify situations God has orchestrated to continue your recovery the way He did for Jane, so that she would stop pigeon-holing all men as untrustworthy and all authority as unreasonable?

4. Write a summary of what you've learned from the book you've read along with *My Father's Love*.

5. What would be necessary for you to consider attending a support group? Have you investigated to see whether there

are any Christian groups in your area? What things could you do to be a contributing member of a support group?

6. If you were going to help begin a support group in your church, what would you do? What principles for leading people in support groups did you notice in this chapter?

7. The apostle Paul taught everything he knew about Christianity and ministry to a young man named Timothy, who followed in Paul's footsteps. If you are a Christian and believe you've become a survivor, who is your Timothy? What does she need to know now? How will you teach her?

Helper's Focus

> If your brother sins against you, go and show him his fault, just between the two of you. If he listens to you, you have won your brother over. (Matthew 18:15)

All kinds of children are abused: fat and thin, rich and poor, girls and boys, outgoing and shy, pretty and ugly, Christians and non-Christians. Therefore all kinds of adults come to abuse recovery support groups. People do not have to be alike to help each other recover. But they have to respect each other and cooperate to make the best use of their time together.

The support group leader has the responsibility to impart the biblical principles that will help the abused to recover and, as much as possible, to provide an environment where each individual can incorporate these principles into their lives and heal. In addition to the methods discussed in the chapters, Stepping Stones leaders use role-play, sheets on which group members fill in missing words, outlines completed in class, surveys and charts on which members track progress. Interaction in the small group and on the telephone is also part of the healing process.

Leaders also help the domineering people in the group to control themselves so that the weak ones will not be intimidated into following their long-accustomed habit of hiding. Many leaders have a difficult time identifying a wolf in sheep's clothing who is looking for a lamb to devour, or admitting that a member of the group is not there to recover but has some hidden agenda. That is why we believe it important that a pastor take direct responsibility for a support group for adults abused as children. As the leaders relate to him, he can help them deal with relationship problems among group members.

People who can't tell how often or how long to talk and those who give unrequested advice or refuse to allow God's Word to change them are a problem for adults trying to recover from abuse. Yet their effects are slight in comparison to the spirit brought into a group by those who become ensnared in adultery or homosexuality. Leaders should not be surprised when formerly abused people choose to find love in immoral relationships. If we go into this ministry with our eyes open to the forces that pull the abused into destructive relationships, we will act responsibly when faced with actual immorality. Point out what God has said and the illogic of these relationships and make every effort to help the person turn from sin. If you succeed, you are indeed a conqueror. If not, the person must leave the group. Recently Stepping Stones has required members to attend a worship service in addition to the weekly meeting to help round out their spiritual lives and assist them in resisting temptation.

We should not confuse a refusal to confront a hostile terrorist for gentleness extended to a misguided lamb. We have learned that a person who comes asking for help, but then demands control, is usually not seeking help, at least not yet. It may take distancing that misguided lamb from the acceptance and growth of the group to make them realize that their determination to have control is incorrect. On the other hand, the hostile terrorist will not admit his fault, even when separated from the group, and thus should not be allowed to return.

The characters of many adults abused as children still include control problems, authority problems and childishness. This should not be held against them, but it must not be tolerated either. We love them when we make them aware of these weaknesses and provide methods for removing them from their personalities. We love the group when we refuse to let these weaknesses keep others from growing.

> God has said, "Never will I leave you; never will I ever forsake you." So we say with confidence, "The Lord is my helper; I will not be afraid. What can man do to me?" (Hebrews 13:5–6)

Bibliography

Buhler, Rich. *Pain and Pretending* (Nelson, 1988).
Discusses seasons of destruction and recovery—stages each abuse victim goes through.

Butler, Sandra. *Conspiracy of Silence: The Trauma of Incest* (New Glide Publications, 1978).
Study of incest includes quotes from victims, aggressors and family members.

Blair, Rita and Justice. *The Broken Taboo* (Human Sciences Press, 1979).
Presents aspects of incest therapy in which the authors were involved.

Crabb, Dr. Larry. *Inside Out* (Navpress, 1988).
Helps reader realize God's approval of human desires and His intent that we meet our desires through love-giving relationships with others. Encourages reader to move away from self-protection and demanding attitudes. A deep book but worth the effort; includes a workbook.

Edwards, Katherine. *A House Divided* (Zondervan, 1984).
An abuse victim shares the stories of victims, relating the dynamics and applying biblical principles.

Forward, Susan and Buck, Craig. *Betrayal of Innocence: Incest and its Devastation* (Penguin Books, 1978).
Forward is M.S.W. who trains mental-health professionals in treatment of incest. Includes many case histories; secular author.

Frank, Jan. *A Door of Hope* (Here's Life Publishers, 1987).
Does a good job of giving a practical path to recovery for the reader who has been sexually abused.

Hancock, Maxine and Maines, Karen. *Child Sexual Abuse* (Shaw, 1987).
Describes the problem of child sexual abuse and how to help an abused person. Contains case histories and ideas for what to do.

Heifrither, Lynn and Vought, Jeanette. *Helping the Victim of Sexual Abuse* (Bethany House, 1989).
A handbook for those wishing to help a child or adult recover from abuse; includes homework and a model for an abuse recovery support group.

Huskey, Alice. *Stolen Childhood* (InterVarsity Press, 1990).
Very good treatment of factors that contribute to abuse; promotes healing for abused and abuser.

Kroth, Jerome A. *Child Sexual Abuse: Analysis of a Family Therapy Approach* (Charles C. Thomas, 1979).
A computerized analysis of participants in the Child Sexual Abuse Treatment Program in Santa Clara, California. Presents the common characteristics of incestuous families.

Landorf, Joyce. *Irregular People* (Walker & Co., 1986).
Explains how to manage ongoing relationships with dysfunctional people.

Mains, Karen. *Abuse in the Family* (David C. Cook, 1987).
A book for helping professionals or non-professionals that discusses profiles of abuse, case studies, questions the abused may ask, how to counsel and more. Very good; we give this book to Stepping Stones encouragement guides.

Martin, Grant, Ph.D. *Counseling for Family Violence and Abuse* (Word, 1987).
Covers spousal, child and elder abuse for the therapist.

Morrison, Jan. *A Safe Place* (Shaw, 1990).
Well-written help for sexually abused teens. Written by a sexually abused woman whose work is helping teens through disclosure and recovery.

Page, Carole Gift. *Hallie's Secret* (Moody, 1987).
Teen fiction on incest.

Peters, David. *A Betrayal of Innocence: What Everyone Should Know About Child Sexual Abuse* (Word, 1986).
Written by a child protective services worker, this book follows the premise that the only way to stop the epidemic of child sexual abuse is to become educated and get involved.

Ricks, Chip. *Carol's Story* (Tyndale House, 1981).
True story of incest, detailing dynamics of family relationships, arrest of the father and healing of the victim.

Russell, Diana E.H., Ph.D. *The Prevalence and Seriousness of Incestuous Abuse: Stepfathers vs. Biological Fathers*, Child Abuse and Neglect, Vol. 8, pp. 15–22, 1984.

Sanford, Linda. *The Silent Children* (McGraw Hill, 1980).
Written by a secular author, this parent's guide to prevention of child abuse contains some good points.

Seamands, David. *Healing for Damaged Emotions* (Victor Books, 1989).
Insightful analysis of self-esteem, perfectionism and depression, and how to apply God's healing to the stresses of modern life.

Sontag, Marie. *When Love Is Not Perfect* (Aglow, 1990).
Explores the "architecture" of abuse and its aftermath with Bible study on the subject of each chapter.

Van Stone, Doris and Lutzer, Erwin. *Dorie, the Girl Nobody Loved* (Moody, 1979).
True story of an abused girl who becomes a missionary.

Vredevelt, Pamela and Rodriguez, Kathryn. *Surviving the Secret* (Revell, 1987).
Therapists explain how abuse happens and how to support victims.

Yokley, James M., editor. *The Use of Victim-Offender Communication in the Treatment of Sexual Abuse: Three Intervention Models* (The Safer Society Press, 1990).

General Issues of Interest to Adults Abused as Children

Carder, Dave; Henslin, Earl; Cloud, Henny; Townsend, John; and Brawan, Alice. *Secrets of Your Family Tree: Healing for Adult Children of Dysfunctional Families* (Moody, 1991).
Helps reader understand influences, interrelationships and events that lead to dysfunction, as well as principles to apply to recover from hurts and build a healthy family.

Crabb, Lawrence, J. *The Marriage Builder* (Zondervan, 1982).
Practical help for developing a balanced marriage relationship of oneness.

Dobson, Dr. James. *Dare to Discipline* (Tyndale House and Regal Books, 1972).
Guidelines to help you avoid abusing your children by taking positive steps to nurture them.

Gundry, Patricia. *Woman Be Free* (Zondervan, 1977).
Biblical analysis of most verses concerning the role of woman in society.

Hendricks, Howard. *Heaven Help the Home* (Victor Books, 1983).
How to develop a family based on God's principles.

Minirth, Frank; Meier, Paul; Hemfelt, Robert; and Sneed, Sharon. *Love Hunger* (Nelson, 1990).
Best book we've found for breaking addictions resulting from childhood dysfunction; concentrates on food addiction.

Packer, J.I. *Knowing God* (InterVarsity Press, 1973).
The perfect foundational devotional for developing a balanced view of God.

Parker, Gary, M.S., Ed.D. *Life Before Birth: A Christian Family Book* (Master Books, 1987).
Help for anyone who finds it difficult to discuss sex with their children.

Smalley, Gary and Trent, John. *The Blessing* (Nelson, 1986).
How to bless the lives of your children and your mate. Excellent for those raised in dysfunctional homes who need a new game plan.

Townsend, Dr. John. *Hiding from Love* (Navpress, 1991).
How withdrawal patterns occur and what to do to change them, since they prevent us from being cared for.

Wheat, Ed M.D. and Gaye, *Intended for Pleasure* (Revell, 1977).
Excellent work for helping husband and wife achieve a fulfilling and biblically-based sexual relationship.

If you would like more information,
Dr. Talley or Art and Jane Baker
welcome your letters and calls:

Dr. Jim A. Talley
4216 N. Portland Avenue, Suite 203
Oklahoma City, OK 73112-6363
(405) 949-2227
Fax (405) 943-3630

Rev. Art and Jane Baker
2025 Dickens Drive
Modesto, CA 95350
(209) 579-5312

Book Outline Form

Name: _____ Date: _____ Pages: _____

Book Title: _____

Author: _____ Publisher: _____

Chapter: _____ Title: _____

A. Introduction or Next Main Heading: _____

    Point 1: _____

    _____

    Point 2: _____

    _____

    Point 3: _____

    _____

B. Next Point or Main Heading: _____

    Point 1: _____

    _____

    Point 2: _____

    _____

    Point 3: _____

    _____

C. Next Point or Main Heading: _____

    Point 1: _____

    _____

    Point 2: _____

    _____

    Point 3: _____

    _____

Real Help for Real Hurts

Released From Bondage by Dr. Neil T. Anderson. An inspiring collection of testimonies from the overcomers themselves—those who have discovered God's restoration in even the most traumatic of circumstances. Includes helpful insights and commentary from Dr. Anderson.

A Door of Hope by Jan Frank. An incest victim, now an experienced counselor, provides hope for victims of childhood trauma, and shares ten steps for healing. An effective group therapy tool.

When Victims Marry by Don and Jan Frank. Help and hope for couples struggling in their marriages due to victimization in their past. Specific steps to rebuild the marriage foundation and to enhance physical, emotional and spiritual intimacy.

Freeing Your Mind From Memories That Bind by Fred and Florence Littauer. Setting forth a biblical basis for inner healing through Jesus Christ, the authors explore emotional dysfunction and the childhood experiences which potentially lead to it.

The Promise of Restoration by Fred Littauer. If you have a past that won't let go, this book can help. Discover God's promise of restoration and be released from the issues that hinder you from being all God created you to be.

At Christian bookstores everywhere.

Or call

Here's Life Publishers
1-800-950-4457

(Visa and Mastercard accepted.)